SHAKESPEARE'S THEATER OF JUDGMENT

SHAKESPEARE'S THEATER OF JUDGMENT

Six Keywords

◆ ◆ ◆

KEVIN CURRAN

EDINBURGH
University Press

Edinburgh University Press is one of the leading university presses in the UK. We publish academic books and journals in our selected subject areas across the humanities and social sciences, combining cutting-edge scholarship with high editorial and production values to produce academic works of lasting importance. For more information visit our website: edinburghuniversitypress.com

The open access version of this publication was funded by the Swiss National Science Foundation.

Published with the support of the Swiss National Science Foundation.

Edinburgh University Press Ltd
13 Infirmary Street
Edinburgh EH1 1LT

Typeset in 11/14 Adobe Sabon by
IDSUK (DataConnection) Ltd, and
printed and bound by CPI Group (UK) Ltd,
Croydon, CR0 4YY

A CIP record for this book is available from the British Library

ISBN 978 1 3995 1636 5 (hardback)
ISBN 978 1 3995 1637 2 (paperback)
ISBN 978 1 3995 1 638 9 (webready PDF)
ISBN 978 1 3995 1639 6 (epub)

https://doi.org/10.3366/CURR6365

CONTENTS

Contents

ACKNOWLEDGMENTS

When I began work on *Shakespeare's Theater of Judgment*, my questions were primarily intellectual historical; it was a project of recovery. By the end, I had come to realize that the topic was of more consequence than this. It had to do not just with Shakespeare's time, but also with our own. Thinking about judgment meant thinking about the terms on which public life operates, the complex ethical calculus involved in managing the relationship between freedom and responsibility, and above all the special place of theater in cultivating moral intelligence and a shared sense of justice. It is a pleasure to be able to thank all those without whom my thinking never would have moved from point A to point B.

Throughout the gestation of this project, I have been fortunate to receive invitations to events that invigorated and challenged me. At the Freie Universität, the University of Western Australia, the University of Sydney, UCLA, Cambridge University, the Université de Montréal, the Moore Institute at the University of Galway, the Università di Padova, Ghent University, the University of Zurich, the Université de Genève, the Université de Neuchâtel, the Université de Lausanne, and the University of Haifa, scholars and artists I would never have been able to get into the same room together on my own provided the banter and provocation essential to the formulation of new ideas. For their central roles in organizing these events, I wish to thank Stephanie Elsky, Robert White, Huw Griffiths, Julia Reinhard Lupton, Subha Mukherji, Joyce Boro, Maria Shmygol, Rocco Coronato, Andrew Bricker, Isabel Karremann, Lukas Erne, Margaret Tudeau-Clayton, Charlotte Dufour, and Alex Feldman.

For conversation, feedback, critique, collaboration, and professional support over the years, I am grateful to Lukas Arnold, Michael Bristol, Sanford Budick, Léonard Burnand, Danielle Chaperon, Douglas Clark, Brian Cummings, Maksymilian Del Mar, Emma Depledge, Meg Duell, Patrick Durdel, Kathy Eden, Marc Escola, Kirk Essary, Rachel Falconer, Georgia Fulton, Indira Ghose, David Goldstein, Jane Grogan, Heather Hirschfeld, Lorna Hutson, James Kearney, James Knapp, Paul Kottman, Vincent Laughery, Zachary Lesser, Dave Lüthi, Céline Magada, Richard Meek, Lise Michel, Beatrice Montedoro, Roelof Overmeer, Andy Reilly, Jane Rickard, Florence Rivero, Kilian Schindler, Liam Semler, Donovan Sherman, Devani Singh, Emily Smith, Emma Smith, Matthew Smith, Sebastien Sobecki, Enit Steiner, Richard Strier, Garrett Sullivan, Josefa Terribilini, Naya Tsentourou, Jennifer Waldron, Greg Walker, Paul Yachnin, Carey Young, and Antoinina Bevan Zlatar.

Paul Yachnin and Julia Reinhard Lupton deserve special mention. Paul took an interest in this project from its earliest days. I benefitted greatly, and over many years, from his deep knowledge of and insatiable curiosity about the public dimension of early modern commercial theater. Julia has always known exactly when to praise, when to question, and when to push, often opening up important vistas for my work that I didn't know were there. She has been an invaluable interlocutor and a constant inspiration. It is a privilege to have colleagues and friends like these. I don't take it for granted.

There are also some organizations and institutions that have played a crucial role in the development of this project. The Swiss National Science Foundation (SNSF) generously funded a four-year collaborative research project called "Theater and Judgment in Early Modern England." This created an ideal context in which to complete my book while also facilitating research on topics that fell outside its specific purview. The SNSF also subsidized an open-access version of *Shakespeare's Theater of Judgment* for which I am very grateful. The Newberry Library in Chicago provided a perfect home for me to write during a well-timed sabbatical in 2023. I am especially grateful to the staff at the Newberry Library's Center for Renaissance Studies for their hospitality. Edinburgh University Press, as ever, has been a pleasure to work with. I wish to thank

Michelle Houston, Emily Sharp, Elizabeth Fraser, Carla Hepburn, Bekah Dey, Fiona Conn, and Eliza Wright for the care with which they oversaw the whole process, from peer-review to production.

Portions of Chapter 4 of this book appear in "Prospero's Plea: Judgment, Invention, and Political Form in *The Tempest*," in *Shakespeare and Judgment*, ed. Kevin Curran (Edinburgh: Edinburgh University Press, 2016), 157–71. An early version of Chapter 5 was previously published as "The Face of Judgment in *Measure for Measure*," in *Face-to-Face in Shakespearean Drama: Ethics, Performance, Philosophy*, ed. Julia Reinhard Lupton and Matthew James Smith (Edinburgh: Edinburgh University Press, 2019), 163–75. I am grateful to Edinburgh University Press for permission to reproduce this material.

Last but by no means least, thank you to Pauline and Stone, for enduring.

A NOTE ON SPELLING

For both practical and intellectual reasons, I have adopted American usage for the word "judgment." That is, a single spelling, without an "-e," to denote all forms of the concept – legal, moral, aesthetic, scientific, rhetorical, and so forth. British usage, by contrast, differentiates between "judgment," for legal contexts, and "judgement" (with an "-e") for other contexts. Though generally speaking a helpful distinction, it proved too cumbersome and constricting for this study which so often highlights the way judgment straddles multiple intellectual and institutional contexts simultaneously.

Picture Macbeth alone on stage, staring intently into empty space. 'Is this a dagger which I see before me?' he asks, grasping decisively at the air. On one hand, this is a quintessentially theatrical question. At once an object and a vector, the dagger describes the possibility of knowledge ('Is this a dagger') in specifically visual and spatial terms ('which I see before me'). At the same time, Macbeth is posing a quintessentially philosophical question, one that assumes knowledge to be both conditional and experiential, and that probes the relationship between certainty and perception as well as intention and action. It is from this shared ground of art and inquiry, of theatre and theory, that this series advances its basic premise: Shakespeare is philosophical.

It seems like a simple enough claim. But what does it mean exactly, beyond the parameters of this specific moment in *Macbeth*? Does it mean that Shakespeare had something we could think of as his own philosophy? Does it mean that he was influenced by particular philosophical schools, texts and thinkers? Does it mean, conversely, that modern philosophers have been influenced by him, that Shakespeare's plays and poems have been, and continue to be, resources for philosophical thought and speculation?

The answer is yes all around. These are all useful ways of conceiving a philosophical Shakespeare and all point to lines of inquiry that this series welcomes. But Shakespeare is philosophical in a much more fundamental way as well. Shakespeare is philosophical because the plays and poems actively create new worlds of knowledge and new scenes of ethical encounter. They ask big questions, make bold arguments and develop new vocabularies in order to think what might otherwise be unthinkable. Through both their scenarios and their imagery, the plays and poems engage the qualities of consciousness, the consequences of human action, the phenomenology of motive and attention, the conditions of personhood and the relationship among different orders of reality and experience. This is writing and dramaturgy, moreover, that consistently experiments with a broad range of conceptual crossings, between love and subjectivity, nature and politics, and temporality and form.

Edinburgh Critical Studies in Shakespeare and Philosophy takes seriously these speculative and world-making dimensions of Shakespeare's work. The series proceeds from a core conviction that art's capacity to think – to formulate, not just reflect, ideas – is what makes it urgent and valuable. Art matters because unlike other human activities it establishes its own frame of reference, reminding us that all acts of creation – biological, political, intellectual and amorous – are grounded in imagination. This is a far cry from business-as-usual in Shakespeare studies. Because historicism remains the methodological gold standard of the field, far more energy has been invested in exploring what Shakespeare once meant than in thinking rigorously about what Shakespeare continues to make possible. In response, Edinburgh Critical Studies in Shakespeare and Philosophy pushes back against the critical orthodoxies of historicism and cultural studies to clear a space for scholarship that confronts aspects of literature that can neither be reduced to nor adequately explained by particular historical contexts.

Shakespeare's creations are not just inheritances of a past culture, frozen artefacts whose original settings must be expertly reconstructed in order to be understood. The plays and poems are also living art, vital thought-worlds that struggle, across time, with foundational questions of metaphysics, ethics, politics and aesthetics. With this orientation in mind, Edinburgh Critical Studies in Shakespeare and Philosophy offers a series of scholarly monographs that will reinvigorate Shakespeare studies by opening new interdisciplinary conversations among scholars, artists and students.

Kevin Curran

INTRODUCTION:
UNDERSTANDING JUDGMENT

This is a book about the ethical and social importance of judgment, which takes Shakespeare as a guide and intellectual travel companion. My basic premise is that Shakespeare offers valuable conceptual and practical resources for recovering a positive, collective, and creative understanding of judgment, something largely lacking in contemporary social and intellectual discourse on the topic. Accordingly, the chapters that follow do not offer "readings" of Shakespeare's plays *per se*, not in the conventional academic sense. Instead, they pursue a series of arguments about various aspects of the theory and practice of judgment carried out with the tools – scenes, vignettes, characters, speeches, theatrical dynamics – that Shakespeare's plays have to offer. To the extent that readings are presented, they are readings of the idea of judgment carried out with the help of Shakespeare, more so than they are readings of Shakespeare's plays from the perspective of judgment. Shakespeare, to put it another way, is not so much an inert object of analysis in this book as he is a collaborator and an interlocutor. Each chapter of *Shakespeare's Theater of Judgment* is organized around a single keyword: Feeling, Objects, Vision, Making, Facing, and Community. Together, these chapters assemble a new lexicon for judgment. It is my hope that this Shakespearean conceptual vocabulary might help us develop new ways of talking and thinking about judgment which place it at the center of collaboration and community-making.

This book fills a conspicuous gap in the critical literature. While recent years have seen a marked interest in the cultural and intellectual history of judgment, scholarship on the topic has neglected the theater of Shakespeare and his contemporaries and the early modern period more generally. Vivasvan Soni's special issue of *The Eighteenth Century* on "The Crisis of Judgment," for example, focuses on eighteenth-century philosophers and novelists in the context of shifting ideas about selfhood and society.[1] Similarly, Hina Nazar's *Enlightened Sentiments* shows how moral judgment connects the seemingly disparate spheres of the eighteenth-century sentimental novel and Enlightenment political philosophy.[2] Thomas Pfau in *Minding the Modern* has produced the most wide-ranging account of judgment as part of a larger study of the roots of modernity. He explores judgment along with personhood and action as the three foundational concepts of Western intellectual history. However, with the exception of some commentary on Thomas Hobbes and John Locke in the latter part of the seventeenth century, Pfau skips the early modern period altogether and makes no mention of theater in any era.[3]

Scholarship centrally concerned with judgment, then, has had little to say about early modern England and nothing to say about the theater of Shakespeare and his contemporaries. When these contexts are addressed, it is in scholarship devoted to other aspects of early modern English culture. The field of literature and law furnishes some examples of excellent criticism in this vein. Richard Strier, for instance, discusses what he views as Shakespeare's skepticism about moral judgment in chapter 3 of *The Unrepentant Renaissance* and returns to the idea in an essay called "Shakespeare and Legal Systems."[4] In *The Invention of Suspicion*, Lorna Hutson discusses the role of judgment within English common law, especially the way ideas about legal judgment are connected to discourses of religion and civility in early modern England.[5] Related to this body of work are books that have considered the place of judgment in the study of early modern rhetoric. This category includes Kathy Eden's *Poetic and Legal Fiction in the Aristotelian Tradition*, Joel B. Altman's *The Improbability of Othello*, and Quentin Skinner's *Forensic Shakespeare*.[6] In a similar mode, Henry S. Turner discusses how rhetorical judgment came to be applied in the context of "mechanical arts," like mathematics, in *The English Renaissance Stage*.[7] The role of judgment in political thought, meanwhile, has been addressed in sections of J. G. A. Pocock's classic work of intellectual history *The Machiavellian Moment*, and to a lesser extent in Andras Kisery's *Hamlet's Moment*, which makes a number of references to the way Senecan tragedy stages the mechanics of political judgment.[8] Julia Reinhard Lupton, engaging closely with Hannah Arendt, takes a more philosophical approach to judgment and politics in *Thinking with Shakespeare*, a line of inquiry she extends in an essay called "Judging Forgiveness."[9]

If this brief critical review demonstrates an ongoing academic interest in judgment, it also demonstrates a general dearth of attention to Shakespearean theater. *Shakespeare's Theater of Judgment* constitutes a first step towards addressing this gap, an undertaking I feel is crucial for three reasons. First, the commercial theater of the early modern period disseminated practical and theoretical knowledge of judgment to a diverse public. If we wish to understand the larger story of how evaluative skills migrated out of the specialized world of schools and universities into the everyday lives of a broad spectrum of men and women, we have to attend closely to plays. Second, judgment in the theater is influenced by a range of cultural practices, including law, rhetoric, religion, early literary criticism, and ideas about social conduct. Accordingly, if we want to understand judgment as a complex, conceptually hybrid phenomenon, rather than as something that belongs only to one or another narrow disciplinary context, we need to attend closely to the theater. Third, and more broadly, re-encountering judgment in its theatrical formation – that is, as something inherently physical and collective – allows us to view it outside the mainstream of the post-Lockean liberal tradition, with its emphasis on reason and individuality. Theatrical judgment involves collaborative deliberation in material, face-to-face environments, the function of which is always, in one way or another, to establish or reinforce a shared sense of truth and value; of the way things are or the way things ought to be. Understood in these terms, judgment lends dynamic form to one's status as a stakeholder, to the simple but crucial idea that what matters for the collective also matters for me.

At this point, you may be asking, *but why Shakespeare?* Indeed, why not Ben Jonson or John Marston or George Chapman or Francis Beaumont, or any of the other early modern playwrights who were attuned to the deliberative power of the audience and who could clearly perceive the place of judgment within social life and the professional cultures of law, politics, and finance? There is much work to be done on early modern judgment and theater, and I hope this book will act as a catalyst for additional projects in this vein. My adoption of Shakespeare as interlocutor in the present study has to do with the fact that unlike so many of his colleagues, Shakespeare does not seem to have had a set view on judgment either in society or in the theater. This may be because his understanding of the topic was less academic than a playwright who had gone to university or studied at the Inns of Court, even if his grammar school education would have introduced him in a basic way to the role of judgment within rhetoric and oratory. Whatever the reason, judgment in Shakespeare, as the following chapters will show, is always a question, a problem, a matter for exploration; never a straightforward answer or solution, nor an object of ridicule. As with so many other recurring preoccupations in his canon, Shakespeare takes a speculative approach to judgment. This makes him ideally suited for a study like this one, which must raise questions about how judgment has developed within the liberal tradition in order to reclaim it as a productive social and political virtue.

What Is Judgment?

With this basic mission statement in place, let me back up and return to our key term: *judgment*. What exactly is judgment? Judgment is difficult to define in part because it signifies across several semantic and cultural fields. A uniquely protean topic, part of judgment's history is legal, with the courtroom serving as its primary institutional home. Part of its history is religious, with divine judgment in particular lending the Abrahamic religions moral force and temporal urgency. The history of aesthetics is also bound up with conceptions of judgment. In the vernacular literary criticism that developed in England over the course of the sixteenth and seventeenth centuries, programmatic descriptions of good writing and right reading by figures such as Philip Sidney, George Puttenham, Samuel Daniel, and Henry Peacham were heavily invested in judgment, citing it as both the faculty responsible for proper discernment and the attribute that stands to benefit from superior writing and oratory. Evolving notions of judgment are central to the development of experimental science just as they are to the emergence of politics as a profession, especially the craft of policy-making. Finally, judgment is also a key term in the discourse of sociality, in which context it is viewed as a practice that knits the individual's sense of self into a larger community of taste. This line of thought begins with Aristotle and the Stoics and is taken up with particular rigor in the eighteenth century when writers like the Third Earl of Shaftesbury, Jean-Jacques Rousseau, and especially Immanuel Kant formulated new ideas about the role of judgment in social and political life. Later, in the twentieth century, Hannah Arendt developed the moral and political implications of Kant's arguments in a series of influential essays. At the time of her death in 1975, Arendt was planning a final volume of her seminal work *The Life of the Mind* on "Judgment."[10] Judgment, in other words, is something *out there* – in the law courts, in the universities, on the tip of God's tongue, and in the codes of socialization. But it is also something *in here*. Judgment is a psychological faculty possessed by each person, even if its effectiveness may vary depending on circumstance and other factors. At once a faculty, a practice, a method, and a skill, judgment transforms as it migrates across the realms of psychology, rhetoric, politics, science, aesthetics, law, religion, and philosophy.

And yet for all its intellectual potency and conceptual malleability, judgment is not a topic we hear a great deal about these days. It tends to be used in very specific institutional contexts, such as law, or in everyday life with a broadly negative connotation, "no judgment" being a common disclaimer to signal the sort of virtuous toleration we are all supposed to be practicing. To judge, in other words, is to be *judgmental*, the latter a term that dates from the mid-twentieth century.[11] In the words of a frequently shared meme attributed to Carl G. Jung, "Thinking is hard, that's why most people judge."[12] Thinking, good; judgment, bad. Not surprising then that the necessary work of discernment and decision tends to fall under the purview of statistics, algorithms, and data-analysis. Who needs judgment when we have math? Numbers, after all, as many would be inclined to posit, are pre-representational and non-interpretive. They are fact incarnate and therefore offer an entirely objective ground for knowledge and choice. Or so the argument goes.[13]

While all this is characteristic of our time, it is by no means a purely modern sentiment. The most famous utterance on the hazards of judgment comes from the Bible, purportedly from the mouth of Jesus himself: "Judge not, lest ye be judged" (Matthew 7:1). In seventeenth-century England, Francis Bacon wrote at length on human bias and the fallibility of judgment in his *Novum Organum* (1620), noting that "the vulgar make up the overwhelming majority . . . and generally allow their judgments to be swayed by passion or prejudice."[14] Each of these instances is slightly different, of course. The biblical injunction is primarily ethical in addressing the importance of shared standards that can be set for a community without hypocrisy. Bacon's concerns are primarily methodological in addressing the challenges of objectivity. Jung's comment hovers somewhere between the moral and the psychological in assuring the reader, *it's not you, it's them*, since the act of judgment is, in and of itself, an expression of intellectual laziness.

What postwar modernity introduces into the discourse on judgment is a particular form of socio-political anxiety, the idea that judgment is a force of normativity, that it polices the boundaries of identity and sets the terms for various kinds of social membership. The two key texts to articulate this view in the twentieth century are Michel Foucault's *Discipline and Punish* (1975) and Pierre Bourdieu's *Distinction: A Social Critique of the Judgement of Taste* (1979). Reflecting on the difference between pre-modern and modern legal judgment, and especially the expanding role of mental health professionals in the trial process, Foucault writes:

> Now quite a different question of truth is inscribed in the course of the penal judgment. The question is no longer simply: "Has the act been established and is it punishable?" But also: "What *is* the

act?" . . . It is no longer simply: "Who committed it?" But: "How can we assign the causal process that produced it? Where did it originate in the author himself?" . . . A whole set of assessing, diagnostic, prognostic, normative judgments concerning the criminal have become lodged in the framework of penal judgment.[15]

He concludes, "The sentence that condemns or acquits is not simply a judgment of guilt, a legal decision that lays down punishment; it bears within it an assessment of normality and a technical prescription for a possible normalization . . ."[16] Foucault's larger point about the normalizing impulses of penal judgment is that it affects far more than courtroom procedure. It is, rather, one institutional iteration of a culture-wide regime of disciplinary power that shapes the psychic world of education and even everyday life. Describing the broader "juridico-anthropological" manifestations of modern penal judgment, Foucault writes:

> It measures in quantitative terms and hierarchizes in terms of value the abilities, the level, the "nature" of individuals. It introduces through this "value-giving" measure, the constraint of a conformity that must be achieved. Lastly, it traces the limit that will define the difference in relation to all other differences, the external frontier of the abnormal . . . The perpetual penality that traverses all points and supervises every instant in the disciplinary institutions compares, differentiates, hierarchizes, homogenizes, excludes. In short, it *normalizes*.[17]

Modern judgment, for Foucault, sets "the external frontier of the abnormal" and incentivizes staying well within that frontier through the promise of punishment – legal, educational, professional, or social. Similarly, Bourdieu, though he is more interested in the aesthetic than in the disciplinary, sees judgment as a boundary maker and manager. "Taste classifies," he writes famously. Taking music as an example, he asserts that "Nothing more clearly affirms one's 'class', nothing more infallibly classifies, than tastes in music . . . there is no more 'classificatory' practice than concert-going, or playing a 'noble' instrument."[18]

Together, Foucault and Bourdieu projected and helped solidify a uniquely twentieth-century attitude towards judgment.

Judgment – whether legal, social, moral, or aesthetic –expresses our internalization of a range of normative divisions at the same time as it contributes to the intensification of those divisions, between natural and unnatural, good and bad, refined and vulgar, smart and stupid, normal and abnormal. These are uncomfortable associations, especially for liberal societies where openness and diversity are to be valued, and prescriptiveness abhorred, above all else. Anxieties of this sort even inform twentieth-century literary criticism. As Vivasvan Soni has shown:

> The effects of the reading practices the New Critics advocate is precisely to produce a suspension of judgment. After all, one of the methodological premises of the New Criticism is that ironies, tensions, ambiguities, and paradoxes pervade good poetry and it is the task of the critic to bring these to light.[19]

In this approach to literary critique, so conventional in today's college classrooms that many have forgotten its origin in New Critical theory, judgment is antithetical to literary analysis. To judge is to have been duped, to have missed the subtleties of the text, or, even worse, to have boorishly ignored them. As Cleanth Brooks explains, discussing Wordsworth's "Ode," "whatever statement we may seize upon as incorporating the 'meaning' of the poem, immediately the imagery and the rhythm seem to set up tensions with it, warping and twisting it, qualifying and revising it."[20]

A similar logic underpins much of deconstruction, which takes as one of its primary hermeneutic commitments the radical suspension of judgment. Deconstructive critical practice seeks to expose those moments in which texts undermine their meaning and defy legibility. As Paul de Man puts it:

> The text both is and is not the theistic document it is assumed to be ... A text such as *Profession de foi* can literally be called "unreadable" in that it leads to a set of assertions that radically exclude each other ... They compel us to choose while destroying the foundations of any choice.[21]

For de Man, since the text is categorically "unreadable" in an interpretive sense, judgment falls outside the parameters of sound critical practice. To live in the aporia of undecidability is not, therefore, some kind of temporary state of intellectual purgatory, but rather the permanent condition of good reading. The modern humanities classroom sometimes hosts a watered-down pedagogical version of this idea which essentially amounts to everybody-is-right-and-nobody-is-wrong. What is undeniable is that two of the most influential movements in twentieth-century literary criticism have made judgment marginal at best to their hermeneutic. This is part of what Soni has called a "crisis of judgment" in the interpretive humanities and in modern culture more broadly.[22] No wonder, then, the memeabilty of quotations like Jung's that indict all critique as judgment and all judgment as bad, or the recurring vernacular disclaimer of "no judgment" issued piously right before an opinion is expressed.

Shakespeare, I propose, can help us unlearn some of our assumptions about judgment. His insights about the topic come from a very different place than those of Jung, Foucault, Bourdieu, and de Man. They come from the world of theater, in which judgment is always, necessarily, collective and embodied; they come from a dramatic imagination that is conjectural rather than clinical, open rather than dogmatic; and they come from the cultural environments of early modern England, the intellectual DNA of which inevitably helps bring Shakespeare's scenes of judgment to life, both in his time and in our own. With this in mind, I want to shift now to early modern England and to the place of judgment within the intellectual and theatrical cultures of Shakespeare's time.

What Was Judgment?

Although there is a difference between how judgment is understood now and how judgment was understood in the sixteenth and seventeenth centuries, neither era possesses an entirely uniform discourse on the topic. The history of judgment does not move in neat, linear increments from one model to another. There is, however, what we may think of as a conceptual center of gravity in each era's account of judgment. My task in this section will be to provide a snapshot of what this looks like in early modern England, while still allowing some of the complexities to emerge.

Towards this end, I am going to advance three general assertions: first, that judgment was central to community formation, including communities of status, profession, expertise, and wit; second, that judgment was both a specialist practice and part of everyday vernacular intellectual culture; and third, that judgment was largely a practical activity, grounded in experience and practically leveraged knowledge. I will address each in turn.

To say that judgment was central to community formation is to stress the fact that it was understood as collective and participatory. This is quite different from mainstream conceptions of judgment now. In early modern England, it is not very likely that judgment would have evoked, say, the condemnation behind the haughty gaze of a difficult colleague at a meeting. That is too internalized and too private. More likely, it would have evoked a skill being put on display in a social environment, especially one in which the ability to muster impressive bits of knowledge or to deploy particular types of language secured membership in a certain community of knowledge, status, or education. These social environments included, but were not limited to, theaters, universities, and private dinners, as well as the many sites of public conversation, including St. Paul's Churchyard, the Royal Exchange, taverns, and, later, the Royal Society. In *A Social History of Truth*, Steven Shapin comments on the communal dimension of knowledge in a way that helps pinpoint the role of judgment in the dynamics of sociality. "Knowledge," he writes,

> is a collective good. In securing our knowledge we rely upon others, and we cannot dispense with that reliance . . . The fabric of our social relations is made of knowledge – not just knowledge of other people, but also knowledge of what the world is like – and, similarly, that our knowledge of what the world is like draws on knowledge about other people – what they are like as sources of testimony, whether and in what circumstances they may be trusted.[23]

Though it goes unmentioned, judgment is crucial to the epistemological transactions Shapin describes. Judgment is the faculty that manages the trust on which knowledge can be credibly received. Trust, and the shared knowledge it facilitates, only obtains upon passing through the threshold of judgment where "what they are like as sources of testimony" is assessed. If shared knowledge forms the grounds of community, judgment comprises the conditions of possibility for such sharing to take place. As Shapin elaborates, "the fate of any particular claim that something 'is the case' is never determined by the individual making the claim." Rather, "truth is a matter of collective judgment" and "it is stabilized by the collective actions which use it as a standard for judging other claims."[24]

Shapin takes as his central example of this process, the formation of scientific communities in early modern England. In this context, social knowledge and natural knowledge are inextricably linked. Who someone is – their education, their status, their command of rhetoric and wit – bears directly on the perceived validity of what they claim to be true of the world. We practice a similar socio-scientific mode of adjudication now: "what we know of comets, icebergs, and neutrinos irreducibly contains what we know of those people who speak for and about these things, just as what we know about the virtues of people is informed by their speech about things that exist in the world."[25] In early modern England, this phenomenon played out in debates about alchemy or the theory of induction. In our time, it plays out in debates about climate change or Covid vaccines. In all cases, judgment manages knowledge according to a social index, and as such it forms the main link between what we know and those with whom we associate.

One mark of a gentleman, whether in a scientific context or otherwise, was the ability to sift through information – academic, rhetorical, literary – and extract what was particularly useful or high quality. Even better was the ability to then redeploy that information – a turn of phrase, a proverb, a historical reference, a piece of evidence, or a nugget of wisdom – in an especially fitting social or professional situation. These skills constitute a form of judgment-in-action which stood at the intersection of a variety of concepts within the rhetorical tradition. They are connected, for example, to the Stoic notion of *modestia* – "the essence of orderliness and of right-placing" – which Cicero calls *collocationis*.[26] They are connected, as well, to the notion of literary *decorum*, the selection of specific characters and forms of speech deployed towards particular affective and generic ends. Discussions of *decorum* could be found in both Aristotle's *Rhetoric* and Horace's *Ars Poetica*, as well as in widely circulated handbooks by sixteenth-century theorists such as Thomas Wilson and Robert Ascham who replaced *decorum* with the English terms "aptness" and "propriety," respectively.[27] The ability to discern among the many things one heard and read and determine "this is valuable and impressive and this is not" was an everyday aptitude evolved from the more specialized adjudicatory skills denoted by terms like *modestia*, *collocationis*, and *decorum*.

The early modern theater was central to this judgment-based knowledge economy because it was one of the main purveyors of the maxims, proverbs, *sententiae*, and witticisms that accrued social capital. There were a variety of ways in which early modern men and women would mine plays for wit and wisdom. Most straightforwardly, they could select good lines and copy them into a table-book while watching plays in the theater. Alternatively, they could write them down from memory into a commonplace book once they got home. They could also memorize or copy such material from other manuscript and print sources, such as playbooks and miscellanies.[28] Commonplace books and miscellanies, whether in manuscript or printed form, assembled short passages of instructive, funny, or morally edifying text from a variety of sources, sometimes under themed headings. John Foxe, for example, published the very successful *Locorum Communium Tituli* in 1557, which left most pages blank except for pre-printed subject headings so the reader could see examples of good extracts and then proceed to find and fill in their own.[29] The point of a text like this is precisely to foster the skill of judgment – the ability to discern and select, and through that, to develop one's own potential for reasoning and moral intelligence. Foxe's project is a morally somber take on Seneca's argument that keeping a commonplace book helps us craft what we might now call an intellectual identity. "We should imitate bees," Seneca explains in Epistle 84,

> and we should keep in separate compartments whatever we have collected from our diverse reading, for things conserved separately keep better. Then, diligently applying all the resources of

our native talent, we should mingle all the various nectars we have tasted, and turn them into a single sweet substance, in a way that, even if it is apparent where it originated, it appears quite different from what it was in its original state.[30]

Laura Estill has traced how the English interest in commonplacing from classical and religious sources eventually led to extracting from vernacular poetry and commercial plays.[31] Marking this vogue was the publication of popular collections such as *Politeuphuia: Wits Commonwealth* (1597), *Palladis Tamia: Wits Treasury* (1598), *Wits Theater of the Little World* (1599), *Belvedére or the Garden of the Muses* (1600), and *England's Helicon* (1600).[32] We also begin to see "commonplace markers" appearing regularly in printed playbooks: inverted commas or asterisks used to indicate lines that are especially good candidates for extraction and copying. This is the case in the 1605 quarto of Ben Jonson's *Sejanus* and the first and second quartos of Shakespeare's *Hamlet* (1603 and 1605, respectively). Between 1600 and 1603 alone, there were thirteen plays printed with commonplace markers.[33] It is also in the first years of the seventeenth century that manuscripts containing extracts from professional plays begin to appear with some regularity. The most well-known of these, Edward Pudsey's commonplace book, contains material compiled between about 1600 and 1609, including extracts from plays written by Jonson, Shakespeare, and Marston, among others. He likely wrote the passages down in a table-book while viewing the plays in the theater.[34]

The point to underline at this stage is that by the time Shakespeare was at the height of his career, the commercial theater was at the center of an ecology of judgment that included playwrights, actors, spectators, printers, and readers. It offered a collective environment in which a vernacular version of the academic skills of selection and categorization could be exercised.[35] As in other knowledge communities, the process of deciphering what information is worthwhile and what is not in the theater was as social as it was epistemic. What we choose to know – or rather, what information we deem of value – is based on criteria keyed to whom we wish to be. *I judge* these lines of sufficient merit to write down, memorize, and then reuse in conversation so I can *be judged* worthy of membership in a certain milieu. As Stefano Guazzo put it in his widely read conduct book *The Civile Conversation* (1581), "The judgment which we have to know ourselves is not ours, but we borrow it of others . . . the knowledge of ourselves, dependeth of the judgment and conversation of many."[36] If Seneca evokes the way good discernment arms us with the tools we need to craft an identity, Guazzo builds on the idea by insisting that identity is always social. It involves not just the judgments we make, but also the way those acts of discernment are then judged by others. Any space of knowledge transaction in early modern England, from scientific communities to theater, participates in this process.

The second assertion I wish to make about early modern judgment is that it was both a specialist practice and part of everyday vernacular intellectual culture. Our discussion so far has already begun to bear this point out. To explore further, let us return to the culture of science in early modern London. Here is the evocative picture painted by Deborah E. Harkness in her groundbreaking study *The Jewel House: Elizabethan London and the Scientific Revolution*:

> London's urban sensibility, along with new trade networks and her growing population . . . made the City an ideal place for new ideas about the natural world to emerge. Shouting to be heard over the din from the market stalls on nearly every street, working in cramped backyards over furnaces and smelting ovens, and operating out of storefronts in the Royal Exchange and other merchant neighborhoods, hundreds of men and women of all nationalities engaged in the work of science, medicine, and technology in London. Some were poor immigrants, like "Dutch Hans," a German metalworker who traded his knowledge of the properties of molten lead for beer in a crowded pub near the Globe. Others were fixtures of London's trade organizations, like the Barber-Surgeon George Baker, who extracted teeth, set bones, and performed surgical procedures in his shop at the gates of the Royal Exchange. The Antwerp native Lieven Alaertes and Londoner Thomasina Scarlet established lucrative medical practices in the City, specializing in treating obstetrical and gynecological complaints despite the best efforts of London's College of Physicians to force women out of the medical market.[37]

Harkness's study assembles a wide range of printed and manuscript sources to recover a thriving world of amateur science in Elizabethan England, "hundreds of men and women of all nationalities engaged in the work of science, medicine, and technology." Thoroughly cosmopolitan and distributed among a variety of shops, offices, stalls, commercial outposts, and spaces of public congregation, the socio-professional world evoked by Harkness centered on judgment-based tasks and activities. This included identifying, classifying, and measuring natural-world phenomena and substances, all of which was the preserve of *prudence*, or "practical wisdom," the virtue tradition's term for judgment.

The shopkeepers of the Royal Exchange and "the Lime Street naturalists," among other communities studied by Harkness, practiced a vernacular version of academic science. It was informal, oriented towards practical ends, and undertaken outside of any official institutional context, decades before the establishment of the Royal Society in 1660. Nevertheless, the habits of thought this work required were enabled by specialist academic skill. Concretely, this could include anything from mathematics and book-keeping to anatomy and herbalism. More generally, it involved a knowledge of rhetoric and a way of understanding the world from within the conceptual parameters of a rhetorical education. Anyone who had been to grammar school would have received a basic training in rhetoric through texts like Cicero's *De inventione*, the anonymous *Rhetorica ad Herennium*, or Quintillian's *Institutio oratoria*.[38] These rhetorical manuals were used to teach, among other things, the relationship between invention and judgment within oratory. If invention denotes the skill of deciding the most apt line of persuasion in a given situation, judgment denotes the skill of choosing and arranging the words, images, and references that best serve that line of persuasion.[39] Judgment can be thought of as a form of design, a way of curating raw materials with a view towards their practical and experiential affordances.[40] Judgment and invention were essential components of what Aristotle termed the *genus iudiciale*, the kind of speech typically found in the law courts.[41] But studying these elements of rhetoric also imparted a more general sense of judgment's crucial role in any form of creation or making. The de-cluttering and refinement of undifferentiated information which was judgment's function formed the foundation on which any craft could be successfully carried out. This is one way in which judgment can be understood as both a specialist practice and part of everyday culture.

One of the main spaces where professional and amateur judgment intersected in early modern London was the theater. The rise of the commercial playhouse during the 1570s and 80s turned playgoers into quasi-judges, unofficial arbiters of taste whose approval or disapproval determined the fate of plays and playwrights. The analogy was readily seized upon by playwrights themselves, who regularly referred to their audiences as members of a theatrical version of the legal profession in performed prologues and epilogues and in prefatory material in the printed versions of their plays. The power of the analogy, which persisted for decades, may have to do not only with the new commercial conditions under which plays were being performed, but also with the very real social link between theater and law in the period. Theaters drew a sizeable portion of their audiences, and even some of their playwrights, from the Inns of Court, the institution that trained young men for careers in law.[42] Marston, for example, was a member of the Middle Temple in the 1590s, as was John Webster. John Ford was admitted in 1602. Ben Jonson did not attend the Inns himself, but he was close friends with prominent jurists such as John Seldon, with whom he corresponded about transvestism on the stage, and John Hoskyns, who was also a respected poet and wit.

It is perhaps not surprising, given the links between the worlds of drama and law, that judgment loomed large in the conceptual landscape of English commercial theater, too. As Leo Salinger has shown, "from about 1599 to about 1613, the keyword in a dramatist's approach to his public was . . . the word *judgment*."[43] In fact, this begins even earlier. John Lyly's *Midas* (1589) tells its audience that the actors are "jealous of your judgments, because you are wise," and in *Doctor Faustus*, Christopher Marlowe invites the "patient judgments" of the playgoers, to give just a couple examples.[44] But 1599 does mark something of a watershed moment in the judicial rendering of theater audiences if we consider how programmatically obsessed with good and bad judgment Jonson's

Every Man Out of His Humour was. Here, Jonson makes a distinction he would continue to make in one way or another throughout his career between "judicious friends" and "envious censors," terms which denote two different modes of theatrical judgment, each with definite social and moral coordinates.[45] A year or so later, Hamlet would lecture the players visiting Elsinore at length about aesthetic and stylistic discernment and how bad theatrical decisions "make the judicious grieve," invoking a class of playgoers roughly similar to Jonson's "judicious friends."[46]

There is clear social snobbery at play in some of these appeals to audience judgment. Lyly's behest for critical feedback – requested "because you are wise" – is aimed at "Gentlemen." And Jonson's view of the deliberative acumen of the average theater audience is consistently sneering. Another oft-quoted example can be found in *The Alchemist* (1610), where he refers to the "vice of judgment" among playgoers who "commend writers as they do fencers or wrestlers; who if they come in robustly, and put for it with a great deal of violence, are received for the braver fellows."[47] Elsewhere, though, we find a more egalitarian treatment of the topic, as in Thomas Heywood's *The Silver Age* (1611), where the playwright offers his work to "this judging nation," a phrase suggestive of theater's role in the democratization of judgment and the formation of a proto-public sphere.[48] Like it or not, to put on a play in early modern London meant submitting your creation not just to the learned, but also to the unlettered workers, shopkeepers, and servants who made up the majority of early modern London's population. As Thomas Dekker put it famously in *The Gull's Horn-Book* (1609):

> The Theater is your Poet's Royal Exchange . . . your Stinkard has the self-same liberty to be there in his Tobacco-Fumes, which your sweet Courtier hath: and . . . your Car-man and Tinker claim as strong a voice in their suffrage, and sit to give judgement on the play's life and death, as well as the proudest *Momus* amoung the tribe of *Critics*.[49]

In using the wonderful image of the "Poet's Royal Exchange," Dekker summons up a picture of the theater as a marketplace of ideas, an environment in which the skills of value assessment were practiced by a wide swathe of the population. To use a different image, we might say that the early modern theater constituted a court of public opinion. But whether you prefer to look at it from the metaphorical perspective of economics or law, the core idea is the same: in early modern England, the theater was a site of intersection among professional and vernacular cultures of judgment.

The third and final assertion I wish to make about early modern judgment is that it was largely a *practical* activity. This should make sense by now since it is an insight that is closely bound up with the other two assertions I have made. Judgment was, to borrow Steven Shapin's evocative phrase, "embedded in streams of practical activity."[50] As we have seen, judgment was not understood to be a purely mental capacity or an exclusively cognitive event. Instead, judgment was something grounded in experience and applied knowledge. It was something you *do*; it involved interaction with the people and things of the world *out there*. If reason belongs to the mind – as a host of thinkers from Aristotle to Locke maintain that it does – then judgment belongs to the body, to what John Fortescue called *usage* in chapter 16 of *De Laudibus Legum Angliae* (c.1468–71), the most influential piece of legal and political theory in sixteenth-century England.[51] Usage, or experience, is the bedrock of judgment. English common law itself was based precisely on usage rather than on codes, and that is what made it distinctive. Laws were customary, and "a custom's goodness," as J. G. A. Pocock puts it, "is not its demonstrable rationality, but the simple fact of it having remained in usage."[52] "A custom," he continues,

> is a particular judgment to which so many men's experience testifies, and which has attained so high a degree of consistency under repeated tests over time, that the probability of its continuing to give satisfaction . . . is very high indeed.[53]

The nature of early modern English legal and political culture was such that judgment was viewed as a skill; it belonged to the collective world of craft, of trial and error, of lived experience. This was no less true of the more quotidian judgment of the shopkeeper at the Royal Exchange; the apothecary on Lime Street; and the playgoers at the Globe Theatre deciding when to clap and when to boo, and in some cases memorizing or writing down key phrases for subsequent transcription into their commonplace books.

This Book

Legal, political, and academic norms do not provide perfect analogies for what we see going on in the streets and theaters of early modern London. But for all the local differences among these various epistemological communities, there are certain things about the way judgment is understood and practiced within each of them that are the same across the board. These similarities – the fact that judgment was collective, the fact that judgment was participatory, and the fact that judgment was practical – are of paramount importance for this book. They allow us to recover a sense of judgment as something fundamentally theatrical in both a formal and conceptual sense, which should also alert us to the way actual theater can provide blueprints for collaborative, creative, worldmaking forms of judgment. The historical dimension of judgment, in other words, is important not so much to read Shakespeare back into an early modern context, but rather to understand the ethical genome that Shakespeare's plays were born with and which they carry forward as the seed of theatrical life in all subsequent eras, including our own. With this as a grounding critical and methodological insight, the chapters that follow will balance between historical and philosophical inquiry in order to pursue this book's central mission: the constitution of a new vocabulary of judgment assembled from the raw materials of Shakespeare's writing and dramaturgy. Towards this end, as I mentioned at the outset of this Introduction, each chapter is organized around a single keyword.

Chapter 1, "Feeling," sets the foundation for the rest of the book by establishing the body as a crucial site for discernment. This basic proposition is returned to again and again in the chapters that follow, in a variety of different ways and with a variety of different kinds of implications. Chapter 1's starting point for thinking about embodied judgment is act 3.4 of *Hamlet*, the closet

scene, in which Hamlet forces his mother to gaze on two portraits, one of her dead husband, Hamlet senior, the other of her
new husband, Claudius. With its sustained attention to perception
and emotion as the bedrock of moral evaluation, act 3.4 offers
fertile ground for an exploration of the way feeling and judging
existed in a close and mutually reinforcing relationship in the early
modern period. The chapter also shows that Shakespeare's feeling–judgment link is part of a much larger genealogy of thought
that runs from Aristotle to the eighteenth century, even if for most
of that time – and still in our own – it jostles with other models of
the judging self.

If judgment is a bodily experience, it necessarily inheres in the
material world. To put it another way, we could say that judgment
is a phenomenological, rather than a purely intellectual, process.
It starts with physical presence; intellection follows on from there.
This is one of the overarching claims of Chapter 2, "Objects."
How, the chapter asks, can real-world artifacts – the bodies and
things we encounter as we move through our lives – function in
the formation of moral knowledge? To help answer this question,
the chapter turns to act 3.2 of *Julius Caesar*, the "forum scene,"
in which Mark Antony addresses the plebeians in the wake of
Caesar's assassination, using the latter's bloody cloak as an object
lesson in civic and moral failure. This scene offers a compelling
case study in prudence, a practical and collaborative form of
judgment that would have been familiar to many early moderns
through the virtue tradition. Tracing how prudence works in a
variety of theatrical, legal, and broader public contexts, in both
Shakespeare's time and our own, the chapter shows how big questions of right and wrong, true and false, and good and bad are
often navigated in material and highly particularized terms, rather
than in the universalizing intellectual terms one might expect.

Chapter 3, "Vision," considers the role of seeing in judgment
and, as such, extends ideas presented in the previous two chapters.
Its main focus, however, is on a subject yet to be addressed in the
book: the way Shakespearean theater invites, indeed requires, a
particular kind of vision that cannot be fully explained by recourse
to any of the dominant intellectual accounts of sight available

in Shakespeare's time. In the course of exploring this topic, the chapter wanders through several well-known scenes of seeing and looking in Shakespeare's canon. Along the way, it maps out the complicated philosophical and intellectual historical landscape of early modern vision and shows the uneven and unpredictable ways in which Shakespeare's plays fit into it. The last scene of *Twelfth Night* eventually emerges as the chapter's central example of how we might think of the relationship between vision, judgment, and knowledge in non-objective, even irrational, terms. The theater, we discover, nurtures a form of visual discernment that depends more on wonder and faith than it does on evidence and fact. What makes this particular mode of judgment so important, the chapter suggests, is its special power to effect social transformation.

The idea of judgment being socially transformational becomes a touchstone, in one way or another, across the next three chapters. Chapter 4, "Making," shows that Prospero's epilogue in *The Tempest* participates not only in the theatrical convention of soliciting audience applause, but also in an intellectual tradition that views judgment and invention as closely related concepts. The rhetorical system at the heart of humanist education held that if you want to create something – whether it is material like a choreography, or discursive like a speech – you must first select the components (steps, movements, words, figures of speech, and so on) that are appropriate to the creation and to the context in which that creation is to function. This process of selecting is the domain of judgment, which could be thought of in this case as ends-oriented discernment conducted according to set criteria. Understanding this conceptual and practical link between judgment and invention is significant because it allows us to view the former as something generative and creative, rather than as something regulatory and punitive. Hannah Arendt was the first modern philosopher to discuss judgment explicitly in these terms and to argue accordingly for the social value of judging. Chapter 4 ultimately suggests that the theater is a place where the humanist and Arendtian accounts of judgment meet, and where the constructive, future-oriented work of judging can take place.

Chapter 5, "Facing," continues to examine judgment's future-oriented trajectory, this time with a particular focus on the way judging can make new forms of social life possible. Unlike the previous chapter, which concentrated on the conceptual foundations of the judgment–invention link, Chapter 5 zeroes in on the theatrical dynamics through which generative judgment takes place. At the center of this discussion is the actor's face and the phenomenon of *facing*. Facing is an action that is physical and dimensional, but also ethical in so far as it entails mutual recognition and acknowledgment. Taking act 5.1 of *Measure for Measure* as a case study, the chapter shows, first, how the collective presencing that facing makes possible is essential to adjudication in theatrical environments, and second, that the spatial and object-oriented grammar of the face invites us to think of judgment less as an individual decision or rational cognitive procedure and more as a material event that involves orientating oneself in space and time. Finally, Chapter 5 shows how putting facing at the center of an interactive choreography of deliberation in act 5.1 plays a key role in creating the preconditions for social change in the world of the play.

Chapter 6, "Community," turns to another play in which judgment creates the preconditions for social change, or perhaps more precisely, social renewal: *The Winter's Tale*. The particular goal of this chapter is to show how the community-making power of judgment is enhanced when it incorporates forgiveness into its procedural and ethical structure. The final scene of *The Winter's Tale* is especially remarkable for the way it provides baseline philosophical resources for a politics of atonement, a way of responding to criminal behavior in which judgment takes the form of a collective ritual of acknowledgment rather than a singular decision, and where the aim of adjudication is to rebuild the community rather than to punish specific persons. There are models for some aspects of this form of judgment within early modern legal culture. We find it, for example, in the principles underpinning the rise of the jury trial in England, in certain writings on the role of judges, and even in some practical guides to trial procedure, all of which are discussed in the chapter. But *The Winter's Tale* is also part of a larger, less historically localized story. The way in which the play articulates the relationship between judgment and forgiveness, and the communitarian ethics through which that relationship is framed, points us forward to the philosophy of Emmanuel Levinas and to more recent instances of atonement-based justice, such as the Truth and Reconciliation Commission in South Africa (1996) and the Good Friday Agreement in Northern Ireland (1998). These contexts, too, are addressed in Chapter 6.

Shakespeare's Theater of Judgment concludes with a Coda that reviews and reflects on the lexicon generated over the course of the preceding chapters. The purpose of doing so is not just to summarize, but also to consider two essential questions that are at the core of the book. First: What is it that this Shakespearean lexicon of judgment allows us to say, think, or imagine about judging? And second: Why does it matter?

I hope it goes without saying that in setting as this book's chief aim the formation of a new language of judgment, I do not literally take six words to constitute a language. What I mean by this claim is that Shakespeare's reflections on judgment take place within certain intellectual parameters, and if we can map this out by naming particular conceptual hubs, we will have a different kind of framework within which talking and thinking about judgment can take place. *Feeling, objects, vision, making, facing,* and *community* are "keywords" in Raymond Williams's sense of that term.[54] That is to say, they are not just individual units of speech, but also rubrics under which certain ideas about experience and sociality gather and certain material and intellectual histories intersect. They are also profoundly connected to one another: sensation, embeddedness, collectivity, and motion form the phenomenological deep-structure that holds these keywords together. This is an inherently theatrical constellation of ideas; together they denote the foundational conditions that make theatrical experience possible. Accordingly, what I hope readers will take away from this book – what I hope this language of judgment will enable them more easily to articulate – is the way in which judgment is, or at least can be, a collaborative and forward-looking act of social creation; and the way theater offers a particularly powerful locale for cultivating it.

CHAPTER 1

FEELING

What does it feel like to judge? This probably sounds like an odd question since we do not typically think of judgment as a sensory experience. Judging is something we do with our minds, not our bodies. We also tend not to think of judgment as an emotional experience. Indeed, most would say that sound judgment is exercised when reason overrides the distorting effects of passion. One of the surest ways for one side of a political debate to shut down the other is to say something along the lines of, "I think we're all getting a bit emotional." This rhetorical maneuver works to discredit important aspects of participatory political culture such as protest and other forms of direct action, which, unlike the anonymous, mechanical, and bureaucratic experience of modern voting, are affective and demonstrative. This maneuver rests not just on the idea that judgment is an essential component of responsible democracy, but also, and crucially, on the idea that judgment should be analytic and disinterested – more computational than emotional.

It is not surprising, then, that we find charges of emotionalism – and therefore of questionable judgment – being leveled most frequently in political contexts where individuals undergo considerable personal distress: abortion rights and questions of bodily sovereignty; harassment and abuse legislation as it relates to issues of consent; immigration policy as it impacts at-risk populations, especially children; and the relationship between environmental protection and public health. These are inherently emotional subjects since they cut to the core of basic questions about human dignity, and in some cases life and death. Part of the reason so much public engagement around these topics takes place in the form of direct action is because it has proven difficult for proponents of reform to reconcile their understandably urgent and emotional positions with a post-Enlightenment political culture that connects responsible decision-making to reason. Reason is of the mind, not the body, and judgment is rational. From this perspective, the question "what does it feel like to judge?" would be met with a haughty cock of the eyebrow and a quick corrective: It doesn't feel like anything. If you're feeling something, it's not judgment.

My aim in this chapter is to overturn this assumption, and I will be enlisting *Hamlet* to help me do so. The play's title character is a perfect guide for this undertaking since he is marked by a special capacity to feel things intensely, an insight that finds its point of origin in the eighteenth century when writers like Johann Wolfgang von Goethe and Henry MacKenzie started describing Hamlet as a *man of feeling*.[1] As Robin Headlam-Wells puts it, "the age of sensibility invented a new Hamlet – sensitive, delicate, distressed."[2] My purpose in returning to this idea is not to resurrect an old-fashioned reading of the play, but rather to think more carefully about what being a man of feeling might mean, in both Shakespeare's world and our own. Feeling, or *sentiment*, was at the time Goethe and MacKenzie were writing closely linked to judgment. It was premised on a specific kind of relationship between the experience of the body and critical participation in the world. We find this linkage articulated with particular force in the sentimental philosophy of David Hume and Adam Smith, which I will return to towards the end of this chapter. What I want to insist on now is the simple but crucial idea that understanding Hamlet as a man of feeling means seeing him as someone for whom sensation and emotion are connected to active adjudication, not to vulnerability or stagnation. In this chapter, Hamlet will help us recover a specifically early modern way of understanding the link between feeling and judging, which we will then be able to situate in a larger genealogy of thought that runs from Aristotle to the eighteenth century. Hamlet will serve as a guide whose particular way of going about the business of adjudication offers us an opportunity to retell the story of modern judgment in a new way. The endgame of this retelling is to begin laying the groundwork for an ethics of collectivity in which judgment – and in particular *theatrical* judgment – plays a key role, an undertaking which will continue to gain momentum across the entirety of the book.

Hamlet's Unreasonable Judgment

Unlike Thinking Hamlet, Feeling Hamlet seems to have fallen between the cracks of modern critical debate. On one hand, there is a tradition associated most closely with Samuel Taylor Coleridge and, later, Harold Bloom which views Hamlet as "The Western hero of consciousness."[3] This is Hamlet the thinker; Hamlet who is a harbinger of modern literary subjectivity and who arrives on the scene with a fully formed inner life. John Lee, for instance, attributes to Hamlet a "self-constituting sense of self," contending that "this sense of self is central to his tragedy," while Marjorie Garber refers to Hamlet as "the premiere Western performance of consciousness."[4] On the other hand, there is the seminal work of Margreta de Grazia which shows how "Hamlet's deep and complex inwardness was not perceived as the play's salient feature until around 1800."[5] Instead, in its own time, and for a good while after, the central theme of *Hamlet* would have been the breakdown of the patrilineal system through the dispossession of a king's only son. *Hamlet*, in other words, is first and foremost a political play, one chiefly concerned with questions of lineage, land, and genealogy. To the extent that Hamlet the character offered particular theatrical pleasures, early sources tell us that this had more to do with his physical intensity – his "antic disposition" – than with verbal disclosures about a putative inner life.

Somewhere between these two Hamlets – the rowdy clown of the Renaissance and the introspective thinker of post-Enlightenment modernity – is the Feeling Hamlet of the eighteenth century. Hamlet feels things with particular intensity – fear, anger, disgust, sorrow – and the theatrical pay-off, so the argument runs, is that he makes audience members feel things intensely as a result. In a 1780 issue of *The Mirror*, Henry MacKenzie describes how Hamlet inspires a unique level of affection in spectators. "We see a man," MacKenzie writes,

> who in other circumstances would have exercised all the moral and social virtues, placed in a situation in which even the amiable qualities of his mind serve but to aggravate his distress and to perplex his conduct. Our compassion for the first, and our anxiety for the latter, are excited in the strongest manner.[6]

MacKenzie's vocabulary of aggravation, distress, anxiety, and excitement points to bodily experience as the grounds for emotional empathy. This would have been amplified in performance through techniques that externalized and exaggerated Hamlet's feelings in ways that audiences could easily grasp. David Garrick, for instance, was famous for the gestures, props, and stage business he would employ to heighten emotionality, including a specially made wig that made it look like his hair was standing on end when he spoke to the ghost of his father. Both Garrick and Thomas Betterton also employed the trick of having a chair suddenly fall over when the ghost entered Gertrude's chamber, an effect that underlined and materialized Hamlet's shock.[7]

For our purposes, though, the most important thing about Hamlet's feelingness is the way it accommodates a facility for good judgment, and it is to this specific link that I would like to turn now. The key moment to consider is act 3.4, the "closet scene." Hamlet impulsively kills a snooping Polonius and proceeds to confront his mother about marrying his uncle so soon after his father's death. The latter passage is structured around a comparison of two pictures, one of Hamlet Senior, the other of Claudius. In the seventeenth century, portrait miniatures would most likely have been used, though Restoration performances established a parallel tradition of using full-size paintings hanging on the wall. In either case, this is a scene that essentially stages *looking*, and more specifically stages the connection between vision and discernment, a topic I will continue to explore in the next two chapters. Hamlet asks his mother to "Look here upon this picture, and on this, / The

counterfeit presentment of two brothers" (3.4.53–54).[8] He starts
by presenting his father:

> See what a grace was seated on this brow,
> Hyperion's curls, the front of Jove himself,
> An eye like Mars to threaten and command,
> A station like the herald Mercury
> New-lighted on a heaven-kissing hill,
> A combination and a form indeed
> Where every god did seem to set his seal
> To give the world assurance of a man;
> This was your husband. (3.4.53–61)

Hamlet then presents Claudius:

>   Look you now what follows:
> Here is your husband, like a mildewed ear
> Blasting his wholesome brother. Have you eyes?
> Could you on this fair mountain leave to feed
> And batten on this moor? Ha, Have you eyes? (3.4.61–65)

What is notably missing from this passage is an appeal to reason.
Interpretation and moral choice are, instead, securely anchored to
the body and its methods of gathering information. Gertrude is
impelled to "see" and to "look" – for this, according to Hamlet, is
how one discerns between "Jove" and "a mildewed ear." Twice he
demands of his mother, "Have you eyes?" The connection between
sensation and judgment becomes more explicit as the passage
progresses:

>   What judgment
> Would step from this to this? Sense, sure, you have –
> Else could you not have motion. But sure, that sense
> Is apoplexed, for madness would not err
> Nor sense to ecstasy was ne'er so thralled
> But it reserved some quantity of choice
> To serve in such a difference. What devil was't
> That thus hath cozened you at hoodman-blind?
> Eyes without feeling, feeling without sight,
> Ears without hands or eyes, smelling sans all,

Or but a sickly part of one true sense
Could not so mope. (3.4.68–79)

It is not a lack of reason or any other higher, disembodied faculty
that has led to Gertrude's misjudgment. It is the fact that "*sense /
Is apoplexed*" (emphasis added). Nor are we to understand that
term "sense" as equivalent to the modern "common sense," a kind
of foundational, self-evident logic. On the contrary, the metaphor
of blindfolding – "What devil was't / That hath cozened you at
hoodman-blind?" – reinforces the physiological valence of the
word. Judgment is a species of spectatorship in Hamlet's speech.
Had the Queen been able to see, she would have been able to
judge. This sort of judgment – good judgment – involves a clear
alignment of perception and emotion. Bad judgment, on the other
hand – Gertrude's judgment – is associated with the misalignment
of these two things: "Eyes without feeling, feeling without sight."
The closet scene places moral decision at the crossroads of sensation
and emotion. It impels Gertrude, along with all the spectators in the
theater who are gazing on with her, to look hard, not with the inner
eye of the soul or the mind, but with the outer eye of the body.

Judging with the Body

Where does this conception of physiologically based discernment
come from? Early modern England possessed a pluralistic notion
of what judgment was and how it worked. The Greek equivalent
for the Latin word *iudicare* (to judge) is *krinein*, meaning to distinguish, discriminate, or, more mechanically, to separate or to select.
This sense is preserved within the early modern rhetorical tradition,
which I will discuss in more detail in subsequent chapters. Running
through the closet scene, however, is a different strand of the intellectual history of judgment, one that has less to do with rhetoric
and more to do with faculty psychology, though both traditions can
ultimately be traced back to Aristotle. In the *Nicomachean Ethics*,
Aristotle observed that ethical behavior "is not easy to determine
by reasoning, any more than anything else that is perceived by the
senses; such things depend on particular facts, and the decision

rests with perception."[9] This observation laid the foundation for a tradition of thought concerned with pre-rational sensate judgment, which influenced writers in the Middle Ages and the early modern period, as well as eighteenth-century theorists of aesthetics. Within this account, judgment was understood to be a faculty that functioned by relating sensible particulars (that is, specific things that we see, hear, and feel) to intelligible universals (that is, broadly applicable notions of good and bad, right and wrong).[10]

Early modern faculty psychology inherited two distinct versions of this Aristotelian scheme. One, closely anchored to Aristotle's own writings, viewed judgment as, in the first place, a collaboration among the senses which over time generates universal principles, or what we now might call "standards of judgment." As Aristotle put it in *On the Soul*, the animal soul – the site of sensory knowledge and the aspect of our being that we share with other nonhuman creatures – is not just the faculty that generates movement, it is also the source of our "capacity to judge, which is the function of thought and perception." "Each sense," he writes, "judges the specific differences of its own sensible object . . . Sight produces upon white and black, taste upon sweet and bitter, and so with the rest."[11]

In the sixteenth century, we find some English scholars rehearsing this account of the relationship between judgment and sensation. Abraham Fraunce, for example, writes in *The Lawyers Logike* (1588):

> For as Aristotle teacheth in the second of his demonstrations, every sensible creature hath a naturall power and facultie of judging, which is called sence; & this sence (2. Topic) is of him sayde to bee a certayne kinde of judgement: and without doubt, the sence is a most upright judge of suche thinges as are properly under his jurisdiction, as the sight of colours, the hearing of soundes, the smelling of smelles (4. Metap)[12]

For Fraunce, following Aristotle, judgment is common to "every sensible creature" because sensation performs a "certayne kinde of judgement." At the heart of this argument is the idea that how you *feel* bears directly on how you discern and, eventually, on how you act. Taken to its logical conclusion, it is an argument that accommodates the notion of passion leading, ultimately, to moral action. This is noteworthy because it runs counter to the mainstream of more than one powerful tradition of thought in the early modern period, including Calvinism, which generally urges the repression of passion, and Stoicism, which generally sees inner virtue rather than sensation or emotion as the source of moral action.[13] As Timothy Hampton has shown, even Montaigne, a writer strongly influenced by Cicero and Seneca, acknowledged in essays like "De l'inconstance de nos actions" and "Apologie de Raymond Sebond" that there were limitations to the Stoic ideal of inner virtue over passion and that direct bodily experience – being disgusted by something you witness or being aroused by a speech, for example – could impel a kind of *applied* virtue (one version of which, prudence, we will explore in detail in the next chapter).[14] This, certainly, is what Hamlet has in mind in act 3.4 when he urges his mother to *see* right, to *feel* right, to *judge* right, and finally, therefore, to *act* right: "Confess yourself to heaven, / Repent what's past, avoid what is to come" (3.4.147–48) and "Not this, by no means, that I bid you – / Let the bloat King tempt you again to bed" (3.4.179–80).

Other writers in early modern England take a very different approach to judgment, describing it as precisely the thing that distinguishes humans from animals. These writers view judgment as an expression of reason, and therefore as a component of Aristotle's uniquely human rational soul, rather than as an expression of feeling, which falls under the purview of the animal soul. According to this model, emotion – conceived of in pointedly physiological terms as "passions" – *impedes* judgment. Thomas Wright explains it like this in *Passions of the Minde* (1601):

> Those actions then which are common with us, and the beasts, we cal Passions, and Affections, or perturbances of the mind . . . They are called Passions (although indeed they be acts of the sensitive power, or faculties of our soul . . .) because when these affections are stirring in our minds, they alter the humours of our bodies, causing some passion or alteration in them. They are called perturbations, for that . . . they trouble wonderfully the soule, corrupting the judgment, & seducing the will . . .[15]

Similarly, Philippe de Mornay in *The True Knowledge of a Man's Owne Selfe* (1602) instructs that "The knowledge of a mans owne selfe, availeth, not onely for preservations of the bodies health, but likewise to moderate the vehemcie of inordinate affections, which hinder and impeach the health of judgment."[16] Wright and Mornay, characterizing judgment as rational and practical and opposed to the operations of the body, are reduplicating a version of the Aristotelian scheme that had been influenced by Platonism, one in which the idea of knowledge and judgment accruing directly from physical contact with the real world was replaced by the idea that knowledge and judgment passed through a hierarchy of faculties. This hierarchy may start with sensation, but it ends with reason.

Boethius, for instance, saw judgment as the result of information ascending through increasingly higher faculties, from sense to imagination to reason. All three faculties were involved in the process, but a judgment that resulted from sense alone would hardly ever be the same – and certainly would not be as reliable – as a judgment that benefitted from the application of reason. This is because, in this model, each faculty has the capacity not only to judge the issue or thing at hand, but also to judge the judgment of the faculty just below it in the hierarchy. Imagination keeps a check on sensation and reason keeps a check on both sensation and imagination. To form a judgment based on feeling alone would, within Boethius's thinking, amount to a blatant disavowal of the rational soul – and to that extent it would, in a sense, be inhuman.[17] Bonaventure proposes a similar scheme. In his *Journey of the Mind to God* (1259), he writes, "the reception of the species depends upon the body, but judgment depends upon the sensible virtue."[18] What he means is that while we must of course see with our real material eyes, evaluative knowledge results from the *soul* working *through* the material sense organs. The body undergoes the action of external objects and the soul reacts. It is this reaction that is judgment.

In the genealogy of thought represented by Boethius, Bonaventure, Wright, and Mornay, Aristotle's materialist definition of sensation, represented most famously by his metaphor of wax impressed by a signet ring, is replaced by a definition of sensation that ultimately serves some kind of disembodied inner vision, the vision of the soul or the mind.[19] Judgment was readily adapted to this model and this version of judgment was to have a long life. Its most canonical iteration in the early modern period comes from John Locke, who cordoned off judgment, and the mind in general, from the passions and the senses. In *An Essay Concerning Human Understanding* (1689), Locke describes how the mind is enclosed within the body, but nevertheless distinct from it since it occupies the role of owner and caretaker of the total self. As a property of the mind, judgment within Locke's scheme is not beholden to bodily experience. He calls judgment a "faculty of the mind" and explains that "the ideas we receive by sensation are often . . . altered by the judgment."[20] Indeed, if we do not "alter" our sensation with reason, we risk judging wrong. "Wrong judgment," Locke writes, is "most commonly" caused by

> The prevalency of some present pleasure or pain, heightened by our feeble passionate nature, most strongly wrought on by what is present. To check this precipitancy, our understanding and reason was given us, if we will make a right use of it, to search, and see, and then judge thereupon.[21]

We can see that for Locke, judgment is a form of practical knowledge within the mind, one that employs particular methods of evaluation. To this extent, judgment, or what would later be called "taste," can even be improved through education, discipline, and training. "Men may and should correct their palates," Locke insists, "and give a relish to what either has, or they suppose has none. The relish of the mind, is as various as that of the body, and like that too may be altered."[22] By putting judgment in the mind and by putting the mind in control, Locke effectively removes the problem of determinism from individual decision-making. This is exactly what his theory of government, and our own ongoing tradition of liberal thought, requires: a subject capable of voluntarily submitting to government and of choosing to conduct themselves according to both their own rights and the rights of others.

Of course, Hamlet does not ask Gertrude to think with the mind. He asks her to see with the body. And in this respect, the closet scene belongs very much to the materialist Aristotelian tradition voiced in vernacular terms by writers such as Fraunce. Hamlet's judgment – sensory, bodily, emotional, unreasonable – is on display elsewhere in the play too. Consider the Mousetrap episode. Hamlet, we will recall, asks a visiting acting troupe to perform the play *The Murder of Gonzago* for guests who will include Claudius and Gertrude. The players agree to let Hamlet interpolate a scene which stages a murder almost identical to the one the ghost accused Claudius of committing. Hamlet dubs this revised version of the play "The Mouse-trap" (3.2.237). His idea is to turn theater into a legal instrument, a living technology of judgment. He recalls that sometimes,

> guilty creatures sitting at a play
> Have by the very cunning of the scene
> Been struck so to the soul, that presently
> They have proclaim'd their malefactions: (2.2.588–92)

As this indicates, the theatrical event is not simply an object of judgment (like the poem that Polonius finds in act 2 or the portraits that Hamlet shows the Queen), but also the conditions under which judgment occurs. That is, the play serves as a catalyst for quasi-legal judgment *among* members of the audience. Thus Hamlet prepares Horatio shortly before "The Mouse-trap" begins with, "*Observe* my uncle . . . And after we will both our judgments join / To censure of his seeming" (3.2.80, 86–87; emphasis added).

Theater and judgment share the same core ingredients in the Mousetrap episode: the same physical setting, the same occasion, the same ensemble of people. They also share a common sensory environment, an elemental requirement that people hear, see, feel, and think together. Hamlet reaches his final verdict through a process of collaborative perception:

HAMLET:	O good Horatio, I'll take the ghost's word for a thousand pound. Didst *perceive*?
HORATIO:	Very well, my lord.
HAMLET:	Upon the talk of the pois'ning?
HORATIO:	I did very well *note* him. (3.2.286–90; emphasis added)

Spoken to Hamlet alone, "the ghost's word" requires the corrob-
oration of seeing collectively ("*Observe* my uncle"; "Didst *perceive?*"; "I did very well *note* him"). It has often been remarked
that perception, especially collective seeing, is central to theatrical
experience, that the Greek word *theatron*, for example, meant literally a "place of seeing." The first occurrence of the word "theatre"
in English, in a Wycliffite Bible manuscript of 1382, carries the
gloss a "commune biholdying place."[23] In the Mousetrap episode,
not only is collective seeing an essential component of theatricality,
it is also the source of legal knowledge and the basis for judgment.

It goes without saying that no English jurist would have recognized in the event Hamlet organizes anything concretely analogous
to the procedures of a common law courtroom. But the episode is
nevertheless consistent with a way of viewing legal judgment that
is unique to early modernity and which was, moreover, influenced
by the same sort of Aristotelian materialism that I have discussed
in relation to the closet scene.[24] In his landmark legal treatise *De
Laudibus Legum Angliae* (c.1468–71), John Fortescue comments
on the core maxims from which legal knowledge is acquired and
judgment is enabled. He insists that the maxims of the laws of
England – like the maxims in mathematics or the paradoxes in
rhetoric – form the "universal, self-evident, and undemonstrable"
principles on which that particular system of knowledge rests. He
insists, moreover, that these maxims are acquired and put into use
"by induction through the senses and the memory" and "are not
known by force of argument or by logical demonstrations." In
fact, Fortescue continues, "there is no rational ground for principles . . . any principle is its own ground for holding it."[25]

In linking legal knowledge and legal judgment to the senses
rather than reason, Fortescue is following the basic tenets of Aristotelian philosophy, and in spots he is even quoting directly from the
medieval texts of Aristotle. Crucial to Fortescue's assertion is the
rule that the faculty of reason only pertains to deductive thought –
the drawing of particular inferences from general principles. But
the maxims of English law, according to Fortescue, are principles
in themselves. And even when judgments are made based on them,
those judgments are not technically deductions. As I noted in

the Introduction, the term Fortescue uses instead for this sort of applied legal knowledge is *usage*. Usage was a very important concept within sixteenth- and seventeenth-century legal theory because it did what neither reason nor logic could do: it legitimated English common law. Here are Fortescue's thoughts on the matter:

> we must examine what are the customs, and also the statutes, of England, and we will first look at the characteristics of those customs.
>
> [XVII] The kingdom of England was first inhabited by Britons, then ruled by Romans, again by Britons, then possessed by Saxons, but finally by Normans, whose posterity hold the realm at the present time. And throughout the period of these nations and their kings, the realm has been continuously ruled by the same customs as it is now, customs which, if they had not been the best, some of those kings would have changed for the sake of justice or by the impulse of caprice, and totally abolished them, especially the Romans, who judged almost the whole of the rest of the world by their laws. Similarly, others of these aforesaid kings who possessed the kingdom of England only by the sword, could, by that power have destroyed its laws. Indeed, neither the civil laws of the Romans, so deeply rooted by the usage of so many ages, nor the laws of the Venetians, which are renowned above others for their antiquity . . . nor the laws of any Christian kingdom, are so rooted in antiquity. Here there is no gainsaying nor legitimate doubt but that the customs of the English are not only good but the best.[26]

Fortescue's concluding mic drop – "the customs of the English are not only good but the best" – feels slightly out of proportion to the rather simple argument that leads to it: old laws are better laws, and since English law is the oldest, it is the best. There is no importance whatsoever given to logic; lines of defense grounded in rationality are completely elided. Reason is neither a source of English law's authority nor a principle of its operation. Authority lies, instead, in the duration and breadth of collective participation in regulatory and organizational principles which are, appropriately, referred to as "customs." In J. G. A. Pocock's words, "the particular laws of particular nations are legitimized by reference not to reason and the knowledge of universals, but to antiquity and usage."[27] Within the English legal imagination, then, judgment does not issue from logic-based forms of intellection, but rather from experience, a crucial distinction in English legal and political theory.[28] Experience is a form of knowing that extends through time and does not belong to any one person. Judgment can thus be thought of as a sort of collation of repeated use-events poised on the cusp between past and present, and managing the relationship between the two. Edward Coke would later describe this kind of discernment as "artificial reason" in his influential case report *Prohibitions del Roy* (1607).[29] True to its name, artificial reason – unlike regular reason – is *artifactual*. It belongs not to abstract universal principles living in the mind, but instead to the material, technical, and relational world of trial and error, action and consequence.

To be clear, there is no direct intellectual-historical line of transmission that can be drawn between *all* the figures and texts I have mentioned above. Shakespeare, Fortescue, Fraunce, Wright, and Mornay work in different forms, in different professional contexts, and with different publics in mind. What they nevertheless all have in common is a generally Aristotelian understanding of the processes and conditions through which judgment takes place. Some of these figures were clearly working directly with Aristotle's texts; Shakespeare was not (at least it is highly unlikely). Shakespeare's plays live in a largely vernacular, rather than academic, intellectual culture, and his ideas about the physical and collective nature of discernment and moral decision could just as easily have derived from the material conditions of theater itself. Most important for our purposes is simply to observe that *Hamlet* iterates in theatrical terms a key insight that we can find scattered across a wide range of intellectual texts, both specialized and popular, in the sixteenth and early seventeenth centuries: the idea that judgment, far from being a product of individual thought, is a product of collective experience – sensory and historical, in the body and in time.

Materiality, Sentiment, and Collectivity

With this context in place, a picture begins to emerge of *Hamlet*'s position among the various genealogies of modernity. We do not find the play where it has often been located, on the path to individuality and interiority. One source for this critical narrative, as I have already discussed, is Coleridge whose ideas have been taken up, consciously or unconsciously, by a wide variety of modern scholars, including Bloom, Garber, and Lee. Another, overlapping, point of origin could be located with G. W. F. Hegel and, later, Jacob Burckhardt, both of whom positioned Shakespeare at the center of what they viewed as epochal historical shifts towards autonomous subjectivity.[30] A. C. Bradley's seminal mid-twentieth-century study of Shakespearean tragedy ushered Hegel's and Burckhardt's ideas securely into the realm of English literary studies.[31] When Stephen Greenblatt wrote, now famously, in 1980, "My starting point is quite simply that in the sixteenth century there were both selves and a sense that they could be fashioned," he was working within an identifiably Hegelian–Burckhardtian–Bradleyan tradition – though he was of course doing so at a high level of intellectual innovation.[32] Decades later, the same premise would underpin Greenblatt's book *Shakespeare's Freedom*, especially the final chapter on "Shakespearean Autonomy."[33] That same year, 2010, Peter Holbrook's *Shakespeare's Individualism* made the case that Shakespeare is "an author for a liberal individualistic culture."[34] Central to Holbrook's argument is an interpretation of *Hamlet* that builds on Søren Kierkegaard and Martin Heidegger, both of whom viewed the eponymous prince as a figure of alienation and radical autonomy.[35] Hamlet, Holbrook asserts, "holds himself back from the world"; his appeal lies precisely in his "aggressive singularity."[36]

It would be incorrect, I think, to say that Shakespeare was not interested in what we now understand as individuality. Holbrook's book is a tour de force of intellectual history, philosophy, and sensitive literary analysis, and it is fully persuasive within the terms of inquiry it sets for itself. The studies I have mentioned by Hegel, Burckhardt, Bradley, and Greenblatt, moreover, are among the most influential works of humanities scholarship for good reason. But what the ideas outlined so far in this chapter have shown is that judgment forms a horizon beyond which arguments that align Shakespeare with individuality, interiority, and philosophical liberalism cease to make sense. Judgment requires engagement with the world; holding back, to borrow Holbrook's phrase, is not an option. To judge is to participate, which means finding a middle ground between autonomy and dependency, speaking and listening. By staging scenes of judgment in *Hamlet*, Shakespeare offers a series of case studies in the sociality of thinking and the intersubjective grounds of moral agency. When looked at from the perspective of Aristotelian judgment, *Hamlet* stands outside the geography of individuality and interiority, inhabiting instead a terrain where discernment, responsibility, and action cohabit with sensation, emotion, and collectivity.

As this suggests, Hamlet's unreasonable judgments have little to do with Locke and his intellectual inheritors. They do, however, speak compellingly to another strand of Enlightenment thought: that represented by philosophers David Hume and Adam Smith and novelists Henry MacKenzie and Samuel Richardson, and usually referred to collectively as sentimentalism.[37] Indeed, the scenes of discernment in *Hamlet* could be thought of as offering a conceptual bridge between the Aristotelianism of early modernity and the sentimentalism of the Enlightenment. This is one respect in which these scenes invite us to tell the story of modern judgment in a new way. Sentimentalism distinguished itself from other paradigms of Enlightenment liberalism by entwining judgment and feeling. In Hina Nazar's words, "judgment emerges under sentimentalism as a worldly and contingent process, one that is inextricably tied to feelings and sociability."[38] It is noteworthy that eighteenth-century dictionaries regularly list "opinion," "thought," and "judgment," as terms cognate with "sentiment." In Hume's *Treatise of Human Nature* (1738), feeling is described as intrinsic to the process of moral and aesthetic deliberation:

> An action, or sentiment, or character is virtuous or vicious; why? Because its view causes a pleasure or uneasiness of a particular kind . . . To have the sense of virtue, is nothing but to *feel* a satisfaction of a very particular kind from the contemplation of a character. The very *feeling* constitutes our praise or admiration . . . The case is the same as in our judgments concerning all kinds of beauty, and tastes, and sensations.[39]

There are two meanings of "sense" activated in Hume's "sense of virtue": *to know* and *to feel*. We *know* things are right or wrong because they *feel* good or bad. He says pointedly in Book 3 of the treatise that morality is always a "matter of feeling." We will recognize this by now as the same broadly materialist, broadly Aristotelian principle from which Hamlet works in the closet scene when he concludes that his mother judged incorrectly because she judged "without feeling."

If judgment is linked to sensation and emotion, it is also, by definition, something that takes place with others – not in the mind's isolation, but in the shared space of the body. The most famous formulation of this idea remains Immanuel Kant's in the *Critique of Judgment* (1790). His *sensus communis*, or "enlarged mentality," refers to a form of decision-making based on a combination of one's own intuitions and the range of other possible intuitions held by those with whom you share a particular space or community. He describes it as "a power to judge that . . . takes account (a priori), in our thought, of everyone else's way of presenting [something], in order as it were to compare our own judgment with human reason in general."[40] In the formation of taste, Kant argued, there is always this projected feeling together. It would await Hannah Arendt in the twentieth century to develop Kant's ideas about aesthetics into a fully realized political theory of judgment.[41] But the basic notion that *feeling together* was at the heart not just of judgments of taste, but also of moral judgment, was already being posited by the sentimentalists. Adam Smith, for example, argues that moral and aesthetic concepts exist only in relational terms, between and among sensate beings living together:

> Were it possible that a human creature could grow up to manhood in some solitary place, without any communication with his own species, he could no more think of his own character, of the propriety or demerit of his own mind, than of the beauty or deformity of his own face. All these objects which he cannot easily see, which naturally he does look at, and with regard to which he is provided with no mirror which can present them to his view. Bring him into society, and he is immediately provided with the mirror which he wanted before . . . It is here that he first views the

propriety and impropriety of his own passions, the beauty and deformity of his own mind. To a man who from his birth was a stranger to society, the objects of his passions, the external bodies which either pleased or hurt him, would occupy his whole attention. The passions themselves, the desires or aversions, the joys or sorrows, which those objects excited, though of all things the most immediately present to him, could scarce ever be the objects of his thought.[42]

The most significant part of this quotation comes towards the end. Outside of a social context, an individual can only experience a raw confrontation with the artifacts of the world. Under such conditions, the feelings those objects trigger are entirely unintelligible, and so judgment is impossible. It is only through "the mirror" of others that "the propriety and impropriety of his own passions, the beauty and deformity of his own mind" become coherent and cognizable. Value, in other words, is emotional before it is rational, and it can never be generated in a vacuum. It is a function of collectivity. Smith's ideas would have made sense to Hamlet. His Mousetrap scheme is, as we have seen, very much *sensus communis* in action, with deliberation and condemnation accruing from Hamlet and Horatio's shared experiences of perception: "*Observe* my uncle"; "Didst *perceive*?"; "I did very well *note* him." Judgment in this scheme has very little to do with thinking to oneself; it is a process centered primarily on feeling with others.

My aim, to be clear, is not to make the Enlightenment beholden to early modernity, or Hume and Smith beholden to Shakespeare, or all three beholden to Aristotle. Who-thought-it-first is of minimal importance to me. Instead, my goal here has been to use *Hamlet* as a starting point for thinking about the history and theory of judgment not so much as a straight line of development, but rather as an evolving constellation of ideas in which sense and emotion move in and out of view. *Hamlet* helps us see this kaleidoscopic process in action by staging scenes of judgment that point us both backward and forward, curating a set of conceptual links between Aristotelian materialism, early modern faculty psychology, and a particular strain of eighteenth-century liberalism. What it leaves us with finally is a set of historical and philosophical coordinates that can help us reframe judgment, not as something that is mine not yours, but rather as a form of collective participation in the-world-out-there, a way of feeling with others, and of translating common experience into action.

This way of thinking about judgment comprises a conceptual and ethical foundation for the rest of this book, with each chapter adding a new keyword that enables us to better speak and think about judgment in material, social, and creative terms. Once we locate judgment in the body, once we recognize sensation as a deliberative experience, and once we understand this deliberative experience as relational and transactional, an ethical blueprint begins to emerge from which a more detailed account of judging as a form of positive, participatory intervention in our shared world can begin to be assembled. In establishing judgment as *un*reasonable, as something that can be done *feelingly*, we align it with phenomenology rather than ontology. Judgment is phenomenological because, as we have seen, it emerges interactively from a larger sensory environment and because it functions as part of a material ecology that includes but also exceeds the individual body.[43] These are the terms in which theater, another intrinsically phenomenological practice, works as well. Both material, both interactive, and both rooted in sensation, judgment produces knowledge in much the same way that theater makes meaning: through the dynamic and sensorial interplay of people and things in a certain time and place. This – the theatricality of judgment, the deliberative affordances of theater – is an idea to which I will be returning regularly in the subsequent chapters. It is of crucial importance for the book's larger ethical project; for if we recognize that judgment is something physical and collective, we have the basic conceptual infrastructure in place to begin freeing it from common contemporary associations with things like subjective bias and personal opinion, or condemnation and blame. Only then can we begin to recover judgment as a positive social and political virtue, and to recognize theater as a vital site for its cultivation.

CHAPTER 2

OBJECTS

The previous chapter showed how we might conceive of judgment as having a physical as well as a rational vector. To judge *feelingly* requires a sensory encounter with the material world and a willingness to trust the body as a source of knowledge. This chapter builds on these discussions by zeroing in on *objects*. Objects have the ability to stand in as a kind of artifactual shorthand for an issue, a question, or an occurrence, and as such form a heuristically potent interface between self and world. Think of Desdemona's handkerchief (which we will return to in Chapter 3) that signifies histories of love and lust, faithfulness and betrayal. Or consider how within Christian devotional contexts the piece of fruit, often thought of as an apple, evokes variously the fall of Man, temptation and sin, the loss of innocence, and the problem of knowledge. Much more than simply symbols, objects of this sort are vectors of interpretation, material anchors for hermeneutic events. The handkerchief and the fruit are questions-made-flesh: Is my wife unfaithful? Is to know evil to sin? This special capacity of objects within the phenomenology of judgment and knowledge becomes especially vivid in formal institutional contexts, such as courtroom proceedings, where the evaluation of material evidence is required to establish a verdict. But in all such cases, whether fictional or real, institutional or informal, we see the same basic phenomenology at play: assessment is necessarily preceded by a sensory encounter with an object. A dagger with blood on it, a gun with fingerprints, a glove that will not fit, a strange mole on the body, a cloak full of holes: first there is the object, then sense perception, and finally the emotional effect that forms the bedrock of an evaluative response.

There are a variety of cultural and intellectual contexts that can help us make sense of object-oriented deliberation. For many readers, no doubt, the term "object-oriented" itself will immediately evoke a certain strand of twentieth- and twenty-first-century philosophy and theory that works in a broadly materialist vein ("materialist" in an Aristotelian and/or Spinozistic sense, more so than in a Marxian sense). I should clarify from the outset that I do not place Graham Harman's "object-oriented ontology" (or OOO) within this lineage, despite the clear verbal echo between this school of thought and my stated interests (and I am sure Harman would agree). Despite the suggestion of the first two Os, the operative term in OOO is "ontology." Though it is concerned with objects, OOO is neither materialist nor phenomenological in any recognizable sense. On the contrary, it offers a new metaphysics which purports to encompass a "theory of everything."[1] More relevant is recent work by Jane Bennett which has explored the ethical and political implications of recovering "a vital materiality" which does away with the artificial partition between lively beings and inert objects.[2] Bennett adopts Bruno Latour's term "actant" to describe any form of matter, human or nonhuman, which is "a source of action . . . which has *efficacy*, can *do* things, has sufficient coherence to make a difference, produce effects, alter the course of events."[3] Bennett's project, as she points out, draws on an established philosophical tradition of theorizing what she calls "vibrant matter," which includes, in addition to Latour, writings by Baruch Spinoza, Friedrich Nietzsche, Henry David Thoreau, Charles Darwin, Theodor Adorno, Henri Bergson, John Dewey, A. N. Whitehead, and Gilles Deleuze and Félix Guattari, the latter of whom coined the closely related term "material vitalism" to model a concept similar to Bennett's.[4]

The work undertaken in this chapter is certainly materialist in general orientation – as is the book as a whole – and I will have occasion to cite both Bennett and Deleuze and Guattari again in subsequent pages. But I am also very much concerned with a rhetorical tradition that understands objects, language, action, and

deliberative thought to circle around each other in complex config-
urations, and which plays little if any role in the work of Bennett,
her "new materialist" colleagues, and her intellectual forerunners.[5]
In my view, the place where this rhetorical context intersects most
compellingly with a materialist and phenomenological notion of
experience is the virtue tradition, especially in its ancient, early
modern, and (to some extent) contemporary formations. For this
reason, I will be particularly concerned in this chapter to think
about object-oriented deliberation in relation to the concept and
practice of virtue. The cardinal virtue of prudence, in particular,
I suggest, sheds light on the way objects function in the constitution of moral knowledge in theatrical, legal, and broader public
contexts.[6] Shakespeare offers an especially rich site for investigat-
ing these issues in act 3.2 of *Julius Caesar*. Here, Mark Antony
addresses the plebeians in the wake of Caesar's assassination using
the latter's bloody mantle (that is, cloak) as an object lesson in civic
and moral failure. This scene, I argue, has something important to
teach us about the theatricality of prudence, including, especially,
the object-specific way in which particular things enable general
moral insights. As this suggests, virtue does not offer a script for
the cultivation of inner qualities so much as a community-oriented
set of practices grounded in the capacity of humans to think, feel,
and discern together. Put another way, virtue is a social logic or
dynamic, rather than a set of personality traits or individual moral
attributes. Like theater itself, it provides a linked set of frame-
works for physical, emotional, and ethical participation in the
world, with judgment at its very center.[7]

This argument will unfold in three parts. The first section offers
a brief overview of how prudence functions as a source of moral
knowledge, including the particular way in which it relates to
the cardinal virtue of justice. The second section situates Mark
Antony's speech within the broader cultural framework of evidentiary thinking, an important historical context for understanding
the theatrical phenomenology of virtue. The third section, finally,
opens up to a broader consideration of how objects and images
foster virtue by creating occasions for collective moral judgment,
in both Shakespeare's time and our own.

Prudence, Justice, and Moral Knowledge

In ancient and early Christian philosophy, the four virtues of prudence, justice, temperance, and courage were seen as so definitive of human flourishing, and each so integral to the right operation of the others, that they eventually became known as "cardinal," from the word meaning "hinge." The scheme finds its source in Plato's *Republic* and is subsequently absorbed into the ethical systems of Neo-Platonism and both Greek and Roman Stoicism. In the late fourth century, Ambrose of Milan, one of a number of early church fathers writing on prudence, justice, temperance, and courage, coined the term *virtutes cardinales*.[8] Later Christian philosophers, most notably Parisian scholastics such as Thomas Aquinas and Bonaventure, integrated the four cardinal virtues with Aristotelian ethics. By the time we reach the early modern period in England, the cardinal virtues had become deeply embedded in intellectual, political, and literary culture with vernacular editions of Cicero's *On Duties* and Aristotle's *Nicomachean Ethics* appearing in 1534 and 1547, respectively. Both went through numerous reprintings.[9] Secular handbooks devoted to the art of governance, such as Thomas Elyot's *A Boke Named the Governor* (1531) and William Leighton's *Vertue Triumphant, or A lively description of the foure vertues cardinall dedicated to the Kings majesty* (1603), made the cardinal virtues central to their system of counsel. Conduct manuals, including Dominic Mancyn's *The Myrrour of Good Maners, conteyning the iiii vertues callyd cardynall* (1520) and Lodowyck Bryskett's *A Discourse of Civill Life* (1606), used the cardinal virtues as touchstones for social comportment. Poets, meanwhile, found in the cardinal virtues a consistent source of moral speculation, from Edmund Spenser's reflections on temperance and justice in *The Faerie Queene* to John Milton's exploration of courage in *Samson Agonistes*.[10]

Of the four cardinal virtues discussed by Plato – prudence, justice, temperance, and courage – prudence (or *phronesis* in Greek) has sometimes been called the virtue of virtues, the baseline competence on which all the other virtues depended. Bryskett, in *A Discourse of Civill Life*, writes that prudence is "aptly called the eye of the mind" and the "conserver" of justice. He continues:

Prudence is most necessary to discern what is just from what is unjust; and a good judgment therein can no man have that wanteth prudence: without which judgment, justice can never rule well those things that are under her government. And . . . if he be not guided by prudence . . . she works more harm than good.[11]

Prudence, in other words, enables ethical action through moral discernment, and in this way forms the foundation of the virtuous life. Bryskett, like so many writers of conduct manuals in the early modern period, is influenced by Cicero, who presents a similar, if more obscurely phrased, perspective on the place of prudence among the cardinal virtues in *On Duties*. "All that is morally right," Cicero writes, "rises from some one of four sources." He continues:

it is concerned either (1) with the full perception and intelligent development of the true; or (2) with the conservation of organized society, with the rendering of every man his due, and with the faithful discharge of obligations assumed; or (3) with the greatness and strength of a noble and invincible spirit; or (4) with the orderliness and moderation of everything that is said and done . . .

Elaborating on this description of the virtues (which he does not actually name at first, but which correspond to prudence, justice, courage, and temperance), Cicero notes that "in that category . . . which was designated first in our division and in which we place wisdom and prudence, belong the search after truth and discovery," and concludes finally by emphasizing that "of the four divisions which we have made of the essential idea of moral goodness, the first, consisting in the knowledge of truth, touches human nature most closely."[12] Prudence, then, is the cardinal virtue most securely grafted into human nature itself. It constitutes a foundation for justice and a platform on which the virtues of courage and temperance can be cultivated. Justice, after all, is a condition produced by the applied moral calculus of courage and temperance, and courage and temperance, in turn, are virtues that can only obtain in situations where choice is involved.

Prudence is usually described in English as "practical wisdom," a type of knowing that is active and collective. It stands in contrast to *sophia*, an abstracted and ideal type of wisdom set in opposition to *praxis* and the operations of the body.[13] One specific way in which prudential knowledge distinguishes itself from *sophia* is that while the latter is broad, universal, and seemingly innate to certain individuals, the former is acquired by using judgment to relate particular things to universal concepts. "Practical wisdom," Aristotle says,

> is concerned with human affairs, namely, with that which we can deliberate about . . . Nor is practical wisdom concerned only with universals. An understanding of the particulars is also required since it is practical, and action is concerned with particulars.[14]

Prudence is a calculative quality. It expresses itself in response to "that which we can deliberate about," and more specifically to particular objects, events, and questions that obtain in the real world of "human affairs." This can take the form of moral deliberation, as described by Bryskett in his discussion of the relationship between prudence and justice, or it can take the form of practical and technical discernment in fields as diverse as building, surveying, engineering, cartography, horse riding, fencing, and dance.[15]

The key thing to stress is that prudence is always a functional virtue. It is to be found in social, material, or otherwise transactional environments, not in solitude. Prudence has less to do with thinking (in our conventional understanding of that term) than it does with making and doing.[16] Aristotle emphasizes that the *phronimos* – the prudent person, or person of practical wisdom – does not, indeed cannot, exist in isolation. One hopes and assumes that the *phronimos* can navigate their private affairs discerningly, but they are characterized above all by practicing the sort of public virtue that leads to *eudaimonia*, or well-being for society in general. As this suggests, prudence only truly obtains when public acts of judiciousness are acknowledged and shared by a larger collective of stakeholders.[17] This is the process that enables justice, which is itself, within the Aristotelian scheme, a state of living temperately according to the golden mean.[18] The key take-away in all this is that contrary to our everyday understanding of virtue as a set of inner, moral attributes, the cardinal virtues, especially within the Aristotelian tradition, are of the world and for the world. They are deliberative in structure and in this respect rely on collaborative dynamics, be they of the Greek agora, the modern seminar room, or the transactional environment of Shakespeare's theater.[19]

Let us turn now to the latter, Shakespeare's theater, and consider how Mark Antony's interaction with the plebeians in act 3.2 of *Julius Caesar* stages prudence-in-action; a scene of collective, hands-on knowledge-making in which practical discernment is used to link a particular thing to a larger concept of justice.

Caesar's Mantle and the Phenomenology of Virtue

Early on in act 3.2, Brutus, one of the conspirators, makes a sharp distinction between private and public duty, explaining that it is "not that I loved Caesar less, but that I loved Rome more" (3.2.22).[20] The plebeians are initially roused by this argument ("Live, Brutus, live, live," "Let him be Caesar" [3.2.48, 51]), but when Mark Antony arrives bearing the body of Caesar, he quickly sways them to a more critical assessment of the assassination and of Brutus's role therein. How does Mark Antony achieve this? The answer has to do with the way he uses material objects to advance his argument: first the body of Caesar, then a piece of parchment (Caesar's will), and finally, and at most length, Caesar's mantle. These object lessons allow for that crucial prudential linkage to be made between the particular and the universal. This is what makes practical wisdom *practical*. Before there is an idea, there is a thing; before there is a thought, there is the world. This basic phenomenological precept forms the foundation of prudence and establishes the material conditions necessary for justice and the virtuous life more generally.

Mark Antony's main object lesson explicitly requires visual engagement. Beseeching all present to "Look," he directs the plebeians' attention to Caesar's mantle, still bloodily caked to the body that lies before him. I quote the passage in full:

> If you have tears, prepare to shed them now.
> You all do know this mantle. I remember
> The first time ever Caesar put it on.

'Twas on a summer's evening in his tent,
That day he overcame the Nervii.
Look, in this place ran Cassius' dagger through:
See what a rent the envious Caska made:
Through this, the well-beloved Brutus stabbed,
And as he plucked his cursed steel away,
Mark how the blood of Caesar followed it,
As rushing out of doors to be resolved
If Brutus so unkindly knocked or no;
For Brutus, as you know, was Caesar's angel.
Judge, O you gods, how dearly Caesar loved him.
This was the most unkindest cut of all:
For when the noble Caesar saw him stab,
Ingratitude, more strong than traitor's arms,
Quite vanquished him: then burst his mighty heart;
And in his mantle muffling up his face,
Even at the base of Pompey's statue,
Which all the while ran blood, great Caesar fell.
O what a fall was there, my countrymen!
Then I, and you, and all of us fell down,
Whilst bloody treason flourished over us.
O, now you weep, and I perceive you feel
The dint of pity: these are gracious drops.
Kind souls, what weep you when you but behold
Our Caesar's vesture wounded? Look you here,
Here is himself, marred as you see with traitors. (3.2.167–95)

Mark Antony starts by drawing collective attention to the thing itself: "You all do know this mantle" (3.2.168). In doing so, he lays the groundwork for a communal and object-oriented knowledge-event, mapped out linguistically through three keywords: "all . . . know . . . mantle."

For the crowd assembled around Mark Antony, as for the audience watching this scene at the newly opened Globe, the invitation to "Look you here" and assess the mantle would have triggered a moment of common evidentiary thinking. The episode models in theatrical terms a way of engaging critically, skeptically, and systematically with information that was becoming more prevalent in early modern England as a result of developments in a range of

social and intellectual contexts, especially political and legal culture. As Perez Zagorin has shown, an increasing number of early
modern men and women "viewed the world they lived in as filled
with duplicity."²¹ Apprehensive of Catholic trickery and distrust-
ful of political policy, many among Shakespeare's audiences would
have practiced an everyday hermeneutic of suspicion. Among the
learned, writers such as Niccolò Machiavelli, Justus Lipsius, and
Francis Bacon offered explorations (and oftentimes justifications)
of royal dissimulation while, on the other hand, a renewed interest
in Roman historians, especially Tacitus, urged skeptical reading
of political news in order to locate the truth behind what things
seemed to be.²²

In the legal realm, meanwhile, a variety of procedures involving
the empirical and objective evaluation of material evidence were
being formalized.²³ Two very different kinds of cases will serve
to illustrate how this might work. Consider, first, the Court of
Great Sessions in Wales where it had become common to bring
livestock into the courtroom in order to determine ownership. In
one such case, two brothers were tried for stealing sheep belonging
to Morris ap John in 1571. Ap John said it could be proven that
the animals in question were his because they bore a specific mark.
The sheep were brought before the judge and the marks displayed,
after which one of the prosecution witnesses confirmed that they
were indeed the marks of ap John's livestock.²⁴ A rather more high-
profile case, and our second example, is *Venetian Ambassador v.
Brooke*. At stake here are merchants' marks on goods rather
than farmers' marks on sheep. In the spring of 1607, an English
merchant ship named the *Husband* pulled into the North African
port of Tunis, where the crew traded gunpowder and other goods
for almost 30,000 crowns' worth of wool, yarn, indigo, and
cinnamon. This was all normal enough, but upon returning to
Dartmouth, the *Husband* was seized by the vice-admiral because
the Venetian ambassador to London, Zorzi Giustiniano, had
lodged a complaint. The goods onboard the ship, he said, were
Venetian. They had been stolen, so the claim went, from a Venetian
argosy called *Reneira a Soderina* by the English pirate John Ward
before making their way to Tunis.²⁵

For our purposes, what is most interesting about *Venetian Ambassador v. Brooke* is the role played by "inartistic proofs" in resolving the issue. Aristotle defines inartistic proofs as "those things which have not been furnished by ourselves but were already in existence." These could be objects, documents, or expert testimony, but will in any case always be forms of evidence that exist "outside the principles of oratory" (1355b).[26] Inartistic proofs lay at the heart of the English merchants' legal strategy. They told the Admiralty Court judges that it was unjust to give the goods to the Venetians if those goods bore no marks of Venetian ownership. The Admiralty judges agreed and demanded that the Venetian merchants produce actual material evidence, "the necessary information and proofs," to confirm the goods' Venetian provenance. It turned out that the appropriate marks were nowhere to be found on the goods, and so they reverted to the English in 1608.[27]

What Mark Antony's speech has in common with these events in legal and political culture is a core investment in the link between *the real* and *the right* – the simple, but nevertheless radical, idea that there is an objective world of things that present themselves to human judgment as reliable guides to decision-making. It is, of course, unlikely that either Shakespeare or his early audiences made a specific connection between act 3.2 of *Julius Caesar* and, say, actual trial procedure. But we do not have to believe this is the case to see how the scene indexes, both conceptually and theatrically, the phenomenon of evidentiary thinking that was one of the most important psychic effects of vernacular legal culture in the sixteenth and seventeenth centuries.[28] As rhetorically sophisticated as Mark Antony's speech is, it is clearly crafted by someone who viewed material evidence as bearing a verificatory power that exceeds pure oratory. The moral impact of the scene assumes, moreover, an audience that shares these views of material evidence. This is a crucial insight since it reinforces the idea that sensible objects and embodied experience form a necessary hinge between prudence and justice, two principal cardinal virtues. In establishing a specifically juridical set of relations among speaker, auditors, and objects, act 3.2 of *Julius Caesar* dramatizes prudence as a fundamentally phenomenological practice and, by extension, suggests how theater offers a particularly effective space for cultivating it.

Perception, Sensation, and Moral Response

The process of moral deliberation that Mark Antony guides the plebeians through is tightly anchored to the holes in the mantle created by the conspirators' blades: "Look, in this place ran Cassius' dagger through: / See what a rent the envious Caska made: / Through this, the well-beloved Brutus stabbed" (3.2.172–74). The latter Mark Antony describes as "the most unkindest cut of all" (3.2.181), and it is from here that he, along with the rest of the assembled crowd, is able to make that key prudential link between the particular (a piece of clothing) and the universal (notions of duty and ingratitude):

> This was the most unkindest cut of all:
> For when the noble Caesar saw him stab,
> Ingratitude, more strong than traitor's arms,
> Quite vanquished him: then burst his mighty heart; (3.2.181–84)

This leads to a final judgment and the knowledge, at once political and moral, that treason has been committed: "O what a fall was there, my countrymen! / Then I, and you, and all of us fell down, / Whilst bloody treason flourished over us" (3.2.188–90). Although these words are spoken by Mark Antony, the intuition they express is shared by the whole crowd. This common awareness is registered, importantly, in the emotional capacities of the body rather than in the purely intellectual capacities of the mind: the crowd starts to weep:

> O, now you weep, and I perceive you feel
> The dint of pity: these are gracious drops.
> Kind souls, what weep you when you but behold
> Our Caesar's vesture wounded? Look you here,
> Here is himself, marred as you see with traitors. (3.2.191–95)

Mark Antony acknowledges the tears that mark this moment of collective understanding and then delves deeper into the objective grounds from which it has sprung, removing the mantle to reveal the wounded body of Caesar itself. Whereas before the plebeians yelled, "Live, Brutus, live, live," "Let him be Caesar" (3.2.48, 51), now they shout, "O traitors, villains!" (3.2.197).

Mark Antony's calculated appeal to the crowd's capacity for prudence is closely bound up with a simultaneous appeal to their capacity for courage – courage, that is, in the Aristotelian sense of cultivating appropriate responses to "the things we fear, evils."[29] The cardinal virtue of courage involves a certain way of coordinating passion and reason such that we appropriately fear those things that should be feared and do not fear those things that should not be feared. The ideal outcome, as always, is action that leads to justice.[30] Mark Antony is *en*couraging his public to fear rightly; to employ prudence, exercised in response to material evidence and rhetorical appeal, such that they become more apprehensive of the conspirators' actions than of the supposed threat of Caesar. This reminds us that what we might typically refer to in a strictly rhetorical sense as "persuasion" is in the context of the cardinal virtues more appropriately referred to as "encouragement," a social process whereby the tools – deliberative, rhetorical, and material – necessary for the expression of courage and the establishment of justice are distributed among a public.

Orators like Mark Antony understand how effective material objects are at establishing the prudential conditions that make courage possible. Of course, political pundits of all stripes – and now marketing firms, too – understand this as well; the line between community-oriented motivation and self-interested manipulation can be a blurry one. Indeed, Mark Antony's speech itself could fall on either side of this line depending on your reading of the character and this particular passage of the play. Jean Fuzier's influential study of act 3.2 from 1974 argued that in comparison with Brutus, Mark Antony uses rhetoric in a "less systematic and more devious" way.[31] Fuzier's assessment of the play grows out of a critical tradition that has viewed Brutus's rhetoric as appealing to reason and Mark Antony's as appealing to emotion. We find the argument in one form or another in studies by John Palmer, Milton Crane, M. M. Mahood, and Ruth Nevo, and it continues to carry weight.³² This alignment of Mark Antony with emotion has sometimes been enough in and of itself to undermine his integrity. Gayle Greene, for example, takes the rhetoric–emotion link as a jumping-off point for a larger reading of the play as deeply skeptical about the relationship between language and knowledge. Greene views Shakespeare's Rome "as a society of skilled speakers whose rhetorical expertise masks moral and political truth."³³ Mark Antony is at the center of this critique. "Unconcerned with morality or truth," Greene asserts, "his energies are undivided, all geared to the manipulation of others."³⁴

It is striking how often this word, "manipulation," comes up in critical discussions of Mark Antony. Lauren Leigh Rollins uses it in various forms three times in the same number of sentences:

> Antony alone understands and successfully manipulates public opinion. Although he shares an understanding of its mutable nature, unlike the others, he does not discount or ignore it but rather learns how to shift and manipulate it to suit his own ends. For this reason, after Brutus and Cassius summon him following Caesar's death, Antony exhibits true authoritarian and Machiavellian strength by manipulating the conspirators not to see him as a threat.³⁵

Rollins's point is not necessarily to cast aspersions on Mark Antony. On the contrary, she describes the character as "integral to Shakespeare's corrective model of effective imperial leadership, as it applies to his own historical moment."³⁶ But whether framed as praise-worthy cleverness or self-interested deception, "manipulation" is a recurring term for describing Mark Antony's conduct in act 3.2. Such characterization finds its way into performance sometimes as well. In John Houseman and Joseph L. Mankiewicz's film version of *Julius Caesar*, produced by MGM in 1953, Marlon Brando was cast as a demagogic Mark Antony, stirring up the critically unsophisticated masses to advance his own ambitions. After the mantle speech, the frenzied crowd erupts in pursuit of the conspirators and the next shot shows Mark Antony leaving the forum with a smug, and slightly devious, smile on his face. He has triumphed. In his discussion of the film, "The Populist *Julius Caesar*,"

Robert F. Wilson, Jr. observes that Antony's "maturing ambition prompts him to *manipulate* the citizenry to do his will."[37]

I am cognizant of this strand of criticism devoted to Mark Antony and act 3.2, and I find some of it perfectly persuasive when taken on its own terms. But none of these studies address the place of objects in the scene, focusing instead on verbal rhetoric. Moreover, they are all chiefly concerned with character and theme rather than with the philosophical implications of theatrical form, which is where my main interests lie. Mark Antony as a character may be a demagogue and a manipulator (or at any rate, such an interpretation of the character may be furnished by the text), and this may be expressive of any number of aspects of early modern English intellectual, political, or literary culture. But in a formal sense – that is to say, in terms of the way various dramaturgical elements are configured and interact – Mark Antony's object lesson in act 3.2 offers a valuable account of the material grounds of moral intelligence and the way particular things open up to general ideas through an affective process of communal judgment. While object lessons like Mark Antony's continue to be used cynically and coercively, they also remain a powerful source of public virtue. One thinks of the well-known pile of shoes at the United States Holocaust Memorial Museum that have triggered moral outrage in generations of visitors. The efficacy of the object lesson as a pedagogical tool lies in its seemingly infallible status as moral evidence and the prudential way in which it holds the particular and the universal in an especially close configuration. Over the last fifteen years, social media has provided a platform especially conducive to object-lesson proliferation: the sad child who evokes the ethical catastrophe of detained migrants on the US–Mexico border; the terrified pig who conveys the abject cruelty of the meat industry. Nilüfer Demir's 2015 photograph of Alan Kurdi, the three-year-old Syrian refugee whose small body washed up on the shores of Bodrum, Turkey in the wake of a failed sea crossing to Europe, not only appeared on the front pages of hundreds of newspapers worldwide, it also translated directly, and almost immediately, into actual policy-making. Within days, Germany committed to admitting thousands of refugees who had up until then been stranded in Hungary, a humanitarian corridor was established in central and eastern Europe stretching from northern Greece to southern Bavaria, and Canada agreed to resettle 25,000 Syrians.[38]

One of the special characteristics of the object lesson is that it collapses the age-old distinction between *episteme* (knowledge) and *doxa* (opinion), the former associated with reason and the mind, the latter associated with sensation and the body. As a technology of judgment, object lessons are visceral and emotional, but also have the empirical force of evidence. The shoes at the Holocaust Museum prompt tears and indignation, but they are also actual shoes worn by actual people who were murdered. Like the bloody mantle of Caesar, they are both fact and feeling, a truth that we know in our body. Aristotle would not have been surprised at the effectiveness of such object lessons, nor by the way that effectiveness resides in a particularly close link between feeling and knowing. The very notion of *pathos*, Aristotle's second principle of rhetorical appeal, rests on the assumption that reason alone is insufficient to successfully communicate a truth-claim.[39] William M. A. Grimaldi explains this well in his discussion of the Aristotelian concept of the enthymeme, a truncated form of syllogism that required auditors to engage emotionally and critically in order to supply the premise themselves. Within legal studies, Maksymilian Del Mar has recently developed a useful equivalent to rhetoric's enthymeme, which he terms "artefact." "Artefacts," Del Mar writes, are "forms of language" encountered in juridical contexts which "call upon us to participate" imaginatively.[40] In involving auditors in the process of their own persuasion, the enthymeme, Aristotle argued, was the most effective aspect of public speech, and the kind of utterance most likely to feel like irrefutable proof. Grimaldi writes:

> Reason does not possess the power of persuasion. Thus Aristotle introduces into the syllogism, the instrument of reason, his psychology of human action. The enthymeme as the main instrument of rhetorical argument incorporates the interplay of reason and emotion in discourse . . . At the heart of Aristotle's theory of rhetoric, the enthymeme brings meaning to the assumed conflict in the

Rhetoric between reason and *ethos-pathos* . . . Like the metaphor
in poetry the enthymeme in rhetoric fuses the knowing in the person, makes the act of knowing a total perception of intellect, emotions, feelings.[41]

Scholars of philosophy and rhetoric, like Valerie J. Smith and Cara
Finnegan, have shown that in our own time enthymemes can take
visual form, like the pile of shoes or the body of Alan Kurdi.[42] The
modern object lesson is something like a material enthymeme, just
as the Aristotelian enthymeme could be thought of almost as an
object lesson in verbal terms. In any case, these concepts, ancient
and modern, testify to the enduring importance of emotion for
judgment and the particular kind of moral knowledge judgment is
involved in producing.

In *Julius Caesar*, the mantle is an instrument that triggers
pathetic engagement among Mark Antony's public, a prop whose
purpose is to occasion emotionally charged visual descriptions
that early modern rhetoricians would have identified as *enargeia*
or *illustratio*:

> I remember
> The first time ever Caesar put it on.
> 'Twas on a summer's evening in his tent,
> That day he overcame the Nervii.
> Look, in this place ran Cassius' dagger through: (3.2.168–72)

Here, the verbal strategies of Aristotelian rhetoric meet the lived
experience of Aristotelian virtue: an object generates rhetoric, rhetoric generates an image, the image generates emotion, emotion generates prudence, and prudence leads to courage and, finally, justice.
A similar process obtained in the public reception of and response
to the photograph of Alan Kurdi in 2015. Shakespeare's Mark
Antony belongs neither to Aristotle's world nor to our own, of course,
but the character's use of Caesar's mantle to elicit cardinal virtues
glances forward and backward at both worlds simultaneously.

Mark Antony's object lesson is a prudential knowledge-event
par excellence: it stages a direct confrontation with the reality of
material life and elicits an equally material response in the form of

bodily experience (weeping, disgust, anger). As theorists of affect will tell us, such bodily experience is valuable precisely for the way it always promises to engender forms of knowing not otherwise available through individual rational thought. This is what Brian Massumi calls "a sock to thought," a sensory jolt which, as Jill Bennett writes, "does not so much *reveal* truth as thrust us involuntarily into a mode of critical inquiry."[43] What neither Massumi nor Bennett discusses, but which act 3.2 of *Julius Caesar* puts on display, is the way prudential judgment plays a crucial role in guiding the purely sensory experience of the "sock to thought" into the rational ambit of "critical inquiry." Theater by its very nature is designed to issue these socks to thought, to thrust spectators into situations of emotionally grounded, but rationally informed, critical inquiry oriented towards moral action and justice. At its most basic operational level, theater curates transactions among objects, emotions, judgment, and knowledge. As an event, a practice, a phenomenon, an experience, theater is one of the clearest iterations of Deleuze and Guattari's famous notion of the "assemblage" which has been so influential within contemporary philosophy and theory.[44] An assemblage, Deleuze and Guattari write, is "an intermingling of bodies reacting to one another."[45] The point of the concept for their project, and for the projects of many of the thinkers they have influenced (like Jane Bennett), is to underline the fallacy of unique or privileged human agency. My chief concern is somewhat different. The assemblage-like quality that links prudential judgment and theatrical experience is significant not just for what it tells us about the sources of agency, but also for what it tells us about the conditions under which the evaluation, moral decision, and active worldmaking that has long been referred to collectively as "virtue" takes place. The crucial observation we are left with is that the human–nonhuman transactions at the heart of theatrical judgment form the material and cognitive ecologies in which virtue thrives.

Mark Antony's prudential use of the mantle in *Julius Caesar* looks forward to the latter-day object lessons of the museum, photojournalism, and social media while also being firmly rooted in an

Aristotelian tradition of rhetoric and virtue. What ties them all together is the particular way in which evidence is used to invoke collective emotion and translate it into the sort of judgment that should lead to knowledge and virtuous action. Combining components of forensic rhetoric that would be recognizable to Aristotle and an affectively honed approach to visual rhetoric that would be recognizable to today's bearers of witness, Mark Antony creates a theater of prudence in which a fragmented public is united around a shared act of spectatorship, a shared confrontation with visceral experience, and a shared emotional response to violence. Indeed, prudential judgment can only be enacted through a certain *mise en scène* of human and nonhuman things. It requires for its unfolding a rhetorical, material, and cognitive environment in which physically instantiated particulars (like a mantle) enable evaluative insights about universal concepts like justice.

The way act 3.2 of *Julius Caesar* is crafted suggests that Shakespeare on some level understood this link between prudence and theater, the fact that they share the same basic conditions (collectivity), rely on the same raw materials (bodies and objects arranged in time and space), make meaning through the same methods (the substitution of part for whole, the invocation of common deliberation), and aim at the same general outcome (the production of knowledge, wisdom, or insight experienced as feeling). With these connections in mind – and to return to a claim I made at the opening of this chapter – the scene serves as a powerful reminder that virtue is a system of social practices that rely on the capacity of humans to think, feel, and judge together. To this extent, the theater offers an especially potent site for fostering the aptitudes of public virtue. For this reason alone, I would suggest, any serious vision for a more just and equitable future must involve vigorous support of theatrical institutions, events, and experiments.

CHAPTER 3

VISION

Mark Antony's speech to the plebians helps us map out the cognitive and epistemological structure of *looking*. It shows us that judgment lives somewhere between the seen and the known, shuttling from vision to knowledge and back again, greeting sensory information with standards of assessment and structuring the undifferentiated blur of sentience with evaluative order. But vision and judgment also have a vexed relationship. At once our most privileged and most mistrusted source of knowledge, the eyes have long been a site of both optimism and anxiety about the accessibility of spiritual, moral, legal, and scientific truth. This was certainly the case in the world in which Shakespeare lived and worked. As Stuart Clark notes:

> Between the Reformation and the Scientific Revolution, vision was anything but objectively established or secure in its supposed relationship to "external fact." Many intellectuals at least . . . seem to have been preoccupied precisely with questions to do with whether human vision did give reliable access to the real world after all.[1]

Indeed, Aristotelian and Copernican optics, both influential in Shakespeare's time, lead us in decidedly different directions. Similarly, the rise of material evidence in law courts seems to tell a story about cultural attitudes towards vision and knowledge that runs counter to the one told by Protestant anti-theatricalism or the revival of ancient skepticism. Vision could be treated as either sensory or spiritual; it could be a subject for either scientific or moral consideration; and discourse in all these veins ranged widely from profound trust and optimism to profound fear and pessimism.[2]

In this chapter, I want to look at the skewed way in which theater lines up with the cultural and intellectual history of vision to understand how Shakespearean theater can help us "see anew," to borrow a phrase from Lorraine Daston and Peter Galison.[3] This will involve reflecting on a number of moments in Shakespeare's plays – from *Othello*, *King Lear*, and *Macbeth* to *Twelfth Night* and *The Winter's Tale* – where the act of seeing or looking is being staged. I will be particularly interested in the way theater fosters a non-objective form of visual judgment, one that embraces interpretive risk and epistemological irrationalism. To put it in plainer language, I wish to suggest that theater models a version of vision-based judgment that can tolerate things being both one way and another way, both there and not there, both real and unreal. This kind of pluralism is difficult to assimilate within mainstream traditions of scientific vision. Theater, I will propose, offers a counter-optics in which judgment transforms what is logical and verifiable into what is impossible and wondrous, rather than the other way around.

Seeing/Knowing/Doing

One of the first things an early modernist will think of when presented with the topic of vision is, quite sensibly, Reformation-era iconoclasm and visual skepticism. Much has been written on this subject, and I will return to it myself later in this section. But I want to start by emphasizing that all such skepticism develops against the backdrop of a deeply entrenched ocularcentrism stemming from both Greek and early Christian understandings of perception. We can trace this still in our own time, linguistically fossilized in common phrases like "See what I mean?"; "Oh, I see"; or even "look," as in "Look, all I'm saying is . . ." These conventional enunciations signal just how merged the notions of seeing and understanding are, as if the former is somehow equivalent to the latter. In the early modern period, sight was frequently presented as first in the order of sensory knowledge, giving us our most direct access to things as they are. Thomas Wilson, in his widely disseminated *The Arte of Rhetorique* (1553), wrote that of all the senses "the eye sight is most quicke, and containeth the impression of things more assuredly."[4] In his influential anatomical manual *Mikrokosmographia* (1615), Helkiah Crooke, court physician to King James, uses the metaphor of "Centinels or Scout-watches in the top of the Towre" to describe the relationship of the eyes to human perception and knowledge more broadly.[5] French anatomist Ambroise Paré similarly prioritizes eyesight over the other senses, for "By this wee behold the fabricke and beauty of the heavens and earth, distinguish the infinite varietyes of color" and "perceive and know the magnitude, figure, number, proportion, size, motion and the rest of all bodyes."[6]

There are a couple related lines of thought that we can extract from this grab-bag of representative quotations on vision. One has to do specifically with the relationship of seeing to knowing. Seeing, the suggestion is, provides more complete and more accurate information than the other senses. We have access to things both near and far, which we do not get with touch, which requires proximity. We get what we might now refer to as a more complete data set for the bodies, forms, and substances we encounter, including not only "magnitude, figure, number," but also "proportion, size, motion," things considerably more difficult, and in some cases impossible, to assess through smell. The range of information available to the eyes means that knowledge or understanding of what is seen requires less processing, less extrapolation. There is a sense of immediacy – "eye sight is most quicke" – which in turn lends itself to a higher degree of certainty about what is and what is not: "eye sight . . . containeth the impression of things more assuredly." All of this suggests that what is seen provides firmer grounds for judgment than what is smelled, felt, or heard. Indeed, seeing and judging have a long history as shared, mutually reinforcing concepts. Long before Jeremy Bentham's more sinister rendering of this idea in the panopticon's synthesis of privileged vision and institutional justice, Proverbs 20 reminded Christians that "A king that sitteth in the throne of judgment, scattereth away all evil with his eyes."[7] Vision in this context is not only the sovereign sense, but also the grounds of sovereignty itself. To see is to possess not only objective, but also moral, knowledge. The beholder is both correct and good – the ideal judge.

Othello is a play that channels both poles of early modernity's attitude towards the visual, a morally inflected optimism about vision's relationship to truth and, conversely, the idea that to believe what you see will ultimately lead to disaster. We observe the former when Othello, skeptical of Desdemona's reassurances about her fidelity, becomes absorbed with a desire to materialize and behold the categorically insubstantial: thoughts. This reaches a troubling apex in act 4.2 when he grabs Desdemona roughly and demands she look into his eyes so he may see what she knows and, more essentially, who she really is: "Your mystery, your mystery – nay dispatch . . . Why, what art thou?" (4.2.30, 34).[8] In his quick shift from "your mystery" to, more essentially, "what thou art," Othello articulates what Martin Heidegger would later observe to be our tendency to give "an existential significance to 'sight,'" the idea that vision "lets entities which are accessible to it be encountered unconcealedly in themselves," and that unlike the other senses, we consider "'seeing' as a way of access to beings and to Being."[9] Heidegger's generalizations may not hold true across the board, but they offer an apt characterization of Othello's slippage from particular to ontological scales of knowledge in this passage. For Othello, the visual is the gold standard of evidence and the sole grounds on which he will issue judgment. This conviction gains momentum over the course of act 3.3 while Iago subtly fuels Othello's suspicions. The latter finally decides, "I'll see before I doubt" (3.3.193), the departure point for an unwavering commitment to "ocular proof" (3.3.362), which Othello finally finds – or thinks he finds – in a resurfaced handkerchief, thought to be lost, which Othello had given Desdemona as a gift in the early days of their courtship.[10]

The trust that the play's title character places in what is seen over what is said is, of course, undermined by Iago's calculated manipulation of that trust. Unlike the mantle on which Mark Antony urges the crowd to "Look" (3.2.172) – an object whose bloody dagger holes materialize the truth of an event – the handkerchief does not present facts to vision. "I saw it in his hand" (5.2.213–14), Othello insists, referring to Michael Cassio, with whom he believes Desdemona to be having an affair. Emilia, devastatingly, shows that what lies behind this observation – Othello's "ocular proof" – is a ploy by Iago, not a gift from Desdemona. The audience knows this all along. They see the disaster unfolding before their eyes. In no other tragedy by Shakespeare is the protagonist's folly laid so bare, so early, for playgoers. How would original audiences have reacted to such heavy-handed showcasing of the tragic hero's shortcomings? We can only speculate of course. But I do think it is easier for twenty-first-century audiences to scorn Othello as naïve or simplistic or, eventually, simply deranged than it would have been for early modern audiences. We live in a world that has learned to be suspicious of appearances, to seek truth behind the deceptive veneer of surfaces. This is a deeply entrenched assumption of post-Enlightenment culture. *Don't judge a book by its cover* is just one colloquial platitude that captures our inversely related conceptions of vision and judgment. In the philosophical realm, René Descartes's *Meditations on First Philosophy* (1641) presents an archetypal formulation of the idea. During his famous commentary on gazing down from a window onto a busy street, Descartes explains, "when looking from a window and saying I see men who pass on the street, I really do not see them, but infer that what I see is men." "What," he asks, "do I see from the window but hats and coats which may cover automatic machines?"[11] This kind of skepticism would propel Europe into the age of modern science, where the gaze of humans is always insufficient and physical seeing never provides a reliable path to knowledge.[12] Like Dorothy pulling back the curtain in *The Wizard of Oz*, Descartes quickly and efficiently undermines the idea that seeing should be believed.

Yet we might speculate that much of the play's original power to horrify and ethically disorient must have stemmed from the fact that for many in the audience, Othello's basic approach to evaluation, at least on a technical level, would have seemed pretty sound. If he is manifestly unfair and dangerously obsessive, Othello is also well within the period's pale of rational thought to say, "I'll see before I doubt" and to weigh material evidence above testimony.

Whatever degree of ocularcentrism he is guilty of would have been more or less in line with Aristotelian theories of perception and knowledge, the normative force of which prior to the scientific revolution cannot be underestimated.[13] From an Aristotelian point of view, humans had, under normal circumstances, direct access to the world as it was through sense perception, especially vision. The mind was not a realm separate from, or at odds with, the sensing body, as it would be in Descartes's later works. On the contrary, and as noted in Chapter 1, Aristotle understood the mind to be the domain not only of intellectual powers, but also of vegetative and sensitive powers, including all forms of internal and external sensation and motion.[14] The truth of the world was transmitted to the human mind through the processes of "extromission" (the eye sending out a force that captured images of the world) and "intromission" (the objects of the world giving off a force that entered the eye). Within this model, the world was essentially what it appeared to be. To see was to know. There was no man behind the curtain.

Later scholastic philosophers in Paris and Oxford, including Roger Bacon, who had a strong influence on sixteenth-century English thinkers like Thomas Harriot and John Dee, refined and elaborated Aristotle's optics, developing a purely intromission-based theory of vision which posited that all objects produced *species*, material substances that radiated out through the air transmitting images into the eye. *Species* were then transmitted from the eye to the brain. Accordingly, the scholastics and the sixteenth-century English thinkers they influenced shared with Aristotle the assumption that thought had a powerful visual component.[15] As Aristotle puts it in *De Anima*, "when the mind is actively aware of anything, it is necessarily aware of it along with an image." Because "the objects of thought are in sensible form," "no one can learn or understand anything in the absence of sense," and vision, as has been pointed out, was first among the senses.[16] Crook affirms this precept when he describes the imagination as that "which conceyveth, apprehendeth and retaineth the same Images or representations which the common sense received."[17] Debora Shuger rightly emphasizes that "Cognition," within Aristotelian thought, "is invariably conceived on the model of vision."[18] All this, as one can imagine, fostered a certain confidence in the correlation between what is seen and what simply *is*. Perception and truth are closely aligned in Aristotelian optics, whereas post-Cartesian optics would generally assume a fundamental rift between the two.

In this, as in so many things, early moderns were phenomenologists *avant la lettre*, living according to vernacular versions of philosophical precepts that would eventually be given new theoretical and programmatic form by thinkers like Edmund Husserl, Martin Heidegger, Maurice Merleau-Ponty, Paul Ricoeur, Hannah Arendt, and others. Merleau-Ponty, for instance, argued rigorously that we can only *conceive* – and therefore evaluate and judge – what we first *perceive*, that thought is largely the product of embodied experience of the world.[19] "All knowledge," he insists, "takes place within the horizons opened up by perception."[20] Merleau-Ponty's arguments are seminal within the history of twentieth-century phenomenology and its critique of transcendental philosophy, but they also gesture back to similarly sense-oriented theories of human cognition within the Aristotelian tradition of philosophy, including scholasticism and neo-scholasticism. Indeed, there is something curiously pre-modern about Merleau-Ponty's sensual account of thought and about the conceptual machinery of phenomenology, more generally. Merleau-Ponty suggests as much when he describes the goal of phenomenology as "re-achieving a direct and *primitive* contact with the world."[21] Robert Sokolowski has traced some of this relationship in detail, noting, for example, the "continuity between Thomistic thought and the early stages of phenomenology," the chief instance of this being the formidable influence of Franz Bretano's neo-scholastic philosophy on Husserl. "Phenomenology," according to Sokolowski, "breaks out of modernity and permits a restoration of the convictions that animated ancient and medieval philosophy."[22]

Othello is an Aristotelian and a phenomenologist by intellectual temperament, convinced that truth lies in the artifacts of the material world made apprehensible to his senses; convinced that if he can see, he will know. But this is a phenomenology gone terribly, terribly wrong. When Othello grabs Desdemona roughly and tells her to gaze into his eyes, demanding, "Your mystery, your mystery – nay dispatch . . . Why, what art thou?," he is indeed trying to achieve direct contact with the world, to paraphrase Merleau-Ponty. He is trying to *perceive* so he can *conceive*, and by extension judge correctly. But there is nothing there. No truth, no knowledge. It does not occur to Othello to pull back the curtain. Had he done so, he would have found Iago frantically pushing buttons and pulling levers.

Such a move is not intuitive within an Aristotelian worldview, but there were other powerful strands of thought developing across the sixteenth century that would have urged just such a method for evaluation and judgment. Copernican astronomy, for example, posed a formidable challenge to the veridical optics of Aristotle and the scholastics. It offered a theory of the universe based precisely on the assertion that it operated in a manner that was at odds with the way it appeared from the perspective of human vision. Among the various impacts of Copernicus's theories in Europe was an interest in optical illusions among natural philosophers in sixteenth-century England. A good example is William Fulke, who argued in his *Goodly Gallerye* that under certain atmospheric conditions, light could be reflected in such a way as to create mirages of things that are not there. He notes the way clouds can act as mirrors, causing people to see more than one sun in the sky, insisting:

> They are nothing els but Idols or Images of the sunne, represented in an equal smooth and watry cloude, placed on the side of the sunne, and sometimes on both sydes, into which the sunn beames being received as in a glasse, expresse ye likeness of fashion and light, that is in the sunne, appearing as though there were many sunnes, where as in dede there is but one, and all the rest are images.[23]

Optical illusions drastically destabilize the vision > judgment > knowledge chain that held together securely within the Aristotelian scheme. Fulke and, a bit later, Dee and his associates Leonard Digges and William Bourse were also interested in man-made optical illusions, such as the famous "brazen head, made by Albertus Magnus, which dyd seem to speake."[24] The world of optical illusions and Copernican concealment is one in which things are quite categorically not as they appear to be. Against this epistemological backdrop, someone like Iago can say "I am not what I am" (1.1.64) and sound sinister and conniving, but not necessarily paradoxical. "I am not what I am" describes a state of deception and illusion, not of meaninglessness or nonsense. Unlike, say, the nihilistic semiotics of René Magritte's famous painting *La Trahison des Images* (1929), in which the words "Ceci n'est pas une pipe" (This is not a pipe) appear under an image of a pipe, Iago's stage declaration evokes a world in which there *is* meaning, there *is* truth – it is just very hard to determine what it is, and you certainly are not going to figure it out just by looking.

For a number of thinkers in early modern England, whether their views derive from the Reformation theology of Jean Calvin or the philosophical skepticism of Sextus Empiricus, this is precisely the problem with images. They can only deceive and mislead. Oxford intellectual George Hakewill writes of this at length in *The Vanitie of the Eie* (1608), but he frames his discussion with a more balanced reflection on the ethical and spiritual conundrum presented by vision:

> Though manie and singular bee the commendations of the nature and frame of the eie, & the use of it in the ordinary course of life bee no lesse diverse then excellent as wel for profit as delight, yet the dangerous abuses which arise from it not rightly guided, are so generall, and almost inseparable, that it may justly grow to a disputable question whither wee should more regard the benefit of nature in the one, or the hazard of grace and vertue in the other.[25]

In other words, being able to see is quite handy for getting things done in everyday life, and much pleasure can be had from it too. But "inseparable" from this "benefit of nature" are the dangers of delusion and sensual excitement. This hazardous side of vision is at the center of the criticism sometimes leveled at theater itself, an essentially visual and illusory undertaking which, in William Rankins's words, "bleareth mens eyes," leading them "with enticing shewes to the divell."[26] *Othello* is a fascinating document in the cultural history of vision and visual judgment because it stages an encounter between what we might call optimistic and pessimistic ways of thinking about vision, the former undergirded by a long history of Aristotelianism and scholasticism, the latter undergirded by more recent intellectual developments in theology, philosophy, and science which, for all their differences, share a basic distrust of human sight. Vision-based judgment ultimately leads to Othello's (and Desdemona's) downfall, but the play would not work as tragedy if this deliberative and epistemological orientation towards the visual was generally viewed as daft from the get-go. The horror of it all is that a man with basically sound instincts ruins his life and the life of his beloved. If the play is a product of a culture increasingly skeptical of sensory knowledge, it also depends for its effect on an audience who would have by and large thought, *I too would have believed the evidence of the handkerchief.*

Some of this ambiguity can be found in other plays by Shakespeare, too, such as *King Lear*. On one hand, there is a committedly skeptical strain in the play, including in its treatment of vision.[27] After being brutally blinded, Gloucester declares, "I have no way, and therefore want no eyes. / I stumbled when I saw" (15.16–17),[28] juxtaposing the fallen vision of the body with the pure vision of the soul, a distinction that can be traced back to Plato. Within the Platonic tradition, the Aristotelian notion of *phronesis*, a practical form of wisdom that assumes action to play an essential role in the acquisition of knowledge, is gradually displaced by *sophia*, which I described in Chapter 2 as an abstracted and ideal form of wisdom set in opposition to *praxis* and the operations of the body. *Sophianic* knowledge is acquired through a new kind of seeing, one that takes place through the eyes of the soul rather than the eyes of the body and which, therefore, carries a sense which would eventually be entrusted to Latin terms like *contemplatio*.[29] With this tradition behind it, Gloucester's utterance has an almost proverbial ring to it, signaling his alignment with the likes of Tiresias and Oedipus, all of whom attain wisdom – intellectual and moral vision – after, or even through, physical blindness. And yet at the end of the play, seeing – real, physical seeing – carries a great deal of ethical freight. Looking, in and of itself, becomes a form taking moral responsibility. "O see, see!" (24.299), Albany exclaims as

Lear stands over the lifeless body of his one loyal daughter, Cordelia. The invocation is directed at all those onstage, and by implication all those in the audience as well. For a brief moment, actors and spectators alike unite simply to bear witness, one of the most powerful ethical (and juridical) affordances of vision – something we saw playing out in a different way in the previous chapter.

Given the intellectual environment in which Shakespeare was thinking and writing, it makes sense that his engagement with vision is varied and inconsistent, both morally and philosophically. One thing is sure, though: beyond questions of skepticism and certainty, deception and trust; beyond the whole issue of right and wrong, there is the overwhelming sense in Shakespeare's plays that *looking matters*; that beyond being a means of assessment, visual judgment forms the phenomenological grounds for action which, for better or for worse, changes lived experience. To see is not just to *know*; to see is also to *do*, to craft the world to come. Some of Shakespeare's most compelling insights about seeing emerge when we stop thinking about visual judgment as a form of assessment and view it instead as a zone of possibility that involves willed belief and the suspension of rational thought. This idea will be at the center of the next section.

Theatrical Vision

Among the various ways of thinking about the value of sight presented in *Othello* and *King Lear*, most can be linked to identifiable historical sources. But Albany's behest to "see!" at the end of the *King Lear* has more to do with the capacity of plays themselves to host shared occasions of witnessing and testimony, an aspect of theater as potent now as it was then. In what follows, I am going to focus on episodes in Shakespeare's plays that while certainly anchored to the thought-world of early modernity are even more valuable for what they teach us about the unique way visual judgment works, or can work, in the theater.

The famous dagger soliloquy in act 2.1 of *Macbeth* is a good place to start. There is real theoretical work being undertaken in this scene. What I mean by that is the material and verbal resources of theater are used to stage a train of thought and finally an *idea* about vision. Consider the very first line: "Is this a dagger which I see before me" (2.1.33).[30] The objective response to this question would be no. There is not an actual dagger floating in the air in front of Macbeth. He is quite right to wonder if what he sees is merely "a dagger of the mind, a false creation, / Proceeding from the heat-oppressèd brain" (2.1.38–39). But the situation is more complex than the rules of objectivity would allow. Two distinct propositions, that Macbeth's "eyes are made the fools o'th'other senses" or that they are "worth all the rest" (2.1.44–45), are equally plausible. In so far as what he sees does not exist materially and cannot actually be seized, it is indeed possible that he is experiencing an illusion. But in so far as what he sees – a dagger with "gouts of blood" on the "blade and dudgeon" (2.1.46) – gives untimely form to a truth soon to be manifest, it is not nearly as straightforward as a simple illusion. Rather, it is an iteration of both intention and action existing somewhere along the phenomenological continuum of immaterial knowledge and material event. The dagger's indistinct ontological status in no way undermines its basic verity. In the world of *Macbeth*, there is no clear taxonomy of what-is-there and what-is-not-there, just as there is no clear taxonomy of present and future. The status of vision, like the status of time, remains fluid in the play.

The wild optics of the dagger soliloquy come from the same world of theatrical speculation as the closing scene of *Twelfth Night*, in which Duke Orsino is confronted by the momentarily inexplicable vision of two Cesarios standing side by side: Viola dressed as a boy and her twin brother, Sebastian. This brief but profound passage is evocative of theater's unique status as a space for visual judgment. To begin explaining what I mean by this, we should first recall that Shakespearean comedy depends for its effects on the careful management of knowledge distribution. That is, what creates the chaos which it is the task of comedy to solve is the fact that some characters know things that other characters do not – about who is who, about who did what, about what happened to whom. A similar unequal distribution of knowledge – the fact that the audience knows more than most, sometimes all, characters on stage – is what triggers laughter. If while watching *Twelfth Night* we were as

ignorant as Sebastian as to why Sir Andrew walks up to him in act
4.1 and out of nowhere strikes him on the head, it would not be
funny; it would just be confusing. Sebastian knows what he knows,
but not what Sir Andrew knows; Sir Andrew knows what he knows,
but not what Sebastian knows. The audience, however, knows both
what Sebastian knows and what Sir Andrew knows. Knowledge is
the raw material from which comic form is assembled and it creates
the conditions of possibility for laughter. Importantly, knowledge,
both true and false, is most often acquired through vision in Shakespearean comedy. Sir Andrew hits Sebastian because he sees (as far
as he is concerned) Cesario. Lucius in *Measure for Measure* knows
he is in trouble ("This may prove worse than hanging" [5.1.361])[31]
because he pulls off the hood hiding the Duke's face. In the comedies, "Ocular proof" may not lead to death and disaster, as it does
in *Othello*, but it can definitely lead to a great deal of disarray and
hilarity before finally providing the revelations necessary for the
re-establishment of order.

   This is certainly the case in *Twelfth Night*, a play in which
Viola, a shipwrecked young woman with a presumed-dead twin
brother, dresses as a boy to secure employment at the court of
Duke Orsino. However, *Twelfth Night* also treats visual judgment
in a way that is different from other comedies of disguise and mis-
taken identity. In these plays – among which we can count, to a
greater or lesser extent, almost all of Shakespeare's comedies –
visual information is interpreted either correctly or incorrectly.
Either you know or you don't. There is no in-between. Characters
believe there is one Antipholus, based on the visual information
available, until they see, in the light of new visual information,
that there are two. Lucius erroneously, but logically, believes he is
addressing a friar; until he *sees*, equally logically, that he has been
addressing the Duke the whole time. The net effect of this is a con-
flicted appraisal of visual judgment, consistent with the period's
divergent accounts of vision within intellectual culture. On one
hand, revelation almost always takes visual form – characters *see*
the truth. On the other hand, vision is consistently the most easily
deceived of the senses. In comedy, this leads to disorder; in tragedy,
this leads to death.

Twelfth Night is remarkable, however, for the way it opens, for a brief moment, a space in which one can be both right and wrong, where vision is both revelation and mystery. This occurs at the moment I mentioned above when, at the end of the play, Orsino is confronted for the first time with the twins, Sebastian and Viola, the latter still dressed as a boy, standing side by side before him. Visually, they are indistinguishable. Orsino says:

> One face, one voice, one habit, and two persons,
> A natural perspective, that is and is not. (5.1.209–10)[32]

I mentioned above how *Macbeth* takes a particularly pluralistic approach to visual judgment in the dagger episode. The scene refuses to commit to an objectively grounded notion of presence. Orsino's response to the twins in *Twelfth Night* operates according to a similar hermeneutic. Just as no clear classificatory threshold exists between what-is-there and what-is-not-there in *Macbeth*, Orsino opens a door of conceptual possibility in *Twelfth Night* when he sees the twins, a door to a world in which things both *are* and *are not*. In this world, reason and objectivity have little purchase; there are no fixed criteria for knowledge. Conventionally, the techniques of judgment within rhetoric – defining, classifying, selecting, ordering (on which, more in the next two chapters) – are leveraged towards minimizing interpretive risk. This in order to ensure that the decision, action, or creation that is the endgame of the deliberative process will be "right"; that is to say, correctly suited to the circumstances and/or grounded in verifiable knowledge. Not so in *Twelfth Night*. Orsino, the court community, and the community of spectators in the theater all bask briefly in the epistemologically risky glow of the impossible made possible.

We linger in this world only fleetingly. For ultimately comedy must do what comedy does: set right; put in order; and lay out clearly, according to shared criteria that everyone can agree on, what has and has not happened and who everyone actually is. That is what takes place next. Viola tells her brother:

> Do not embrace me till each circumstance
> Of place, time, fortune do cohere and jump

That I am Viola, which to confirm
I'll bring you to a captain in this town
Where lie my maiden weeds (5.1.243–49)

We are returned with these lines to a set of procedures through
which judgment establishes clearly what *is* and what *is not*,
placing them in two separate baskets rather than allowing
them magically to coexist. Viola, that is, brings us back to the
world of rational, indeed forensic, discernment in which various circumstances ("place," "time") are determined and ana-
lyzed, and material evidence ("my maiden weeds") is secured for
verification.[33]

The appearance of the indistinguishable twins, two Cesarios,
is like a bright shaft of light that comes screaming through a door
pushed open just a crack and then promptly closed. It is a moment
of interpretive and experiential possibility marked with wonder; quite literally so when Olivia exclaims, "Most wonderful!"
(5.1.221). Olivia's line is of course a joke – two Cesarios instead of
one! – and usually prompts laughter in the audience. But it is also
an utterance of awe, even reverence, which holds in suspension
this tableau of wondrous irrationality. Sebastian evokes a similar sentiment in act 4.3 of *Twelfth Night* when he finds himself,
remarkably and inexplicably, showered with gifts and waited on
hand and foot in Olivia's home:

This is the air, that is the glorious sun,
This pearl she gave me, I do feel't and see't,
And though 'tis wonder that enwraps me thus,
Yet 'tis not madness, (4.3.1–4)

Like Macbeth, Sebastian must consider seriously if his "eyes are
made the fools o'th'other senses":

though my soul disputes well with my sense
That this may be some error but no madness,
Yet doth this accident and flood of fortune
So far exceed all instance, all discourse,
That I am ready to distrust mine eyes (4.3.9–13)

As illogical as it all may seem, he *does* "feel't and see't," and therefore, "'tis not madness." It is "wonder." Wonder in the early modern period was not an effect produced by illusion or error, but rather, in Michael Witmore's words, "a response to some novel situation or object, the result of a lack of understanding that invited further engagement."[34] Wonder is a concept built on the assumption that the world contains things that are obscure to us, that defy prescriptive categories and even language. Most important of all, the realness of wondrous things is not diminished by our inability to comprehend them. More to the point, as T. G. Bishop explains, wonder creates "a dynamic space of flux between the real and the impossible, between belief and skepticism, between reason and feeling."[35]

How do passages like these, which hold seeing, judging, and knowing in such a strange configuration, and which place all three in such an unfamiliar relationship to conventional understandings of concepts like "truth" and "fact," fit in with the larger history of vision, some of which I have outlined above? Rather than returning to Aristotelianism, Skepticism, Calvinism, or any number of other intellectual-historical contexts which offer only limited resources for understanding what is important about the final scene of *Twelfth Night*, I want to take up this question by thinking about theater itself as both a visual and epistemic practice.

Seeing Anew

In their monumental study of modern scientific vision *Objectivity*, Lorraine Daston and Peter Galison discuss how the atlases produced by various "sciences of the eye" between the eighteenth and twentieth centuries (geographical, radiological, bacteriological) asked their publics "to 'see' anew."[36] I would propose that theater, too, is a science of the eye of sorts, and one that likewise asks its public to see anew. In this section, the final section of the chapter, we will explore how this works.

In Chapter 1 I pointed out that theater, as both a practice and a concept, has deep roots in visual experience. We will recall that the Greek word for theater, *theatron*, means literally, a place for

viewing, and that the first occurrence of the word "theatre" in English, in a Wycliffite Bible manuscript of 1382, carries the gloss, a
"commune biholdying place."[37] However, the theater is not simply
a site for passive looking. More precisely, it is a place of knowledge-making in visual terms and through visual means. The word
"theory" (*theorein*), in fact, derives from the same etymological
root as "theater": the Greek verb *theaomai* (to look).[38] To theorize,
in other words, was to observe intensely the outward appearance
of something. To go to a "commune biholdying place," a theater,
was to theorize – to speculate, to develop ideas – together. This
conceptual proximity, preserved in ancient Greek words like *theatron* and *theorein*, persists in early modern humanist conceptions of
knowledge-making and knowledge-management. In the sixteenth
century, the Latin word *theatrum* could refer either to a place
for viewing spectacles or to a wide-ranging, encyclopedic book,
so that by the time The Theatre was built in London in 1576, its
name evoked works of scholarship like Pierre Boaistuau's *Theatrum mundi* (1561), Theodor Zwinger's *Theatrum vitae humanae*
(1566), and Abraham Ortelius's *Theatrum orbis terrarum* (1570).[39]
The Theater, like other London playhouses established after it, was
not only a place of entertainment, it was also a learning environment where one could watch ideas and see thinking in action.
Thomas Elyot draws on this conception of theater when in *The
Image of Governance* (1541) he has his ideal educational facilities
include not only a library shaped like a theater, but also an actual
theater where people could "dispute openly . . . some matter of
philosophy."[40] William N. West explains:

> For Elyot, the areas of the theater and the library are contiguous
> and complementary . . . In fact, the circularity of the library and
> the vivid statues and images with which it is decorated mark it as
> a kind of asymptomatic ideal for the theater as a perfectly legible
> *spectacle of knowledge.*[41]

Theater, at base, is a collaborative knowledge-making practice
grounded in visual judgment, a science of the eye in which seeing is essential to knowing. But theater is also – it goes without

saying – different from astronomy, geography, radiology, bacteriology, and other disciplines which Daston and Galison call sciences of the eye. The relationship in the theater between seeing and knowing, a relationship which is managed by judgment, works differently than it does in a field committed to the principles of objectivity, or even reason. Theater asks us to see anew, not just with the eyes of interpretation, but also with the eyes of wonder. It asks that we suspend our disbelief, repudiate fact, and consent to the proposition that this place is a different place than the one it clearly is and that these people are different people than the ones they actually are. Theatrical fictions require the consent and collaboration of their audiences and, accordingly, demand a form of judgment grounded in *disknowledge* rather than *knowledge* in its conventional, rational sense. I borrow the term "disknowledge" from Katherine Eggert, who describes it as "the conscious and deliberate setting aside of one compelling mode of understanding the world – one discipline, one theory – in favor of another." "To know something literarily," she notes as an example, "is a conscious choice over knowing it factually."[42] The same can be said of theater. To know something theatrically – whether it is an audience watching a play or Orsino watching Viola's performance of Cesario next to her twin – is different than knowing it factually. In the theater, what we see and feel is true; what we ratiocinate is not. Theater is *make-believe*, in the most literal and artisanal sense of that term.[43]

The point has been made before in this book, but it bears repeating and emphasis now: in the context of Shakespearean theater, judgment is not purely, or even predominantly, a rational exercise. It is not data-management. It involves deliberation, but also the willing avoidance of logic and at times outright faith. It can accommodate something being two things at once – impossible and real, there and not there. Truth, for Shakespeare, is something different than what we would now call fact. Though in our own time, the two concepts have largely collapsed into one, truth can be a more open, improvised, and communally determined category. There is a shrewd exploration of this topic in sonnet 138, in which Shakespeare reimagines truth as something *made* collaboratively, rather than as something absolute, transcendent, and singular. The opening lines declare:

> When my love swears that she is made of truth,
> I do believe her though I know she lies,
> That she might think me some untutored youth,
> Unlearnèd in the world's false subtleties. (1–4)

Truth (the woman is faithful, the man is young) is not keyed to what the individual knows factually, but instead to what the social unit actively chooses to believe. Collective participation is the substance of truth and its necessary condition. Sonnet 138 invites us into a scene where the content of each individual's claims – the question of whether they are correct or not – is less important than the conditions of mutual recognition under which those claims are made. Truth, the sonnet proposes, is not a thing in itself; it is an effect of shared judgment and common acknowledgment, a matter of form, not of substance.

Of course, for all its optimism, there could also be a cynical streak in this poem, the suggestion that if truth can be assembled from anything, it can also be assembled from lies. On the stage, however, this radical openness to the extremes of possibility becomes one of theater's most powerful "epistemic virtues," making feasible forms recognition, acceptance, and even healing not achievable in an either/or world of prescriptive reality.[44] One thinks immediately of the statue scene at the end of *The Winter's Tale*, a miracle that has no rational explanation and yet is true, something that is and is not. Describing "the play's central epistemological dilemma" as "the relationship of the seen to the truth," James Knapp has written illuminatingly on the way Leontes's confrontation with a revivified statue of his long-dead wife can be read as a scene of "ethical judgment."[45] Knapp continues:

> His [Leontes's] willingness to affirm the unknown constitutes a risk that is the guarantor of an ethics freed from the restrictions of prescriptive thought (prescriptions, for example, of conventional epistemology or institutional religion). To proceed is to risk choosing in favor of what cannot be known in the present but will have

full consequences in the future. To accept the unknown is not to remain at the moment of undecidability; it is to act in the face of the indeterminate in order to make meaning.[46]

Knapp's last words in this passage seem crucial to me. Responding positively or proactively to the obscure, the wondrous is not to accept that meaning is unattainable or that there is no meaning to attain. Rather, it is a decision to *make meaning* through action and acknowledgment, to take the visually opaque and perplexing as an invitation to plot a course forward or create something new. Visual judgment, in the theater and in a number of Shakespeare's worlds, is essentially a creative impulse, not a mechanism for testing claims or verifying data.

The relationship among vision, judgment, and knowledge takes different forms across Shakespeare's plays, tapping into various aspects of the conceptually variegated, and sometimes contradictory, intellectual currents of his time. But Shakespeare also thinks about vision as a playwright; that is to say, from the perspective of someone for whom seeing generates meaning in a different way than it does in the context of everyday life or other vision-based disciplines. For theater to work, an audience must look trustfully and collaboratively; there must be a certain degree of shared interpretive consent; and there must, on some level, be a common feeling that this kind of looking matters, that there is *added value* (to borrow a popular phrase from the world of business) – experientially, ethically, emotionally – that accrues from suspending disbelief and accepting and entering the world that is temporarily given to you. Not every play earns its audience's commitment to this demand, and not every audience (or audience member) is willing to consent. Plays fail, plays are poorly received. But the basic condition from which any play can have a chance at success is the broad acceptance of an invitation to see anew. In this environment, judgment must organize thought and lay the groundwork for decision and action based on the world as it is given, not on some other version of that world behind a curtain; it must orient the subject towards wonder rather than certainty; and it must operate according to the principle that truth can exist between the poles of pure fact and pure fantasy.

The dagger scene in *Macbeth* is Shakespeare's most purely philosophical meditation on this version of visual judgment. It takes
the appropriate form of a soliloquy and leads troublingly to the
murder of the king and his attendants. In *Twelfth Night,* on the
other hand, it allows the marvelous to be held in suspension, opening a space between confusion and closure in which the impossible
suddenly seems possible. In *The Winter's Tale,* the marvel is held in
suspension much longer, never to be resolved within the horizons
of the play, leaving characters and audience members alike with a
sense that they have experienced a miracle. There are few moral
parallels we can draw between these examples. Each one serves the
formal, thematic, and tonal requirements of the genre to which it
belongs. Structurally and conceptually, though, they have something in common, something that has to do with the way the visual
judgment of Macbeth, Orsino, Olivia, Sebastian, Leontes, and any
committed theater audience allows things to happen which would
not otherwise have taken place.

This chapter has spent a good deal of time talking about in-
between spaces: the space between there and not there, impossible
and possible, fact and fantasy, confusion and closure. These are
the spaces nurtured by Shakespeare's counter-optics, the spaces
curated and animated by theatrical judgment. And it is from
within such in-between spaces that we are most likely to find ourselves capable of the leaps of imagination that make revelation and
change possible. We will continue to explore this latter idea in a
variety of ways over the course of the next three chapters.

CHAPTER 4

MAKING

As a way into describing this chapter's specific mission, I want to consider a general question: Is judgment an ending or a beginning? Does it finish something or create something new? The question is both conceptual and practical. That is, it has to do with judgment as a philosophical idea, but also with the role judgment might play in actually doing something. The culture in which Shakespeare lived offers more than one answer to the question. Within Christianity, for example, judgment figures most prominently as an ending. It is final, after all, among the Last Things of Christian eschatology. In the extensive sermon literature on the topic, there is considerably more emphasis placed on endings, punishment, and what will happen to you if you are a sinner than there is on new beginnings, salvation, and what will happen to you if you are devout. Preachers are at pains to stress that the "court" of the Last Judgment is not like earthly courts: there are no intercessors, rhetoric will not help you, you cannot buy off the judge, and there are no reprieves. It is absolute, conclusive, and no one can hide. In the words of preacher George Bury:

> mony may do much with earthly Iudges; it may turne iudgement into mercy, and mercy into iudgement: but it is not the multitude of gifts (saith *Iob* in his 36. chap. and 18. verse) that can deliuer thee from the wrath of the Iudge of heauen.[1]

From this perspective, the temporality of judgment seems to be decidedly backward looking. It concludes, it determines, it breaks rather than makes.

And yet a close reader can find traces of generativity, renewal, and futurity even within the body of exegesis connected to the Last Things. For all its finality, the Last Judgment is the necessary prelude to a new heaven and new earth: the World to Come. In a series of sermons printed in 1613, for instance, Robert Horne stresses that Christ's role as judge and as savior cannot be neatly separated. Christ will come on "The day of the last judgement" as a "Sauiour, and as a Iudge"; "He alone is the Sauiour: and therefore he alone must be Iudge. He that saueth his elect, must condemne the world." For the elect, Horne notes, Christ "will be their aduocate, not Iudge, except to acquit them."² In this scenario, judgment takes on the attributes of advocacy. It becomes the gateway to a new a life, just as it would for someone acquitted in an earthly courtroom. The judge speaks, the handcuffs are removed, and out the former defendant walks blinking in the sun, a life on pause set suddenly back in motion.

The English clergyman, scholar, and noted preacher Robert Bolton goes into more detail, explaining that for the righteous, the Last Judgment will form new communities among those whom time, space, death, and circumstance – burdens of the fallen world – have kept separate:

> Society is not comfortable, without familiar acquaintance: Be assured then, it shall not be wanting in the height and perfection of all glory, blisse, and joy. Nay, our minds being abundantly and beatifically illuminated with all wisdome and knowledge, we shalbe enabled to know, not onely those of former holy acquaintance; but also strangers, and such as we never knew before; even all the faithfull, which ever were, are, or shall be. We shall be able to say: this was Father *Abraham,* this King *David,* this Saint *Paul:* this was *Luther, Calvin, Bradford,* &c. this my Father, this my Sonne, this my Wife, this my Pastour.³

This passage gives us a sense of judgment's dual nature within Christian doctrine, its bi-temporal orientation towards both the past and the future. In the work of evaluation and selection, it looks backward; in the work of community-making, it looks forward.

The legal realm, referred to so derisively by George Bury, has its own way of fostering a creative conception of judgment.

A specifically early modern development of English common law is the uniquely generative social role of judicial decision-making. Over the course of the sixteenth century, there is a gradual shift in emphasis from legal doctrine to judge-made law, or *jurisprudence*, which meant that the role of judgment in creating the law expanded significantly.[4] Whereas in the fifteenth century, Thomas Littleton's landmark *Tenures* (1481) relied almost exclusively on doctrine, or common learning, William Staunford, holding the same judicial office as Littleton less than a century later, wrote, in J. H. Baker's words, "books so crammed with references and quotation that he seemed incapable of venturing an opinion unless it could be derived from someone else."[5] Staunford, in other words, in books like *Les plees del coron* (1557) and *An exposicion of the kinges prerogative* (1561), drew heavily on past judicial decisions to lend his own claims authority. Edmund Plowden's later sixteenth-century law reports exhibit the same tendency, but with more methodological rigor and decisiveness. Plowden was very selective when it came to choosing which cases to report. Unlike more typical yearbooks of the period, he would leave out any courtroom debate that was inconclusive, publishing only those cases in which a specific point of law had been settled by a final judgment of record.[6] These shifts resulted, gradually, in a more authoritative judiciary, and judgment came to loom larger in the conceptual landscape of English common law.[7]

With these contexts in mind, it is probably starting to become clearer how "making" might be deemed one of judgment's affordances, even if at first glance the two terms seem to evoke quite different impulses. The aim of this chapter is to delve deeper into the idea of judgment as making. My touchstone in this endeavor will be Prospero's concluding epilogue in *The Tempest*. Though this is a "last judgment" of sorts, my purpose will be to focus less on how the scene functions as a conclusion or an outcome and more on how it functions as a new beginning. In other words, I want to show how Prospero's epilogue invites us to think about judgment as a form of creation. This, as we will see, is an idea that starts to make more sense when we consider two important contexts: first, the way theatrical epilogues link critique to creativity, and second, the way judgment worked in tandem with invention within the rhetorical tradition that was so central to early modern education. With these contexts in place, the last section of the chapter will consider the larger ethical implications of this connection between judgment and making. For this part of the discussion, I will turn to a selection of writings by Hannah Arendt which provide an indispensable intellectual resource for thinking about the way theater's political potency lies precisely in its capacity to create occasions for judicial creation.

Prospero's Plea

I begin by quoting Prospero's epilogue in full. A particularly well-known example of the epilogue form, this speech has become a standard feature of the play in performance. It occurs in the final moments of the play, just after Prospero has released the island castaways and set his servant Ariel free. Addressing the audience directly, Prospero says:

> Now my charms are all o'erthrown,
> And what strength I have's mine own,
> Which is most faint. Now 'tis true
> I must be here confined by you,
> Or sent to Naples. Let me not,
> Since I have my dukedome got,
> And pardoned the deceiver, dwell
> In this bare island by your spell,
> But release me from my bands
> With the help of your good hands.
> Gentle breath of yours my sails
> Must fill, or else my project fails,
> Which was to please. Now I want
> Spirits to enforce, art to enchant;
> And my ending is despair
> Unless I be relieved by prayer,
> Which pierces so that it assaults
> Mercy itself, and frees all faults.
>   As you from crimes would pardoned be,
>   Let your indulgence set me free. (5.1.319–38)[8]

Prospero presents his case to the playgoers, who are expected to consider two related questions: (1) Was the play good? (2) Has Prospero behaved in an ethical manner? In considering these questions, the audience is being asked not simply to pass judgment, but more precisely, to imagine *through* judgment a future for Prospero, an imaginative addendum to the fiction presented on stage. If the audience disapproves and does not clap, Prospero will remain imprisoned on the island. If they approve and do clap, he will return to Milan.

This moment both is and is not typical of theatrical epilogues, which were a common feature of early modern English commercial drama. What I mean by this will become clear if we spend some time reviewing what theatrical epilogues were and how they conventionally worked. Put in the simplest terms, theatrical epilogues were onstage speeches addressed to the audience at the end of a performance. They were typically read rather than memorized, sometimes by a character in the play, sometimes by someone else. An epilogue asserts the merits of the play it punctuates and asks for audience approval in the form of applause. Far more epilogues occurred in performance than survive in print, and of those that do survive, most were occasional. That is, they were designed for particular venues, particular audiences, or particular performances, though some epilogues may have been more permanent features of the plays they accompanied. What all epilogues have in common is their ability to effect what Robert Weimann describes as a "redistribution of authority in the playhouse."[9] When an epilogue speaker requests applause, this changes the relationship between actors and audience and between fiction and life. Playgoers are now expected to do something, to respond based on the kind of emotional and intellectual experience they have had up to that point. The epilogue, in other words, draws attention to the active and participatory nature of theatrical spectatorship and the degree to which audiences were implicated in the imaginative world of the plays they attended.

Printed epilogues in playbooks are an important component of the archive of early modern judgment, but they present certain interpretive challenges as well. In particular, these printed texts can give the misleading impression that epilogues were stable and enduring features of the plays for which they were written when, in fact, they were usually composed with a first performance in mind. Because they carried a higher-than-usual entrance fee, first performances attracted a different kind of audience than one might find at a play later in its run. First-performance audiences were composed of educated playgoers – precisely the sort of people who might think themselves in possession of superior powers of discernment. Moreover, as Tiffany Stern notes, many at first performances would have felt that the high price of admission granted them a right to critique. "At publique Stage-Playes," writes Dudley North in 1645, "whosoever censures" is "entitled to it . . . for his money."[10] This sense of entitlement was fueled by the promise of a very real form of theatrical authority since audiences at first performances largely determined the fate of the plays they watched. Usually, a new play would only be granted a second performance if the audience responded encouragingly to the epilogue.

Epilogues, then, constituted the ritual core of a broadly adjudicatory set of conditions that were central to the culture of professional theater. Playwrights make frequent reference to this phenomenon. The Prologue to John Marston's play *The Dutch Courtesan* (1604), for example, admonishes playgoers as follows:

> know that firme art cannot feare
> Vaine rage: onely the highest grace we pray
> Is you'le not taxe, until you judge our Play.
> Think and then speake: tis rashnesse, and not wit
> To speake what is in passion, and not judgment fit.[11]

The audience may acquire a right to judge when they pay their entrance fee, but as far as Marston is concerned, judgment also requires a certain level of responsibility and skill. It is part of a larger rational procedure that originates in thinking and culminates in speaking and leaves no place for rash emotionalism. Marston clearly harbors some latent skepticism about the ability of theater audiences to judge well. Ben Jonson goes further, expressing outright derision at being held in thrall to the tastes of playgoers. In his epistle to the 1612 quarto of *The Alchemist*, he opines:

> How out of purpose, and place, doe I name Art? When the Professors are growne so obstinate contemners of it, and presume on their owne Naturalls, as they are deriders of all diligence that way, and, by simple mocking at the termes, when they understand not the things, thinke to get of wittily with their Ignorance. Nay, they are esteem'd the more learned, and sufficient for this, by the Multitude, through their excellent vice of judgment. For they commend Writers, as they doe Fencers, or Wrastlers; who if they come in robustly, and put for it with a great deale of violence, are receiv'd for the braver fellowes.[12]

This is the sort of contemptuousness that Jonson is famous for, but his attitude here becomes more understandable when we recall that his play *Sejanus* (1603) was rejected by its first Globe audience and never made it past its opening performance.

With their rituals of evaluation, public-theater epilogues bore a striking resemblance to the procedures of law courts. As was noted in the Introduction, playwrights sometimes even described their relationship to their audiences in overtly legal language. In *The Novella* (1632) by Richard Brome, for example, the playwright is imagined as a defendant in a law court: "Hee'll 'bide his triall, and submits his cause / To you the Jury."[13] The prologue to Thomas Dekker's *The Wonder of a Kingdom* (1631) frets about "what Judges sit to Doome each Play."[14] And *The Coxcomb* (1608–10) by Francis Beaumont, John Fletcher, and Philip Massinger features the sarcastic declaration, "Now 'tis to be tri'd / Before such Judges, 'twill not be deni'd / A . . . noble hearing."[15] These legal references would have made sense to the community of theatergoers in Shakespeare's time, a sizeable portion of which was affiliated with the Inns of Court, the institution that trained young men for careers in law.[16] A number of playwrights, too, we will recall, had connections with the Inns: John Marston was a member of the Middle Temple in the 1590s, as was John Webster; John Ford was admitted in 1602; and Jonson, though he did not attend the Inns, was close friends with prominent jurists such as John Seldon and John Hoskyns. There was significant overlap between the culture of theater and the culture of law in Shakespeare's time, and epilogues constituted a formally compact instance of this crossing.

This much we know, then: Prospero's invocation of audience judgment is part of a larger theatrical convention, one which has clear legal coordinates. What about his invocation of audience *imagination*? I quote the relevant lines once again:

> I must be here confined by you,
> Or sent to Naples. Let me not,
> Since I have my dukedome got,
> And pardoned the deceiver, dwell
> In this bare island by your spell,
> But release me from my bands
> With the help of your good hands. (5.1.322–28)

One way of looking at this passage is as a bid for creative input, and to this extent it fits comfortably under the umbrella of epilogue convention. As Stern writes, "From a time in theatrical history hard to date precisely, some plays on their opening performances were offered as mutable texts ready for audience revision."[17] There is evidence of this practice in printed playbooks. For example, the prologue to John Marston's *Antonio and Mellida* (1602) invites the audience to "polish these rude Sceanes."[18] Similarly, in Thomas Heywood's *Mayden-Head Well Lost* (1634), the audience is told, "Our Play is new, but whether shaped well / In Act or Seane, Judge you, you best can tell."[19] These sorts of invitations made playgoers collaborators in the fiction. Most often, this took the form of cutting. Spectators would communicate which parts of the play they did not like and these sections would be excised for subsequent performances.[20]

In Prospero's epilogue, however, there is something slightly different going on. Here, playgoers are not being asked to "polish" or cut; they are being asked to elaborate and expand. This difference is important because it means their charge is not to perfect something that is already there, but rather to make something that is not: namely, a future for Prospero. Judgment, in other words, leads to invention in Prospero's epilogue. Understanding the link between these two concepts requires us to look beyond the walls of the theater to a larger tradition of rhetorical thought and practice.

Judgment and Invention

The idea that judgment and invention are fundamentally connected would have been familiar to many in Shakespeare's time, including a considerable number of playgoers and playwrights. The link finds its source in a long tradition of rhetorical learning. Thomas Blundeville's commentary in *The Arte of Logicke* (1599) is fairly standard. While "invention finds matter," Blundeville explains, judgment "frameth, disposeth, and reduceth the same into due forme of argument."[21] This formulation derives from Roman rhetorical theory, which has deeper roots in Aristotle. Texts like Cicero's *De inventione*, the anonymous *Rhetorica ad Herennium*, and Quintilian's *Institutio oratoria* describe invention (*inventio*) as the skill of deciding which line of reasoning is most likely to strike a particular audience as especially compelling. Judgment's role is to break that line of reasoning down into component parts and then arrange them in a sequence calculated to achieve maximum persuasiveness.[22] Judgment, in other words, turns ideas into arguments by lending them organizational form. As noted in the Introduction, in Shakespeare's time, anyone with a grammar school education was likely to have encountered rhetorical handbooks like *De inventione*, *Rhetorica ad Herennium*, and *Institutio oratoria*, or vernacular manuals like Thomas Wilson's *The Art of Rhetorique* (1553), which drew on the Roman handbooks.[23] Accordingly, Blundeville's simple description of judgment would have sounded familiar to many early moderns, including Shakespeare, who would have been exposed to rhetorical texts as a student at the King's New School at Stratford-upon-Avon.[24]

With this in mind, we can begin to see how judgment might be conceived as one crucial point along a continuum of creative endeavor. For those with some training in rhetorical theory, judgment was a form of making or *poiesis* rather than a form of decision, as we would now tend to view it. This creative component of judgment is even more apparent in the vernacular literary criticism of sixteenth- and seventeenth-century England, which was heavily influenced by, and sometimes indistinguishable from, rhetorical theory. Central to literary critical judgment was the notion of *decorum*, which involved following carefully proscribed rules about, for example, how certain types of characters require the use of certain kinds of language, how certain styles of argument require particular metaphors, or how a given genre necessitates a specific type of plot.[25] These precepts reached early modern readers through either direct or mediated exposure to the ideas in Aristotle's *Rhetoric* and Horace's *Ars Poetica*, as well as through grammatical and rhetorical commentaries attached to the comedies of Plautus and Terence, which were among the mainstays of elementary and intermediate education in Latin.[26] For early modern critics and theorists writing in this vein, the aesthetic quality and even the moral viability of imaginative writing depended on how well the rules of *decorum* were followed. In *The Arte of Rhetorique*, Wilson uses the word "aptness" for *decorum* and stresses that writers must choose "words most apt for their purpose. In weighty causes grave words are thought most needful, that the greatness of the matter may the rather appear in the vehemency of their talk."[27] Robert Ascham, in *The Schoolmaster* (1570), prefers the word "propriety," and tells his readers that it applies at all levels of a composition, "in choice of words, in framing sentences, in handling of argument, and use of right form, figure and number."[28] George Puttenham goes on to lay out these precepts in impressive detail in *The Art of English Poesy* (1589). Consequently, for many readers in the sixteenth and seventeenth centuries, the process of appraising the aesthetic worth and the moral viability of imaginative writing was guided by simple questions that linked reading to judging: Were laws broken or adhered to? What are the implications? Within this general interpretive framework, someone like Sir John Harrington can defend Ariosto against charges of obscenity by pointing out that "there is so meet a decorum in the persons that speak lasciviously, as any of judgment must needs allow."[29]

Philip Sidney's *The Defense of Poesy* (c.1580; printed 1595) is the first attempt at sustained literary criticism in English. In it, Sidney expands on the idea that judgment forms the basis of sound reading to argue, in addition, that our ability to judge well can be sharpened by good poetry. All the wisdom that philosophy has to offer, Sidney says, "lies[s] dark before the imaginative and judging power if they be not illuminated or figured forth by the speaking picture of poesy."[30] Sidney goes on to describe how religious scripture "inhabit[s] . . . the judgment" precisely because it functions like poetry, which is neither wholly conceptual (as philosophy is) nor wholly particular (as history is), but something in-between, which illustrates universal precepts with specific instances and images:

> Even our Saviour Christ could as well have given the moral commonplaces of uncharitableness and humbleness as the divine narration of Dives and Lazarus, or of disobedience and mercy as that heavenly discourse of the lost child and the gracious father, but that his through-searching wisdom knew the estate of Dives burning in hell and of Lazarus in Abraham's bosom *would more constantly, as it were, inhabit both the memory and judgment* (truly, for myself, me seems I see before my eyes the lost child's disdainful prodigality turned to envy a swine's dinner), which by the learned divines are thought not historical acts but instructing parables.[31]

The charge of English poetry, then, is to help build a community of rational, moral, right-thinking people. Samuel Daniel, for instance, tasks poetry with "setting up the music of our times to a higher note of judgment and discretion" in *A Defense of Rhyme* (1603).[32] It is also true, though, that bad poetry can weaken judgment. The Scottish poet, courtier, and statesman William Alexander has a method for avoiding such problems:

> When I censure any poet, I first dissolve the general contexture of his work in several pieces, to what sinews it hath, and to mark what will remain behind when that external gorgeousness, consisting in the choice or placing of words, as if it would bribe the ear to corrupt the judgment, is at first removed, or at least marshaled in its own degree.[33]

Good poetry builds and fortifies judgment; bad poetry erodes it. And since, as Wilson, Ascham, and Puttenham show us, judgment is the cornerstone of responsible reading – of being able to discern what is good and what is bad – the whole process is circular. The more good poetry one reads, the better equipped they will be to identify other examples of good poetry, and the better disposed they will be to produce good (moral, decorous) poetry themselves. This last point is important. For it is sound judgment, Henry Peacham tells us in *The Garden of Eloquence* (1577), that transforms wisdom, through the application of rules of decorum, into the kinds of eloquent and persuasive verbal packages that affect people:

> Many, not perceiving the nigh and necessary conjunction of these two precious jewels [wisdom and eloquence], do either affect fineness of speech and neglect the knowledge of things, or, contrariwise, covet understanding and contemn the art of eloquence. And therefore it cometh to pass that such take great pains and reap small profits; they ever seek and never find the thing they would fainest have – the one sort of these speak much to small purpose, and the other (though they be wise) are not able aptly to express their meaning. From which calamity they are free, that do use a right judgment in applying their studies so that their knowledge may be joined with apt utterance: that is to say, that their eloquence may be wise, and their wisdom eloquent.[34]

Each of the writers mentioned above has a slightly different way of invoking judgment, a slightly different way of positioning it in relation to the ethical affordances of English poetry and rhetoric. What is clear across the board, though, is that judgment is a practice suspended within a larger web of ideas about literary evaluation and invention: it is part of the reading process since all art is, or should be, rule-bound; it is a faculty that stands to be strengthened or weakened depending on what one chooses to read; and it is a mediating force between pure ideas and the embodiment of those ideas in a structured expressive form. Prospero's epilogue articulates a similar set of associations. The request for judgment is also an appeal to the audience's capacity for literary invention, specifically their ability to craft an imaginary afterlife for Prospero: "release me from my bands / With the help of your good hands," he implores; "As you from crimes would pardoned be, /

Let your indulgence set me free." According to the terms set by Prospero, then, clapping is an act both evaluative and generative, a verdict on the past and a vision for the future.

Judgment and Responsibility

Theatrical judgment is creative judgment. It is judgment as making and shaping, a form of assessment that serves the larger endeavor of invention. This observation, as we have seen, and as we will continue to see in the next chapter, has a number of cultural-historical coordinates in the early modern period. But it also tells us something more broadly significant about the political and ethical value of theater. To begin with, we may note that bringing judgment and invention together as Prospero does gives theatergoers a different kind of ethical stake in the play they are watching than would otherwise be the case. As fellow makers, rather than just consumers, the audience's collective sense of the good, of what is right and what is wrong, is implicated in the play's imagined conclusion, and all the more so for the moral freight Prospero so insistently attaches to the epilogue. Viewed from this perspective, judgment develops less out of an evaluative impulse and more out of a sense of responsibility to communal norms – norms which are both moral and aesthetic. Not to judge, accordingly, would be a failure of responsibility.

This link between judgment and responsibility is key to what makes the theatrical dynamics of Prospero's epilogue politically potent. It is the idea that in judging you give expression to your role as a stakeholder. You judge because it matters, because you are a collaborator in the ongoing work of making and managing a world you find yourself sharing with others. In order to explore this idea further, I am going to shift our attention temporarily away from Shakespeare and early modernity and over to the twentieth-century philosopher Hannah Arendt, whose writings offer a unique series of reflections on guilt and culpability in the aftermath of the Holocaust. Though this may seem a far cry from Shakespeare's world, Arendt is the thinker who more than anyone else sought to understand the conceptual relationship between judgment and responsibility, and so her observations bear directly on the dynamics we have observed in Prospero's epilogue, which I will return to before concluding.

Arendt became interested in judgment when she covered the 1961 trial of Nazi leader Adolf Eichmann for *The New Yorker*. Her articles were later expanded into the book *Eichmann in Jerusalem: A Report on the Banality of Evil* (1963). Arendt was profoundly underwhelmed by Eichmann. She thought he was forgettable, unintelligent, unfrightening. She was also critical of the trial itself. It seemed to her a show trial, one that used Eichmann as a proxy to condemn and punish anti-Semitism in general. Against this method of retribution, Arendt argued that the Holocaust called for specific and nuanced forms of condemnation, mostly of Nazis, but also of Jewish leaders who cooperated with the Nazis. That this did not happen represented for her a "fundamental problem" common to "all these postwar trials," which had to do with "the nature and function of human judgment." She writes:

> What we have demanded in these trials, where the defendants had committed "legal" crimes, is that human beings be capable of telling right from wrong even when all they have to guide them is their own judgment, which moreover happens to be completely at odds with what they must regard as the unanimous opinion of all those around them. ... Since the whole of respectable society had in one way or another succumbed to Hitler, the moral maxims which determine social behavior and the religious commandments – "Thou shalt not kill!" – which guide conscience had virtually vanished. Those few who were still able to tell right from wrong went really only by their own judgments, and they did so freely; there were no rules to be abided by, under which the particular cases with which they were confronted could be subsumed. They had to decide each instance as it arose, because no rules existed for the unprecedented.[35]

Judgment for Arendt, in other words, is not an expression of external social or legal norms, but rather an expression of personal responsibility. So long as you are human, there is an expectation that you will be able to tell "right from wrong."

What postwar trials like Eichmann's threw into sharp relief for Arendt was the degree to which so many were willing to shirk this responsibility, either by refusing to judge or by issuing a sort of judgment that was so broad, so resistant to the concrete threshold between right and wrong, that it amounted to non-judgment. Arendt describes the phenomenon as follows:

> Another such escape from the area of ascertainable facts and personal responsibility are the countless theories, based on non-specific, abstract, hypothetical assumptions – from the *Zeitgest* down to the Oedipus complex – which are so general that they explain and justify every event and every deed . . . Among the constructs that "explain" everything by obscuring all details, we find such notions as a "ghetto mentality" among European Jews; or the collective guilt of the German people, derived from an *ad hoc* interpretation of their history; or an equally absurd assertion of a kind of collective innocence of the Jewish people. All these clichés have in common that they make judgments superfluous and that to utter them is devoid of all risk.[36]

Arendt understood the reluctance of both Germans and Jews to examine closely what took place in Europe between 1933 and 1945, to pinpoint definitively the many groups and individuals – Nazi officers and bureaucrats, "Christian churches," members of "the Jewish leadership" – who had a hand in what she calls "the totality of moral collapse." However, she concludes that "this understandable disinclination is insufficient to explain the reluctance evident everywhere to make judgments in terms of individual moral responsibility."[37]

In the years following her coverage of the Eichmann trial, Arendt finally did arrive at an explanation. In an essay called "Personal Responsibility Under Dictatorship," she recalls, "I was told that judging itself is wrong: no one can judge who had not been there."[38] At the heart of this fiercely neutral stance, Arendt decided, was deep skepticism about the possibility of human freedom:

> There exists in our society a widespread fear of judging that has nothing whatever to do with the biblical "Judge not, that ye be not judged," . . . For behind the unwillingness to judge lurks the

suspicion that no one is a free agent, and hence the doubt that anyone is responsible or could be expected to answer for what he has done . . . . we're all alike, equally bad, and those who try, or pretend that they try, to remain halfway decent are either saints or hypocrites, and in either case should leave us alone.[39]

What Arendt does brilliantly in her writings on judgment is triangulate between three large, difficult concepts – judgment, responsibility, and freedom – in a way that deepens our understanding of all three. Judgment is an articulation of responsibility, and responsibility, in turn, is a condition of being a free agent capable of moral decision and active worldmaking. Viewed thus, judgment is a way of manifesting our status as free agents in moral terms – in terms, that is, of a collective obligation to the good that only a free agent could enter into. The refusal to judge is troubling to Arendt because it indicates an unwillingness to be accountable for the world we all must share. It rehearses a vision of politics as something that works upon rather than through human actors and in this way advances precisely the sort of detached acquiescence that forms the necessary conditions for totalitarian disasters like the Third Reich. That "judgment itself is wrong was Eichmann's own argument against the district court's judgment," Arendt is careful to remind her readers.[40]

It is not so much the historically specific elements of Arendt's work on judgment – those having to do with Eichmann himself, the Holocaust, or the experience of living under dictatorship – that are important for this chapter. Rather, it is the way Arendt extracts from those particulars a framework for thinking about judgment that can help us uncover some of the political deep-structure of Prospero's epilogue. Specifically, Arendt equips us with a vocabulary and a set of concepts that allow us to think about the audience's evaluative response at the end of *The Tempest* as an iteration of responsibility rather than authority, and therefore as something grounded in sociality and active collaboration. Judgment, in Arendt's view, is about having a stake in something. To judge is to participate, with all the potential risks and rewards that always attend participation. Judgment is the place where the freedom and determining power of the individual meets the obligation to something larger than the individual (an Other; a group; a shared experience; a shared future; a shared community; a shared set of norms, be they moral or aesthetic, or as in Prospero's epilogue, both at the same time). On one side, there are the "hands" of the playgoers, which can cast a "spell" and break confining "bands." There is their "breath" that can fill sails and chart a new course. There is their power of "prayer," of pardon, of "indulgence" that holds the promise of "mercy" and "release." On the other side there is Prospero's "project" – a complicated, and at times ethically dubious, undertaking in the name of justice, which has involved calling to account those who have wronged him and seeking reconciliation through selective forgiveness and the restoration of property and titles. There is, more broadly, his freedom – at once spiritual and physical – which is referred to twice in the last three lines of the epilogue: the playgoers' prayer "frees all faults" and their indulgence will "set [Prospero] free." Between these two sides there is the event of judgment, which solders the mind, will, body, and moral intelligence of the adjudicating self to the new, shared set of conditions created through that act of adjudication. As a form of stakeholding participation, judgment is a door perched at the threshold between individual and collective experience – a door through which Shakespeare's audience is compelled to pass at the end of *The Tempest*; a door through which too much of European society, according to Arendt, refused to pass during the Third Reich.

Judgment, we might say, is a sort of event-horizon for political association, a process that translates personal choice into shared consequence. This is the process initiated by Prospero's epilogue when he asks playgoers to evaluate his actions and in so doing determine the final contours of the world that the performers and the public alike have co-created over the course of two or so hours. Accordingly, when I assert that Prospero's epilogue is political, I mean that statement in formal rather than in referential or functional terms. It is the latter two modes of politicization that are most commonly invoked within literary scholarship, but Prospero's epilogue does not work in that way. On a referential level, there is no particular political situation being gestured towards or commented on in the epilogue specifically.[41] On a functional level, meanwhile, the clap-to-free-me-from-my-island conceit is simply a trick to help ensure that the audience will indeed clap. Early modern commercial drama is full of such ploys.

On a formal level, however – that is, in terms of the relationship among the various elements of dramaturgical representation – Prospero's epilogue assembles a theatrical blueprint for participatory politics by changing, through judgment, the nature of the playgoers' creative and ethical involvement in the fictional world with which they have been presented. Jacques Rancière offers a helpful formulation for why this sort of politicization is significant. In *The Politics of Literature*, he writes:

> It is not enough that there be power for there to be politics . . . It is not even enough that there be laws regulating collective life. What is needed is a configuration of a specific form of community.[42]

Rancière points to aesthetic experience as a source of this form of community. Rather than being referentially or functionally political, the aesthetic creates something he calls the "sensory fabric of 'being together,'" which is the foundation of political life and of the human as a political animal.[43] Prospero's epilogue, with its collaborative community of playgoers and performers, fits securely into this scheme. I think this is what Christopher Pye has in mind when he observes – very much in a Rancièrean vein – that Shakespeare's "late plays self-consciously present themselves as works whose inclusive aesthetic form incorporates the audience in its unstable, performatives effects."[44] The claim I am making here is more specific; and while it is certainly Rancièrean in spirit, it owes more to Arendt. The politics of Prospero's epilogue, I wish to suggest, lies not only in the broad way it creates a "specific form of community" through "the sensory fabric of 'being together,'" nor in the general manner in which its "inclusive aesthetic form incorporates the audience." Related to all this, but more particularly, the politics of Prospero's epilogue lies in the fact that the community assembled is a community of judgment – a community, therefore, as Arendt's work clarifies for us, founded on shared responsibility and the collective freedom to craft a world. Indeed, at the heart of Prospero's judgment–invention linkage is an implicit assumption that the playgoers assembled in the theater are free agents and therefore not just able to judge, but also expected to judge. For it is through judgment that they shape the moral contours of the future – Prospero's future.

Brief as it is, the final passage of *The Tempest* offers us a compelling case study in judgment as making; that is to say, in judgment as an act of creation and a point of departure. This is not irreconcilable with an understanding of judgment as evaluation, decision, and completion, but it does reframe those three ideas as part of something larger, and in doing so changes their temporal, ethical, and practical character. Once we start talking about judgment as a form of making, then evaluation, decision, and completion start to look purpose-driven in a more productive, and less punitive, way. Judgment starts to take on a positive social and political role. This aligns Shakespeare's theater with Arendt, who agreed with Immanuel Kant that "judgment presupposes the presence of others," that the very phenomenon of "the public realm," which is necessary for political life, "is constituted by the critics and the spectators."[45] By contrast, Shakespeare's theater is much less aligned with Michel Foucault, who, we will recall, described judgment as a symptom of the "perpetual penality" pervading modern life. It "differentiates, hierarchizes, homogenizes, excludes," according to Foucault. "In short, it *normalizes*."[46] However, if the treatment of judgment in Prospero's epilogue is Arendtian *avant la lettre*, it is also very much of its time. Judgment as a form of making is an idea that is crucial to the most basic principles and methods of English common law, and it can even be detected in some of the sermon literature on the Last Judgment. Above all, though, judgment as making – as what I have referred to above as *one crucial point along a continuum of creative endeavor* – is essential to the rhetorical training that formed the core of early modern education. In translating this basic humanist habit of thought about judgment into theatrical ritual, Prospero's epilogue offers a striking model for collaborative worldmaking – one which (if we take Arendt's insights seriously) we would do well to foster in our own time.

CHAPTER 5

FACING

At this stage in the book, we have developed a fairly robust narrative about what judgment is, or can be, in the theater and in everyday life. We have seen that judgment is rooted in sensation and the vital ecologies of bodies and objects, and that it is active, collaborative, and creative.[1] I will delve deeper into these ideas over the course of the remainder of the book, but in the present chapter I also want to shift my point of entry from the question of *what judgment is* to the question of *how judgment works*, especially in the theater. I choose the phrase "point of entry" carefully because the distinction between these two vectors of the topic is far from absolute. In exploring the sensory grounds of judgment in theoretical terms in Chapters 1 and 2, we also observed the nuts and bolts of how perception functions in the acquisition of knowledge. In exploring the epistemological infrastructure of vision-based judgment in Chapter 3, we also observed how the actual material conditions of theater foster a certain kind of visual ethics. In exploring the conceptual relationship between judgment and invention within rhetoric in Chapter 4, we also observed quite concretely how the deliberative impulses of theater audiences contribute to the process of fiction-making. No matter which side of judgment we start on – *what it is* or *how it works* – we inevitably end up on the other. Be that as it may, this chapter makes a point of leaning deeper into the tangible dynamics of theater and stage action in order to develop a sense of the actual physical choreography of judgment. There is, to be sure, a serious philosophical and intellectual historical component to this topic, as we will see, but the lynchpin of it all is the most basic expressive and interpersonal resource that actors (and humans more generally) have at their disposal: the face.

As Bruce Smith has noted, "face" is both a noun and a verb – a thing and an action.[2] Accordingly, the word denotes two different kinds of physicality. First, it names an object, one that can be seen, touched, and listened to. Second, it describes a way of orienting oneself in space and in relation to other objects (face me, face the wall, face forward, face each other). This verbal use of the word face – in which its noun-form, its thing-quality, is also always active – frequently carries some kind of ethical freight, a sense of being called to account, of taking responsibility, or of acknowledging what has yet to be acknowledged. We see this most vividly in common figurative uses of the word, such as "face the facts" or "face the music." In these phrases, face and facing have something to do with judgment and the kind of moral, social, and practical calculus we all practice every day, and which hopefully leads to the good, the right, or at least the expedient, outweighing the bad, the wrong, or the undesirable.

This connection between facing and judging will be central to this chapter. Specifically, I am interested in how the spatial, object-oriented grammar of the face invites us to think of judgment less as an individual decision or rational cognitive procedure and more as a physical, dimensional event that involves orientating oneself in space and time. I will be referring to this as the "physics of judgment" and my case study will be Shakespeare's *Measure for Measure*, in particular act 5.1 in which two faces – Mariana's and Duke Vincento's – are crucial to the play's final scene of condemnation and forgiveness. The theater provides an especially compelling locale for thinking about the physics of judgment. Indeed, judgment shares with theater its most elemental components: people and things arranged in space and time. The face is crucial to this discussion because in *Measure for Measure* it stands at the crossroads of theater and judgment, indexing their shared fields of location and duration and their common orientation towards the future. This is a set of connections that would have been much more explicit within Latin culture, where *vultus* (the face) was one of three key aspects of oratory, and the one that linked *actio* in the legal sense

(a legal "action") to *acting* in the theatrical sense.[3] Facing, in this
sort of linguistic and rhetorical environment, was intimately related
to doing, making, and creating, terms which, tellingly, share a common etymological root in the Latin verb *facere*.[4]

In attending to the futurity of judgment, I am building on the
work of the previous chapter, but this time with more attention to
the mechanics of acknowledgment and revelation that are essential
to adjudication in theatrical environments. In the terms of performance theorists like James Thompson and Hans Ulrich Gumbrecht,
judgment is a "presence-effect," an event or process made possible
through active, mutually recognized human cohabitation of physical space.[5] Within this model, facing becomes both the physical and
ethical ground zero of judgment. To borrow the lucid formulation
of Mathew James Smith and Julia Reinhard Lupton, facing is a
"pre-semantic" mode of sociality that "cultivates forms of perception and cognition" that are essential to transformation at a social
scale. Judgment is just such a form "of perception and cognition."[6]
Act 5.1 of *Measure for Measure* iterates these theoretical observations in concrete and dimensional terms, situating facing at the
center of an interactive choreography of deliberation that creates
the preconditions for social change. My aim in the pages that follow, then, is to use the dynamics of facing in the final passage of
Measure for Measure to deepen and reinforce the idea that theater
can involve us in the affirmative and creative work of judgment.

Before going further, I should acknowledge that some readers
may find it strange that a Shakespearean *dénouement* known for
courting arbitrariness, ambiguity, and authoritarianism is being
enlisted in the project of recovering a positive version of judgment.
Modern critics have been uneasy about several aspects of the final
scene of the play, including the unexpected betrothal of Isabella
and the Duke and the near executions of Angelo and Lucio. As
early as 1972, Harriett Hawkins described act 5.1 of *Measure for
Measure* as "not only aesthetically and intellectually unsatisfying,
but personally infuriating." She continues:

> Duke Vincentio learns nothing. He admits no limits to his power
> and he never once analyses the total situation. And so, in defiance

of all our critical efforts, Duke Vincentio, in the second half of *Measure for Measure*, remains outside any meaning, an external plot-manipulator, a dramatic engineer of a comic ending, who never sees beyond his single theatrical goal.[7]

Around the same time Hawkins was writing, actors and directors began finding creative ways to give dramatic form to the sort of dissatisfaction registered in her analysis. Perhaps most famously, the Isabella of John Barton's 1970 RSC production of the play "shocked audiences," in Michael D. Friedman's words, "by silently refusing to acquiesce to the Duke's proposal."[8] With this precedent set, productions that opted for a more conventional happy ending risked coming across as naïve, conservative, or even irresponsible. Commenting on Michael Boyd's 1998 RSC production of the play, for example, Pascale Aebischer writes:

> What Boyd seemed all too keen to gloss over is the way the open silences of Angelo and Isabella point to a view of marriage not as a happy comedic resolution but rather as both a form of state control and a kind of rape.[9]

Driving the point home, she concludes:

> Isabella seems to escape rape by the Duke's deputy only to be tricked into having sex with the Duke himself . . . Seen from this point of view, a happy ending of the way imagined by Michael Boyd and, to a lesser extent, Adrian Noble [RSC 1983], seems rather contrived and quite naively conservative in its politics.[10]

These are serious charges and not to be taken lightly. Friedman's solution is historicization. He points out that the critical debate over the betrothal of the Duke and Isabella may miss the fact that marriage in Shakespeare's time was rarely conceived as an institutionalization of love, but more often as a legal or economic transaction.[11] The marriages at the end of *Measure for Measure*, he argues – the Duke and Isabella's included – are forms of recompense for wrongs committed against women. They belong to the world of legal satisfaction rather than consensual mutual attraction. This is indeed consistent with what we know about early modern marriage, and it offers a helpful way to footnote Shakespeare's text. But when it comes to performance, I am inclined to agree with Aebischer that some form of interrogation or subversion of what the text gives us is called for. Theater is not antiquarianism, but a living art that must necessarily inhabit, physically and ethically, the present of its performance.

So, on what grounds do I pursue an affirmative interpretation of act 5.1 of *Measure for Measure*? It is my hope, of course, that the justification for this position will emerge from the details of the discussion to follow, but I will clarify from the outset that in arguing that the close of *Measure for Measure* models a positive version of judgment, I am not proposing that the *dénouement* itself is uniformly positive. Instead, and more precisely, I wish to suggest that the play of faces in act 5.1 helps us redescribe adjudication as a physical and ethical choreography of mutual recognition, and that such mutual recognition constitutes the conditions of possibility for any new social formation. If this is a very different insight from the one arrived at by Hawkins, that is because her assessment is anchored to a notion of judgment that is (1) almost entirely juridical in nature, and (2) associated solely with the Duke.[12] However, as I will show, if we start with the reflexive and interactive rhythms of facing rather than the procedural scripts of law, and if we think of the calling to account at the end of the play in collaborative rather than unilateral terms, then we stand to learn something valuable about the way theater fosters a form of judgment that is creative and participatory.

Mariana's Face and the Physics of Judgment

Let us begin by mapping out how the physics of judgment works in act 5.1. The scene brings together two deception plots. In both cases, the deception is justified by the greater good for which it is committed. The first of these involves Duke Vincento, who throughout the play dresses as a friar to observe the behavior of his subjects undetected. The other involves Mariana, a woman who was betrothed to, then abandoned by, Angelo, the hypocritically puritanical deputy filling in for the Duke. Mariana, Isabella, and the Duke trick Angelo into consummating his marriage to Mariana by sending her to a garden-house where Angelo thinks he is having a tryst with Isabella. The collision of these two plots in the final scene of the play leads to a series of revelations in which the face plays an essential role.

The first of these revelations occurs when, in the wake of Isabella's accusations of sexual blackmail, Mariana is led onstage, supposedly to absolve Angelo of Isabella's charges. Here is the initial part of the scene:

> DUKE: Give us some seats.
> *Two seats are brought in.*
>   Come, cousin Angelo,
> In this I'll be impartial: be you judge
> Of your own cause.
>   *The Duke and Angelo sit*
>   *Enter Friar Peter with Mariana veiled*
>   Is this the witness, friar?
> First let her show her face, and after speak.
> MARIANA: Pardon, my lord, I will not show my face
> Until my husband bid me. (5.1.165–70)[13]

This is clearly a scene of arbitration. A charge has been made and a witness is being brought in to testify. The Duke even has some seats set up to make the exchange feel more like a trial with judge and jury presiding.[14] We should also note that Mariana's face is at the center of this judgment-event. The Duke's command, "First let her show her face, and after speak," seems to assume that the forensic and moral evaluation integral to judgment is only possible under certain baseline conditions of collective ethical orientation: the mutual acknowledgment and recognition intrinsic to the face-to-face encounter.[15] But Mariana refuses: "I will not show my face / Until my husband bid me." A little further on, Angelo echoes the Duke's request, at which point Mariana finally acquiesces:

> ANGELO: This is a strange abuse. Let's see thy face.
> MARIANA: My husband bids me, now I will unmask.
>   *She unveils*
> This is that face, thou cruel Angelo,
> Which once thou swor'st was worth the looking on; (5.1.204–7)

There are two aspects of this exchange that are important for understanding the physics of judgment. To begin with, the component parts of this judgment-event consist predominantly of actions and reactions centered on Mariana's veiled face. This stage business is marked verbally throughout: "give," "come," "show," "not show," "let's see," "*unveils.*" That is to say, Mariana's face indexes the way the judgment-event unfolds in space. In addition – and this is the second aspect – Mariana's face indexes the way the judgment-event unfolds through time. All terms pertaining to temporal positioning – what linguists call "time deixis" – are used in reference to Mariana's face: "first," "after," "until," "now."[16] Here is the relevant passage once again, this time with time deixis marked in bold and references to Mariana's face underlined:

> Is this the witness, friar?
> **First** let her show her <u>face</u>, and **after** speak.
> MARIANA: Pardon, my lord, I will not show my <u>face</u>
> **Until** my husband bid me. (5.1.165–70)
> . . .
> ANGELO: This is a strange abuse. Let's see thy <u>face</u>.
> MARIANA: My husband bids me, **now** I will unmask.
> *She unveils* (5.1.204–5)

Marking the exchange in this way highlights the peculiar theatrical role played by the face in this scene. Though obviously part of the actor's and character's body, the face also functions almost like a prop. It is instrumentalized in a way that exceeds the demands of character in order to advance elements of plot and theme. To this extent, the face muddles some of the standard categories of theatrical semiotics established by scholars such as Patrice Pavis, Erika Fischer-Lichte, and Keir Elam. Consider some basic examples of these categories: linguistic signs, paralinguistic signs, kinesic signs, and proxemic signs. Linguistic signs function both rhetorically and acoustically. They comprise both the meanings of individual words spoken on stage and the tone and pace of delivery. Paralinguistic signs, meanwhile, include such things as props, music, scenery, and lighting. Kinesic signs are self-contained bodily movements, such as gestures. Proxemic signs, on the other hand, are movements of bodies through the space of the stage.[17]

Mariana's face does not fit in a straightforward way into any of these categories. Instead it performs two different kinds of signification simultaneously – kinesic and proxemic – while also challenging received wisdom about how these signifying units are supposed to work. Mariana's face is a kinesic sign in the way that all faces always are on stage, but the fact that it remains veiled for most of the exchange seriously undercuts its ability to do what kinesic signs are supposed to do: express or gesture. Mariana's face is a proxemic sign to the extent that it occasions the scene's primary actions and reactions. Indeed, it is at the center of the scene's orbit of movement. And yet it does very little in the way of significant movement through space itself.

We might instead think of Mariana's face from the perspective of the subfield of proxemics itself, leaving aside for a moment the way it has been taken up within theatrical semiotics. Edward T. Hall, the founder of proxemics – which has influenced disciplines as varied as human ethology, social and environmental psychology, sociology, human geography, and environmental design – defined it as "the study of how man unconsciously structures microspace."[18] The face, for Hall and for his many transdisciplinary successors, is essential to this structuring. Within the eight-point measurement system of proxemics, "zero represents two subjects face to face (maximum sociopetality)" and "eight represents two subjects back to back (sociofugal)," with two to seven denoting points of facial interaction between these two extremes.[19] The notation system, designed to provide an objective means for describing sociality, essentially indexes the physical orientation of faces, or what is referred to within proxemics as an "F-formation . . . sometimes known as Face or Facing formations."[20]

Mariana's face is certainly a proxemic sign from this disciplinary perspective, and in the moment of her unveiling, the scene is propelled from an eight to a zero with no stops in-between. But proxemics is a science of description rather than a method of speculative thought. While the very premise of the field is underwritten by a conviction that modes of facial co-presence are critical components of social behavior and cultural identity, it is ill-equipped to

deal overtly with the ethical implications of the dynamics it measures, or with the complexities of revelation and duration that are
unique to both theater and judgment. For example, a full reckoning with Mariana's face would require the addition of a new
sign-category that neither theatrical semiotics nor proxemics makes
available: something we could call the "chronemic," which would
allow us to isolate the face's time-indexical function in the scene.
As a chronemic sign, Mariana's face is consistently pointing to the
temporal context in which it appears. It creates a scene of judgment which does not manifest itself in a flat present of decision, but
rather unfolds sequentially through a linear process of action and
response: "**First** let her show her face, and **after** speak"; "I will not
show my face / **Until** my husband bid me"; "**Now** I will unmask."

The face in *Measure for Measure* bursts the seams of our received
systems of theatrical interpretation. It demands a more flexible and
expansive set of critical concepts. As the material anchor in the
final scene's culminating moments of punishment and forgiveness,
it offers a vantage point from which we can observe the physics of
judgment at work, the way in which adjudication unfolds through
the space and time of a mimetic environment comprised of bodies,
voices, and objects. From this perspective, judgment takes the form
of a collaborative event. It has less to do with individual evaluation
than it does with the collective application of knowledge towards a
specific end. And, as we have seen in the previous chapter, all forms
of applied knowledge – geometry, mechanics, rhetoric, theater –
use judgment to *make* something: in this case, a livable future, a
shared sense of truth, and new conditions of social possibility in
Vienna. We see the beginning of this process unfolding gradually
during the scene of Mariana's unveiling: collective appraisal of the
situation evolves as false knowledge and misperception give way to
true knowledge. The revelation of Mariana's face is the hinge on
which the former swings towards the latter. Here is the scene with
references to knowledge – first false, then true – set in bold:

> MARIANA: Why, just, my lord, and that is Angelo,
>   Who thinks he **knows** that he ne'er **knew** my body,
>   But **knows**, he thinks, that he **knows** Isabel's.
> ANGELO: This is a strange abuse. Let's see thy face.

MARIANA: My husband bids me, now I will unmask.
    She unveils
    This is that face, thou cruel Angelo,
    Which once thou sworest was worth the looking on;
. . . .
DUKE: **Know** you this woman?
. . . .
ANGELO: My lord, I must confess I **know** this woman, (5.1.201–7,
213, 217)

This moment – the first phase of act 5.1's extended judgment-
event – marks the beginning of a shared coming-into-knowledge
that I will continue to trace in the next section of this chapter.
Mariana's unveiling and the acknowledgment it triggers – "I know
this woman" – establishes a new truth about the relations among
the characters on stage that will lead eventually to fundamental
changes in the social fabric of Shakespeare's Vienna. Like Prospero's
epilogue in *The Tempest*, the dynamics of the face in *Measure for
Measure* show us a version of judgment that is collective and creative, and which has as much to do with the future as with the past.

Judgment and Knowledge-Management

So far, I have made two connected claims. The first is that in *Measure for Measure*, the face is at the center of something we might
call the physics of judgment. The second is that by looking closely
at how this process works on stage, we can recover a version of
judgment that is social and worldmaking. In this section, I will give
more attention to the second claim. I will show, in particular, how
theatrical judgment functions as a form of collective and purpose-
ful knowledge-management, and conclude with some thoughts on
the face as the source of judgment's future-oriented trajectory.

On the early modern stage, judgment creates communities of
knowledge. It does so by realigning the varying levels of information possessed by characters and playgoers around a single,
shared truth. The friar is actually the Duke; there are two young
men named Antipholus in town, not just one; this person whom
you thought was a boy is actually a young woman: these are all

things that are disclosed through scenes of judgment. These particular examples also indicate that creating, maintaining, and
finally redressing disparities in knowledge is especially important
in comedy. At a basic mechanical level, humor is generated in stage
comedy through the uneven evolution in the way sensory information is distributed among characters and playgoers. What makes a
play like *The Comedy of Errors* funny is the disconnect between
what audience members see (Antipholus of Syracuse) and what
characters on stage see (Antipholus of Ephesus). The relationship
between sense perception and knowledge is different for each of
the two groups that together constitute theatrical experience. The
same can be said for act 3.2 of *A Midsummer Night's Dream*,
in which Robin Goodfellow hides while imitating the voices of
Lysander and Demetrius. Humor, again, is generated by a simple
sensory disconnect: the playgoers can hear and see everything;
Demetrius and Lysander can hear but not see. Typically, this disconnect is remedied in the play's *dénouement*. The end of *The
Comedy of Errors* feels like a resolution because characters and
spectators at last see and hear the same thing (*this* is Antipholus
of Syracuse, *that* is Antipholus of Ephesus). Likewise the end of
Twelfth Night when Duke Orsino slowly comes to terms with the
truth about "Cesario," or the final act of *All's Well that Ends Well*
when vision and hearing are once again revelatory. Shakespearean
comedy depends for its effects on this carefully managed economy
of perception and knowledge.[21]

In *Measure for Measure*, perception and knowledge are framed
by the dynamics of judgment. That is, judgment is both the impe-
tus for and the result of the facial revelations that finally distribute
knowledge evenly among each character on stage and the playgoers
in the audience. The faces of act 5.1 – the first unveiled, the second
unhooded – reinforce the observation made in Chapter 2 that judgment is an essentially sensory and communal event: it begins with
showing or revealing and ends with seeing, *really* seeing, together.
We will recall that in the final scene of *Measure for Measure*, the
Duke says of the veiled Mariana, "First let her show her face."
Angelo agrees: "Let's see thy face." When Mariana concedes, she
says bitingly, "This is that face, thou cruel Angelo, / Which once

thou swor'st was worth the looking on." First perception, then judgment, and somewhere in-between a coming-into-knowledge for all present and the establishment of a new truth. Something similar happens when Lucio demands of the Duke (whom he thinks is a friar), "Show your knave's visage . . . Show your sheep-biting face" (5.1.354–55). When he *pulls off the Friar's hood and reveals the Duke,*" the latter says, "Thou art the first knave that e'er mad'st a duke" (5.1.357). In a brief moment that cannot quite be parsed into sequential units, judgment descends on Lucio, a shared truth is established, and a new community of knowledge is formed.

In our own time, in everyday contexts, to judge is to make a decision in response to information. But what we tend to miss is the way judgment also involves managing and distributing that information. As we have seen, this dimension of judgment would have been familiar to many early moderns whose understanding of the concept derived primarily from the Aristotelian rhetorical tradition that was so central to humanist education. There are a variety of subspecies of judgment within the rhetorical system, some of which, like *modestia,* show us how judgment's core functions of framing and disposing, managing and curating, were not restricted to oratorical or compositional contexts, but were also essential to an orderly and ethical life-practice.[22] In Cicero's *On Duties,* for example – which was along with Aristotle's *Nicomachean Ethics* the most influential study of virtue in the early modern period – *modestia* is described as "the essence of orderliness and of right-placing." Cicero also invokes the Stoics' definition of *modestia* as the "'science of disposing aright everything that is done or said' . . . 'the arrangement of things in their suitable and appropriate places.'"[23]

The concept of *decorum,* which we have already encountered, carries a similar set of ideas. In the previous chapter, I discussed the compositional sense of *decorum,* the way it involved following rules of formal alignment, such as suiting particular kinds of speech to particular kinds of characters or deploying certain kinds of metaphors for a given genre of argument. But rules of *decorum* applied in the realm of human speech, action, and *inter*action as well, part of what Stephen Pender has aptly characterized as the "intimate connection" that developed in the early modern period "between

virtue, its rhetorical canons, and the perceived demands of citizen-
ship."[24] Hannah H. Gray offers this neat formulation for *decorum*:

> [The] idea of speaking appropriately, of suiting style and man-
> ner to subject, aim, and audience is treated as the exact analogue
> of behaving with *decorum*, of choosing the actions and responses
> which are best in harmony with and most appropriate to indi-
> vidual character and principles on one hand, the nature of circum-
> stances on the other.[25]

Gray's description resonates closely with what we still call "social
decorum." But in more essential terms, we can also see how *decorum*, like the notion of *modestia*, is about the correct alignment
of part to part and of all parts to whole. It denotes a procedure
of assemblage, an artisanal sensibility, and, in the most practical terms, a way of making something that works. *Decorum*,
like *modestia*, involves the application of discernment in real-
world contexts. It is an active and dimensional form of judgment
which involves not only an architectural sense of the way virtue
is achieved through the appropriate configuration of various units
of meaning, but also, as James S. Baumlin has shown, a temporal
sense of when to do or say what.[26] As an art of both arrangement and timeliness, *decorum* offers us another way into thinking
about the physics of judgment. Cicero brings this idea down to
its most basic level when he writes in *On Duties*, "So, in standing
or walking, in sitting or reclining, in our expression, our eyes, or
the movements of our hands, let us preserve what we have called
propriety (*decorum*)."[27]

Decorum, then, is "the virtue which links the bodily and the
social, uniting them by emphasizing their equal investment in har-
mony and formal coherence."[28] In 1531, English scholar and dip-
lomat Thomas Elyot described *decorum* in his influential *A Boke
Named the Governor* as "the knowledge or opportunity of things
to be done or spoken, in appointing and setting them in time or
place to them convenient and proper."[29] Elyot was writing in a consciously Ciceronian vein in this treatise, but Cicero himself would
often use yet another rhetorical term for the sort of "right-placing"

and "disposing aright" of which we have been speaking: *colloca-tion* (*collocationis* and *collocandarum*, respectively, in Latin). For Cicero, *collocation* is a practice at once technical and ethical. It aims concurrently at correctness and goodness, and it is essential to his notion of *modestia* as "the science of doing the right thing at the right time." "Such orderliness of conduction," he continues in *On Duties*, "is, therefore, to be observed, that everything in the conduct of our life shall balance and harmonize."[30] In *Measure for Measure*, the face is at the center of a process of *collocation*, of setting things right. The unveiling of Mariana and the unhooding of the Duke provide object lessons in accountability and occasion the redistribution of knowledge that restores order to Vienna. This also reminds us how, in a general sense, comic *dénouements* are always moments of embodied collocation – *modestia* and *decorum* in action and at a social scale. They represent one of several ways in which the rhetorical tradition of judgment became part of the genome of theatrical form.

Judgment, Form, and Futurity

We have established that the face of judgment in *Measure for Measure* is part of a dynamic, dimensional process of knowledge-making and knowledge-management. This process involves both actors and audience and, as such, is inherently collective and col-laborative. There is nothing in these observations that intrinsically saves the ending of the play from being "aesthetically and intel-lectually unsatisfying," showcasing "a form of state control," or even enacting "a kind of rape," as the critics discussed above have variously asserted. But they do shift attention away from what the characters do to cast light instead on how they do it, a trade-up which leaves us with more optimism and less distaste. In mov-ing our critical gaze from the particularities of plot to the gen-eral mechanics of judgment, we exchange a mode of assessment that starts with content for a mode of assessment that starts with form. I use these two terms, "content" and "form," in their con-ventional, everyday senses, but I am also thinking here of Georg Simmel's influential distinction between content and form in "The

Problem of Sociology."[31] What Simmel's pioneering work on social
form has in common with the project undertaken in this chapter
is an intellectual and critical commitment to the idea of relational-
ity; that is to say, to the precise way in which units (individuals,
characters, or faces, as the case may be) interact with each other to
make some kind of whole; rather than to the psychological, moral,
or cultural characteristics of those interactions.[32] The point of such
a method is to be able to focus on process, and to understand process as something transactional and eco-systemic.

Looking at things from this angle has significant implications
for how we understand the ethics of the *dénouement*. In particular,
it throws into sharper relief the role of judgment in changing the
underlying conditions of social possibility in the play-world. With
this in mind, I want to usher this chapter towards a conclusion by
reflecting on how act 5.1 models the creative and future-oriented
dimension of judgment. This connection between judgment and
futurity can, at least to some extent, be traced back to Aristotle – so long as our focus is on the broadly deliberative rather
than narrowly institutional sense of that term, judgment.[33] In the
Rhetoric, Aristotle identifies three types of oratory – deliberative,
judicial, and epideictic – and to each assigns a time dimension.[34]
The judicial, within Aristotle's scheme, actually concerns the past
since it looks to rules that have already been established. The
deliberative, however, concerns the future. It mobilizes prudence
to craft a world that is attuned to the public good. (Epideictic oratory, lest we leave it out, treats matters in terms of their present
value.)[35] A similar conceptual scheme inhabits the English legal
imagination. Within common law, judgment is a form of time-
management, a Janus-faced process whose customary component
looks backward, via accumulated experience, towards tradition,
while its policy- and precedent-making component looks forward
towards the outer horizons of a legal system that is always evolving, never finished.[36] In temporal terms, judgment's role in such
a system is to curate the relationship between past, present, and
future, with a necessary thrust towards the latter, towards making
new case reports, new precedents, and new customs; and in this
way creating a lived world – phenomenologists would use the term

Lebenswelt, or "life-world" – in which social conditions slowly, but inevitably, transform.[37]

What makes act 5.1 of *Measure for Measure* so compelling as an artifact of deliberative futurity is the way it subsumes this general legal sensibility within the formal and ethical framework of facing. Let us return to the exchange between Lucio and the Duke to further explore these links between facing, judgment, and social change:

> LUCIO: . . . you must be hooded, must you? Show your knave's visage, with a pox to you. Show your sheep-biting face, and be hanged an hour. Will't not off?
> *He pulls off the Friar's hood and reveals the Duke*
> DUKE: Thou art the first knave that e'er mad'st a duke. (5.1.354–57)

The revelation of the Duke immediately changes the epistemological, legal, and social conditions of the play-world: Mariana and Isabella are confirmed as truthful while Angelo is confirmed as false; Angelo and Lucio are promptly assigned punishments; and marriages are arranged for Angelo and Mariana, Lucio and Kate Keepdown, and the Duke himself and Isabella. For the characters assembled on stage, then, the judgment occasioned by the Duke's face completely remakes the world they had known. It leads to a new truth, a new source of moral authority, and a new set of social relations. Judgment takes the raw materials of one world – people, ideas, connections, and obligations – and reassembles them to form another. Through an extended judgment-event that begins with showing ("let her show her face"; "*she unveils*"; "show your knave's visage"; "show your sheep-biting face": "*He . . . reveals the Duke*") and ends with adjudication, condemnation, and forgiveness, the lines of inclusion and exclusion are redrawn to form a version of community that did not exist when the play opened. Bastards are accommodated (the child of Lucio and Kate Keepdown), the forsaken are acknowledged (Mariana), the guilty are forgiven (Angelo), the condemned are welcomed back (Claudio), and – more dubiously – the self-exiled are reintegrated (Isabella).

This is the sense in which judgment is creative and forward-looking in act 5.1 of *Measure for Measure*. Unfolding consistently in the wake of facial revelations, it is inextricably bound up with instances of interpersonal acknowledgment that reset current social relations. Judgment is also rooted in moments of recognition, which means it makes legible through speech and action changes in the epistemological fabric of the community. At once a response to and an instantiation of what-we-did-not-know-before-but-do-know-now, judgment participates in the alteration of assumed realities about hierarchy and membership. Finally, judgment inheres in the theatrical (and especially comic) rhythms of exposure, reversal, and self-manifestation, and in this way is necessarily kinetic and dynamic, a vital force that contributes to the organismic nature of human collectivity, its homeostatic impulse to grow and change, and so survive. Adjudication may, in one sense, be concerned with assessing the past (past actions, past claims), but in so far as it triggers changes in behavior, social arrangements, and (in a juridical setting) legal precedent, judgment is also always directed towards the future; it is always generative.

My aim in this chapter has been to determine what we can learn about judgment by attending to the dynamics of the face in *Measure for Measure*. As we have seen, the face functions as a deictic component of judgment, an action-object whose verbal and nominal capacities transform judgment into theater by orienting it in time and space. Indeed, the face reminds us that judgment is intrinsically theatrical, though not in the ways typically asserted by cultural criticism: judgment is not theatrical simply because courtrooms are kind of like theaters or because juries are kind of like play audiences.[38] Instead, judgment is theatrical because it is constituted by the same basic raw materials as theater: time, space, and action. The face indexes this shared physics of experience which was essential to the rhetorical tradition, in which terms like *modestia, decorum,* and *collocation* describe judgment as an art of arrangement, curation, and configuration which was both publicly and proportionally minded. As a component of theatrical form, judgment's role, therefore, is not simply to end things, but also to create the conditions for starting things anew, to plot a future course and craft another world – a world that must finally take shape beyond the fictional parameters of the play itself.

When we attend to the facial dynamics of judgment, in which transactional acknowledgment and physical co-presence are so essential, we are once again presented with the idea that judgment is not simply a unidirectional administrative procedure (the legal cliché) or a singular confrontation with absolute authority (the religious cliché). More accurately, judgment is a participatory practice that forms communities by translating common sensory experience (seeing, showing, looking, hearing) into common axes of value (a shared sense of right and wrong, good and bad). In the arch of its unfolding, judgment starts as *evaluation* and ends as *values*, reminding us that the etymological link between those two words finds its source in a common conceptual space where calculation and community are neighbors. The particular determinations of act 5.1 – Mariana is owed something, Lucio owes something to others, Claudio is innocent, Angelo is guilty – reinforce general ethical principles of obligation, responsibility, and justice that make social life possible. The close of *Measure for Measure*, in other words, shows us how assessment can generate the shared standards that form the moral scaffolding of community.

CHAPTER 6

COMMUNITY

In each of the previous chapters, we have seen the dramaturgy of judgment articulating some larger question or idea. Sometimes that question or idea is epistemological in nature, having to do with what we can know and how we can know it. Sometimes it is political-philosophical in nature, having to do with the participatory grounds of social change. Other times still, it is jurisprudential in nature, having to with basic principles of responsibility, obligation, and justice. And of course there is considerable bleed-through and overlap among all these three categories. In all cases, though, judgment points us to something conceptually and ethically greater than the particular determinations being undertaken. This chapter, which focuses on *The Winter's Tale*, is no exception, but the nature of the larger questions being posed is different from what we have seen so far. They include the following: What do we do about crimes that seem too great to punish? Through what legal processes might making amends achieve legal standing? If we break the conceptual and procedural link between judgment and condemnation, to what socially affirmative uses might judgment be put? These questions, all closely related to each other, are central to law's moral and political capacities. They probe the outer reaches of what legal procedure can accommodate and they test the limits of law's role in the management of human crisis and the promotion of human flourishing.

Such questions have resonated with particular force among modern-day legal professionals, politicians, and religious leaders who, in the wake of humanitarian disasters, have been involved in debates about "restorative justice."[1] One thinks of the establishment of the Truth and Reconciliation Commission in South Africa in 1996, the Good Friday Agreement in Northern Ireland in 1998, and the twentieth- and twenty-first-century reparations movements – some realized, some not – for the descendants of slaves in the United States and for indigenous populations in Hawaii, Canada, and Australia.[2] With these larger contexts in mind, this chapter will argue that *The Winter's Tale* provides baseline philosophical resources for a politics of atonement, a way of responding to criminal behavior in which judgment takes the form of a collective ritual of acknowledgment rather than a singular decision, and where the aim of adjudication is to rebuild the community rather than to punish specific persons. Specifically, my reflection on these topics will be anchored to the two adjudicatory events in the play that frame the action subsequent to Leontes's famous descent into paranoid jealousy: the judgment passed on Hermione by Leontes in the trial scene of act 2 and the judgment passed on Leontes by the court community, including Hermione, at the end of the play in accordance with the oracle of Apollo. The first of these two events is juridical: Hermione is placed on trial for adultery. The second event is, in the first place, aesthetic since it is built around collective admiration for what appears to be a statue of Hermione. However, the statue scene is also a moral and legal event since it occasions a final assessment of Leontes's crimes and the possibility of legal satisfaction. The miraculous vivification of the statue becomes the centerpiece of a ritual of political and social renewal in which the line between judgment and forgiveness blurs.

These two scenes of judgment in *The Winter's Tale* shape and are shaped by the play's larger tragicomic form: in act 2, we witness judgment as tragedy; in act 5, we witness judgment as redemption and reconciliation. In addition to their formal affordances, these two models of judgment collectively introduce a distinct ethical vision into *The Winter's Tale*. The key difference between the tragic judgment of act 2 and the restorative judgment of act 5 is that the former is entirely, and pathologically, individual. Leontes ignores other voices and forsakes the legal scene of which he is, or should be, a part. He even disregards the divine voice of the oracle of Apollo. Leontes's judgment is egocentric, and this ego-centrism leads to pain, death, and despair. The healing and rec-onciliation achieved through the judgment of act 5, by contrast, derives from the fact that adjudication has become a shared prac-tice rooted in collaboration and clemency. In what follows – and in a methodological vein that should be familiar by now – I will be putting these two adjudicatory events into conversation with both historical and philosophical sources: on one hand, early mod-ern ideas about legal judgment; on the other, modern philosophi-cal accounts of judgment and forgiveness, some by thinkers we have encountered already (Hannah Arendt), others by those we have not (Emmanuel Levinas). By the end of the chapter, I hope to have shown how *The Winter's Tale* facilitates through its treat-ment of judgment a broader reflection on the hazards of extreme individualism and the restorative powers of a legal communalism grounded in forgiveness.

How To, and How Not To, Judge

The onset of Leontes's jealousy occurs in act 1.2: "Too hot; too hot! / To mingle friendship far is mingling bloods" (1.2.108–9).[3] Observing his wife, Hermione, successfully persuade his childhood friend, Polixenes, king of Bohemia, to extend his visit in Sicilia, Leontes rapidly assembles a narrative of adulterous lust which spurs him to actions that, by the end of the second act, have resulted in the apparent death of Hermione; the death of his son, Mamil-lius; the loss of his daughter, Perdita; and a seemingly irreparable political rupture between Sicilia and Bohemia. Leontes's jealousy transforms into a dangerous and delusional form of egocentrism which Julia Reinhard Lupton has characterized as a "foreclosure of all attachments." Lupton shows how Leontes, who "disavows his dependencies on his wife, friend, son, and unborn child," exem-plifies the psychotic foreclosure studied by Freud and Lacan in the case of Judge Schreber.[4] The King's behavior, she explains, drags "the coordinates of his world into the annihilating vortex of divest-ment":[5] Hermione is a "hobby-horse" (1.2.276), Polixenes is an

"enemy" (1.2.317), his children bastards, and his counselors traitors. Leontes never doubts these convictions for a moment:

> How blest am I
> In my just censure! in my true opinion!
> Alack, for lesser knowledge! How accurs'd
> In being so blest! (2.1.36–39)

Rhetorically, Leontes expresses dismay at being so knowledgeable –
if only I knew less! But even more important than the notion of *bur-
densome* knowledge is the notion of *exclusive* knowledge: Leontes is
in singular possession of the truth, an appraisal of reality keyed precisely to his anti-sociality and actualized in his repeated and unwavering repudiation of competing truth-claims:

CAMILLO:	Good my lord, be cur'd
	Of this diseas'd opinion, and betimes,
	For 'tis most dangerous.
LEONTES:	Say it be, 'tis true.
CAMILLO:	No, no my lord.
LEONTES:	It is: you lie, you lie! (1.2.296–99)

There is a similar exchange between Leontes and Antigonus in act
2.3 when the King accuses the old counselor of conspiring with his
wife, Paulina, to aid Hermione:

LEONTES:	Thou, traitor, hast set on thy wife to this.
. . .	
ANTIGONUS:	I did not, sir.
	These lords, my noble fellows, if they please,
	Can clear me in't.
LORDS:	We can. My royal liege,
	He is not guilty of her coming hither.
LEONTES:	You're liars all. (2.3.131, 142–46)

In this exchange between Leontes, Antigonus, and the Lords,
the King's paranoid foreclosure functions as a rejection of the
sort of collaborative knowledge-making essential to secular legal

determination. Whereas judgment in a common law court is participatory and social, for Leontes it is about alienation and individual will. "Not guilty" is the lords' position; "You're liars all!" is Leontes's response. In *Measure for Measure*, Shakespeare imagines judgment as something one necessarily does with others. In the first three acts of *The Winter's Tale*, by contrast, it is the force that keeps self and other, the one and the many, utterly apart. Observe, for example, Leontes's first specifically juridical action against Hermione: "Away with her, to prison! / He who shall speak for her is afar off guilty / But that he speaks!" (2.1.103–5). This act of judgment is tyrannical, of course, but it is also, and more specifically, profoundly anti-social. It is a legal expression of individualism in its most reckless and irresponsible form.

By contrast, judgment in early modern English courtrooms was, with few exceptions, a *process* involving multiple parties. We get a sense of how this worked in the manuals produced for Justices of the Peace in the period. Essentially printed how-to guides, these manuals were aimed at the gentlemen charged with presiding over the Quarter Sessions – county courts that met four times per year (Epiphany, Easter, Trinity, and Michaelmas) – though they were no doubt consulted by other legal amateurs, too. Justices of the Peace were appointed annually and the primary qualification for the job was local standing, not legal expertise. They would hear cases having to do with comparatively minor offences, such as trespass, assault, licenses for alehouses, and theft.[6] Cases involving the most dangerous felonies, such as murder, were typically heard at the Assizes, which met twice per year and were presided over by professional barristers from the central courts. Responding to a clear need among England's many legal amateurs for procedural guidance, Justice of the Peace manuals began being printed in the late sixteenth century and increased steadily in popularity over the course of the seventeenth century. Almost all Justice of the Peace manuals went through multiple print runs and successive editions, so we can assume that they were in demand. Small books ranging in size from octavo to sixteenmo, they were meant to be carried around and referred to while on the job or shortly beforehand. Accordingly, the tone and style of the Justice of the Peace manuals tend to be practical and concise. From the mid-seventeenth century, in particular, a premium seems to have been placed on usability. The anonymously authored *The Complete Justice* (1637), for example, simply lists alphabetically a series of key technical terms and procedures followed by brief descriptions. This is a manual designed for quick and easy reference. The same format is adopted in *The justice of peace, his clarks cabinet* (1654), written by the prolific William Shepherd, who also produced law lexicons and manuals for parsons, constables, and other minor legal professionals.

All of these texts show legal judgment to be a process involving various individuals working in close partnership. Take William Lambarde's *Eirenarcha: or the office of the justices of the peace* (1581). As an early example of the genre, *Eirenarcha* is more discursive and descriptive than its later-seventeenth-century counterparts. Lambarde overviews the duties of Justices to their community, the central courts, the king, and God, and tries to differentiate between those situations in which strict conformity to certain recorded statutes is appropriate and when more discretionary judgment is called for.[7] Significantly, during the lengthy discussion of the protocols of trial and sentencing, Lambarde describes this "Session of the Peace" as "An assemblie," and he stresses the fact that not one, but "two (or moe) Justices" must be present "to heare and determine" a case.[8] This plurality of adjudicators is essential, and "if any of them be absent," Lambarde explains, "their fellow justices cannot amerce them . . . for . . . the auctoritie of all the Justices of the Peace at the Sessions is equall."[9] Lambarde goes on to describe in some detail each of the other figures who must be present for a trial to go forward and judgment to be passed: the "Shirife," the "Baylifes," and the "Juries," which "ought to containe 12. in number at the leaste."[10] *Eirenarcha* presents judgment as a participatory "assemblie," one in which complex bureaucratic procedures knit together a diverse network of both amateur and professional legal agents. Michael Dalton, a member of Lincoln's Inn, stresses this point, too, opening his manual, *The Countrey Justice* (1618), with a narrative sketch of where the Justice of the Peace stands within the larger legal hierarchy and what that position affords in terms of specific duties, obligations, and dependencies.[11]

At the heart of these Justice of the Peace manuals is a fascination with breaking the legal process, especially adjudication, down into its most essential component parts. This concern with itemization and procedural detail can be found in other kinds of writing, too. Richard Bernard's stunningly dense allegory *The Isle of Man, or, The legall proceedings in Man-shire against sinne* (1627) is a good example. In this narrative, self-examination, self-management, and self-regulation are figured through the collaborative procedures of common law. Conscience is represented by the Judge, but this judge operates within a diverse cluster of Justices and other officials:

> The Justices of Peace in the Countrie are there, and doe sit with the Judge and are in Commission with him. Of these some are of the Quorum, and of the better ranke, some are meaner Justices and take their place lower.
>   The Justices of Peace in the Soule of better ranke are Science, Prudence, Providence, Sapience: the inferiors are Weake Wit, common Aprehension, and some such like.
>   These Justices have their Clerkes, there ready with their examinations and recognizances. Justice Science, his Clerke is Discourse: Justice Prudence, his Clerke is Circumspection, Justice Providence, his Clerke is Diligence; Justice Sapience, his Clerke is Experience: Justice Weake-wit, his Clerke is Conceit: and Justice Common-Apprehension, his Clerke is onely Sense.[12]

In addition to offering a vivid representation of cognitive process and spiritual struggle, Bernard's allegory demonstrates the power of common law adjudication as an emblem of collaborative decision-making and as a figure for the concatenation of forces involved in moral choice.

Rather than playing into this positive model of legal judgment, Leontes, whose ruthless egocentrism is matched only by his apparent lack of discernment, would have embodied some of early modern England's primary anxieties about the topic. Lorna Hutson has shown that in the fifteenth century, writing associated with the Church frequently presented secular judgment as severe and dangerously fallible in comparison with the equitable and restorative principles of Christianity.[13] One such text is *Jacob's Well* (c.1450), a sequence of penitential sermons composed for oral delivery between Ash Wednesday and the Vigil of Pentecost, now widely recognized as an early source for the morality play *Mankind* (c.1465).[14] Each sermon fits into a larger allegorical scheme in which the soul struggles out of a pit of corrupt waters into the pure well of Jacob, assisted by various tools that represent contrition, confession, and satisfaction. The aim of these sermons is to urge parishioners to make confession and embrace the Church's penitential system for managing and purging sin. The diabolical alternative is the secular common law courts in which "thou schuldst be convict in thi cause, for thou art gylty in wrong . . . and the sentens of dampnacyoun shulde be gouyn agens the." Better to go "to the juge of god, that is, to the preest."[15] Whereas God's justice offers a shot at redemption, the inflexible justice of the common law courts leads directly to death and damnation. Hutson explains that in *Jacob's Well*,

> jury trial emerges as no kind of trial at all, and salvation is imagined as a repeated escape from the rigors of Common Law Hell, first by the priestly judge's absolution, and then by Purgatorial pains, figured as our escape, by pleading clergy, to the canonical purgation of the spiritual courts.[16]

The attitude towards secular judgment in *Jacob's Well* is indicative of a deeply entrenched habit of thought, a core distrust of secular law that persisted even despite the momentous shift in jurisdictional authority from spiritual to temporal institutions over the course of the sixteenth century. As late as 1578, Thomas Garter's dramatic interlude *The Commody of the most virtuous and Godlye Susanna* portrays a miscarriage of justice in a secular court set right at the last moment by divine intervention. Here, the concern is less with the diabolically stringent, either/or conditions of common law courts than it is with the basic competence of human judges, fallen and imperfect as they are, to identify truth and arbitrate accordingly. The Judge in Garter's interlude, persuaded by the false testimony of the elders, sentences Susanna to death. However, as "*she is led to execution . . . God rayseth the spiritte of Danyell,*" who insists that "*they return all backe to judgment.*"[17]

In due course, Susanna is proclaimed innocent and the other participants in the trial roundly condemned. Garter's interlude is comforting to the extent that it portrays a caring God that intercedes on behalf of the downtrodden, but it certainly would not have left readers with much confidence in temporal judgment.[18] Daniel refers to the members of the legal community in the interlude as "foolish folke . . . that know not ill from good"[19] – hardly an endorsement of the efficacies of English common law.

Anxieties about the role of judges and the effects of their decisions can be found issuing from *within* the legal community, too. Edward Coke, for example, though confident enough that a judge would not completely misinterpret evidence and testimony, nevertheless urged those charged with the task of adjudication not to overstep their bounds. The role of the judge, Coke insisted, is to declare law, not to make it:

> for that which hath been refined and perfected by the wisest men in former succession of ages, and proved and approved by continual experience to be good and profitable for the commonwealth, cannot without great hazard or danger be altered or changed.[20]

He returned to the issue in his *First Institutes*, noting that "commonly a new invention doth offend against many rules and reasons of the common law, and the ancient judges and sages of the law have ever . . . suppressed innovation and novelties in the beginning."[21] Coke was not the only one to weigh in on the "hazard" of judicial innovation. John Davies makes a similar point in the preface to *Le Primer Report des Cases en Ireland* (1615), and Francis Bacon opens his essay "Of Judicature" with an extended statement on the matter:

> Judges ought to remember that their office is *jus dicere*, and not *jus dare*; to interpret law, and not to make law, or give law. Else it will be like the authority claimed by the church of Rome, which under pretext of exposition of Scripture doth not stick to add and alter; and to pronounce that which they do not find; and by show of antiquity to introduce novelty. Judges ought to be more learned than witty, more reverend than plausible, and more advised than confident. Above all things, integrity is their portion and proper virtue.[22]

Judgment, Bacon asserts, is a strain of applied scholarship, not a maverick performance. He urges a kind of learned modesty and deference to legal doctrine. As long as the laws themselves speak through the judge, rather than vice versa, there is minimal risk of corruption and error.

Leontes, Paulina, and Participatory Judgment

In the context of what I have outlined above, Leontes looks like a poster child for everything that Coke, Davies, and Bacon warn against. Paulina, on the other hand, represents a more reassuring model of judgment, one closer to the world evoked in the Justice of the Peace manuals and, allegorically, in Bernard's *The Isle of Man*. Paulina persistently and forcefully takes Hermione's side and tries to steer Leontes off the dangerous course on which he is set. In the prison where Hermione is held, she declares herself the Queen's "advocate" (2.2.37), the first of a number of juridical gestures on Paulina's part. Then, in act 2.3, forcing her way into Leontes's presence with the infant Perdita, she argues for the child's legitimacy:

> Behold, my lords,
> Although the print be little, the whole matter
> And copy of the father – eye, nose, lip,
> The trick of 's frown, his forehead, nay, the valley,
> The pretty dimples of his chin and cheek, his smiles,
> The very mould and frame of hand, nail, finger. (2.3.98–103)

Paulina seeks a counter-ruling by appealing to *communal* judgment: "Behold, my lords," she begins, beseeching all present to participate in interpreting the evidence at hand. The drive in Paulina's lines is towards collectivity and the restoration of a *scene* of adjudication. Unlike Leontes's enraged decisionism, a worst-case-scenario of judge-made law, Paulina's conduct is closer in spirit to the way legal judgment was actually supposed to work in early modern England. As we have seen, common law trials were designed to be participatory in Shakespeare's day. Queen Elizabeth tried to reinforce this principle by setting up a special office for collecting defaults by jurors.[23] King James subsequently issued a "Proclamation for Jurors" which insisted that "all persons which have Free-hold, according to the Law, shall be returned to serve upon Juries, as occasion shall require."[24] If these measures indicate a certain level of reluctance or apathy among would-be jurors, they also remind us that the system was at least premised on collaboration and productive agonism. Historians such as Thomas Andrew Green and Cynthia Herrup have confirmed this.[25] Documents related to the courts of early modern Sussex, for example, reveal constant, uneven negotiation among judges, justices, and juries, similar in nature to the transactions described, or implied, in the Justice of the Peace manuals. Herrup writes:

> judges, magistrates and petty jurors had generally complementary, but not identical, ideas about justice. Judges, justices and juries seem to have agreed as to the proper sentence in the vast majority of cases convicted in the Assizes or the Quarter Sessions. Each group was willing to intervene when necessary and the Bench, not the jurors, seems to have had the greatest reservoir of patience.[26]

The work of judgment may have been contentious, but it was always fundamentally collaborative. It involved collective thinking and participatory action. These are the attributes that give Paulina's arbitrational practice a kind of procedural and moral authority absent from Leontes's blinkered allegations.

Hannah Arendt, we will recall from Chapter 4, viewed judgment in social and productive terms, and felt strongly that it should be defended and preserved as such. "Judgment," she insisted, "must liberate itself from the subjective private conditions"; a basic element of social existence, judgment ties the individual to a larger community of values, thought, and action.[27] Paulina knows this very well, but Leontes learns it too late. In act 3.2, Hermione is brought in for a formal trial, the strict collaborative procedures of which should mitigate Leontes's unwaveringly subjective censure. Leontes says as much himself at the opening of the "sessions" (3.2.1):

> Let us be clear'd
> Of being tyrannous, since we so openly
> Proceed in justice, which shall have due course,
> Even to the guilt or purgation. (3.2.4–7)

A formal indictment is then read by an Officer and Hermione is given the opportunity to mount a defense. In another gesture of commitment to what Leontes insists is "a just and open trial" (2.3.205), the King submits the case of Hermione to divine judgment. Two Sicilian lords, Cleomenes and Dion, are sent to Delphos where they will receive the oracle of Apollo.[28] Ostensibly, then, at the opening of act 3.2, we have a scene of judgment consistent in spirit with early modern courtroom practice. There are officers and lords contributing to the adjudicatory process. There is also a larger religious framework, something frequently invoked in Justice of the Peace manuals as part of their emphasis on distributed authority. Lambarde, for instance, asserts:

> Such as occupy Judicial places ought to take heed what they doe, knowing (as Jehosaphat saide) that they exercise not the judgements of Men onelie, but of God himself, whose power, as they doe participate: So he also is present on the Bench with them.[29]

Even so, Leontes's egocentric judgment slices through the collaborative conditions he has established. Ignoring testimony and evidence, Leontes condemns Hermione to "no less than death" (3.2.91) in a proceeding that the Queen aptly calls "rigor and not law" (3.2.114).

By far, though, Leontes's most sensational act of adjudicatory egocentrism is his refutation of divine judgment. When Hermione submits herself to Apollo – "refer me to the oracle: / Apollo be my judge!" (3.2.115–16) – she is promptly proclaimed innocent. Leontes reacts by declaring, "There is no truth at all i' th' oracle. / The sessions shall proceed; this is mere falsehood" (3.2.140–41). This is a key moment in the play's shifting topographies of egocentrism, self-sacrifice, and communalism. The ethical and legal-philosophical implications of the episode emerge with more clarity if we view them through the lens of Levinasian philosophy, a body of thought uniquely situated at the intersection of selfhood and justice.[30] In Emmanuel Levinas's ethical scheme, the founding relationship – prior to contract, prior even to Being – is *responsibility* for the other. It is pre-juridical and pre-ontological, the bedrock on which all other forms of obligation stand. With this in mind, Levinas's philosophy can be understood, in the broadest sense, as an attempt to formulate a non-ontological account of Being; that is to say, an account of Being which is open and social rather than bounded and inward looking. His two most influential books, *Totality and Infinity* (1961) and *Otherwise Than Being* (1974), present a radical ethics of selfhood founded on the idea that subjectivity is relational, a property not of hermetic cognitive experience but of the self's encounter with, extension towards, and welcoming of an absolute other.[31] Selfhood, to put it another way, is not a form of enclosed dwelling or sealed off at-homeness, as Martin Heidegger, for example, envisioned it, but rather a state of homelessness, a form of hospitality so complete that it calls into question what, if anything, is properly mine.[32]

Levinas makes this argument in opposition not only to Heidegger, but to Western philosophy from Plato to Kant, more generally. While the mainstream of metaphysics explores Being from the perspective of the singular, self-identical ego – "I think therefore I am"[33] – Levinas, by contrast, proposes a mode of inquiry which prioritizes hospitality and neighborliness. "Philosophy," he famously averred, "is an egology," and as such, he was convinced, a dangerous intellectual manifestation of precisely the sort of systematized egotism that led to the horrors of the Holocaust.[34] Levinas, by investing himself in exteriority rather than interiority and in ethics rather than ontology, expresses a radical hope that we might dislodge the deeply ingrained habit of thought that prioritizes the one over the many, the same over the different, the self over the other, and which ultimately leads to violence. The kernel of Levinas's ethics, his core challenge to "the egoist spontaneity of the same,"[35] is his assertion of an elemental responsibility we bear to the other, understood simultaneously in personal and non-personal terms as that which is different from and outside of ourselves. This, for Levinas, is the most basic and pure relationship, an original and non-negotiable duty towards the not-you.[36] In the political realm, Levinas's ethics have proved unwieldy. As Simon Critchley points out, in Levinas's world, "the ethical subject is . . . a *split subject* divided between itself and a demand that it cannot entirely fulfill," and thus pragmatic political action is "always usurped by the heteronomous experience of the other's demand."[37] For legal philosophy, though, Levinas's vision of absolute and infinite obligation remains compelling.[38] It is the fulfillment of this primary responsibility that Levinas calls *justice*. The term, for him, describes a moral event rather than an institutionally enforced principle. If the latter kind of justice constitutes the *body* of law, then the former type of justice – Levinasian justice – might be thought of as the *soul* of law (to borrow Desmond Manderson's term).[39] The establishment of the Truth and Reconciliation Commission in South Africa, to which I will return below, and the procedures involved in reparations for indigenous peoples are examples of juridical events that stem from the soul of law rather than the body of law. The legal-philosophical arch of *The Winter's Tale* could even be thought of as one that moves gradually towards a practice of judgment that actualizes this soul of law, the mutual and interdependent responsibility that constitutes justice.

Leontes's repudiation of Apollo and his decisive condemnation of Hermione, however, places us very much on the other side of this arch. Leontes crosses a threshold when he defies the oracle, beyond which his own egocentric judgment plays out in precisely the way Levinas would have predicted.[40] For the moment he declares the oracle "falsehood" (3.2.141), a servant enters to report that Mamillius has died out of consternation over his mother's fortune, news which, in turn, causes Hermione to collapse. We soon learn from Paulina that she, too, has perished: "the Queen, the Queen, / The sweet'st, dear'st creature's dead" (3.2.200–1). Leontes's egocentrism has exceeded the bounds of shared discourse and shared belief; Hermione and Mamillius are the casualties of this explosive rupture in the fabric of the spiritual and legal commons.

Forgiveness and the Community of Justice

The rupture I have just described also marks a point of transition, one distinct from, yet coterminous with, that between tragedy and comedy, culture and nature, and "things dying" and "things newborn" (3.3.113, 114), all of which have offered critics useful ways of thinking about the movement from the punitively delusional world of Leontes's court to the festive, fertile world of Bohemia, where Perdita is left by Antigonus in act 3.3.[41] The shift I have in mind involves the legal topography of the play. I alluded to it when I mentioned the passage from the body of law to the soul of law. We witness one adjudicatory event draw to a close in act 3.2 and a second appear on the horizon. The first adjudicatory event has Leontes in the role of judge, and judgment in his hands is experienced as social tragedy. The second adjudicatory event seems, at first glance, to distinguish itself from the previous one by turning the judge into the judged. Indeed, Leontes recognizes the role reversal the moment news of Mamillius's death is delivered: "Apollo's angry, and the heavens themselves / Do strike at my injustice" (3.2.146–47). But this is not itself the adjudicatory event. The oracle of Apollo reads as follows: "Hermione is chaste, Polixenes blameless, Camillo a true subject, Leontes a jealous tyrant, his innocent babe truly begotten, and the King shall live without an heir, if that which is lost be not found" (3.2.132–36). The sentence – "the King shall live without an heir" – is almost passed, but the "if" makes it conditional. The possibility of finding "that which is lost" presents an opportunity for at least partial satisfaction for Leontes's transgression. It also defers the actual adjudicatory event to the final scene of the play.

Those familiar with *The Winter's Tale* know that that which is lost *is* found. Having survived abandonment as an infant on the shores of Bohemia, Perdita returns to Sicilia with Polixenes's son, Florizel, her husband-to-be, in act 5. The two young lovers have eloped and are pursued by a number of others, including Polixenes himself (who disapproves of the marriage), Camillo, an Old Shepherd, a Clown, and the trickster Autolycus. Everyone eventually arrives at the Sicilian court in the company of Leontes and Paulina, and through a series of remarkable revelations it is discovered that Perdita is Leontes's lost daughter and the oracle has been fulfilled. This along with Hermione's apparent revivification in the last scene of the play comprise the final adjudicatory event of *The Winter's Tale*, bringing to completion the suspended, conditional judgment issued by the oracle in act 3.2.

Importantly, these concluding events also reimagine judgment, transforming it from something that proceeds according to the principles of retribution into a process that includes forgiveness and responsibility.[42] This final scene invites us to return to the concept of restorative justice, which I gestured towards at the opening of this chapter. Desmond Tutu, writing in the context of the South African Truth and Reconciliation Commission, describes restorative justice as a system of arbitration that focuses on building and repairing relationships among perpetrators, victims, and society.[43] Tutu, who chaired the commission, writes at length about how those who were involved in finding a path forward in the wake of apartheid needed an alternative to what he calls the Nuremberg paradigm. At post-Holocaust trials, "perpetrators of gross violations of human rights" were made to "run the gauntlet of normal judicial process."[44] This, Tutu explains – possibly with Arendt's analysis of the Eichmann trial in mind – is victor's justice.[45] It can work fine in cases where an actual war has been fought. But what about situations where there has not been a war, where neither side has won *per se*, and where the goal is establishing some kind of shared future for both perpetrators and victims of crimes? "While the Allies could pack up and go home after Nuremberg," Tutu writes, "we in South Africa had to live with one another," and so some kind of balance needed to be struck between the requirements of accountability and the requirements of reconciliation.[46] Similar issues lay at the heart of Northern Ireland's Good Friday Agreement and the ensuing peace process for which it cleared the way.

What legal-political events such as the Truth and Reconciliation Commission or the Good Friday Agreement share with the final scene of *The Winter's Tale* is an interest in reimagining the rituals of judgment as something collective and affirmative. Forgiveness plays a crucial role in this process. Philosophers who work on forgiveness often distinguish between its private, interior dimension ("forgiveness of the heart") and its public, exterior dimension ("performative forgiveness").[47] Political forgiveness, though it may very well include forgiveness of the heart, is first and foremost of the performative sort. It takes place through a public language of expiation and exoneration, and official rituals or procedures of settlement. The goal of political forgiveness is the intrinsically cooperative outcome of reconciliation. So, whereas egotistical judgment is exclusionary and punitive, judgment that includes forgiveness is inclusive and restorative. It aims at creating a single community of justice, both in Levinas's sense of that term and in the broader everyday sense. As Desmond Tutu puts it, the practice of forgiving reminds us that "a person is a person through other persons."[48] This, indeed, is the great lesson Leontes learns by the end of *The Winter's Tale*. As Sarah Beckwith explains, Leontes comes to understand "enough about the grammar of forgiveness to know that he cannot forgive himself, that the grammar of forgiving yourself is, in fact, nonsensical." "Forgiveness," Beckwith continues, "requires the presence of others; and in the acknowledgment of that mutuality lies the truth that others have reality in a past that is no one's individual possession."[49]

Judgment that embraces forgiveness, then, is necessarily premised on a community-oriented vision of legal process. In practice, this version of judgment actualizes an ethics of otherness that is antithetical to Leontes's retributive egocentrism. Let us take a closer look at how this ethics works in the final scene of *The Winter's Tale* where there is both aesthetic discernment and quasi-legal arbitration taking place at the same time. When Paulina "*draws a curtain, and reveals Hermione standing like a statue*," she bids all present to judge on aesthetic grounds: "Behold, and say 'tis well . . . but yet speak. First, you, my liege; / Comes it not something near?" (5.3.20, 22–23). Leontes's extended response marks the moment as both elegiac and sublime, a scene charged with both guilt and wonder. He is in awe at the figure's "natural posture" (5.3.23) and pronounces it a "royal piece" (5.3.38). Likewise, Polixenes exclaims, "Masterly done!" (5.3.65). But Leontes also describes the presence of the statue as "piercing to my soul," and aesthetic approval soon gives way to self-condemnation: "I am asham'd" (5.3.37), he says, and continues:

There's magic in thy majesty, which has
My evils conjur'd to remembrance, and
From thy admiring daughter took the spirits,
Standing like stone with thee. (5.3.39–42)

Aesthetic and moral judgment are carefully wound together in the statue scene. It is through the contemplation and evaluation of beauty that Leontes again confronts his crimes on the psychological terrain of shame and memory. But guilt and remorse do not remain matters of inner turmoil long. Camillo and Polixenes set into motion a process whereby Leontes's self-censure is ushered into the participatory and recuperative ambit of forgiveness:

> CAMILLO: My lord, your sorrow was too sore laid on,
> Which sixteen winters cannot blow away,
> So many summers dry. Scarce any joy
> Did ever so long live; no sorrow
> But kill'd itself much sooner.
> POLIXENES: Dear my brother,
> Let him that was the cause of this have pow'r
> To take off so much grief from you as he
> Will piece up in himself. (5.3.49–56)

Camillo and Polixenes offer Leontes the opportunity to experience the culmination of Apollo's oracular judgment as something curative rather than punitive, and Leontes's acceptance of this is signaled, finally and sensationally, by Hermione's reanimation and embrace. It is true that, as Stanley Cavell has noted, all is not restored in these romantic reversals of fortune. Some losses are permanent. Mamillius and Antigonus are dead and their absence casts a long shadow over the otherwise optimistic conclusion of the play.[50] Nevertheless, there is a profound contrast between the way judgment is imagined in the first half of the play and the way it is imagined at the end. In comparison with the first adjudicatory event in *The Winter's Tale*, in which reckless egocentrism leads to death and the breakdown of both family and service bonds, the second, extended adjudicatory event leads finally to the emergence of a participatory community.

This new community, a community of justice, unfolds along four axes. It is apparent, first, in the collective agencies essential for forgiveness. We see this in the verbal and physical acts of Camillo, Polixenes, and Hermione in response to Leontes's disclosures of guilt and shame. It is apparent, as well, in the kind of mutual presencing that takes place through acts of recognition and acknowledgment: Leontes's and Hermione's recognition of Perdita; Leontes's recognition of Hermione; Hermione's recognition of Leontes. It is apparent in the sociality of aesthetic experience, in which Paulina's invitation to judge is met by an interplay of responses from Leontes, Polixenes, and Perdita. And when Hermione breaks into motion and steps forward to embrace Leontes, it is apparent even in physical action, which becomes in this scene a communal substance, the animated source of an enveloping awe and wonder, rather than an individual force or energy. Hannah Arendt could have been speaking directly to this climactic moment of *The Winter's Tale* when in *The Human Condition* she asserts that "Action, the only activity that goes on directly between men without the intermediary of things or matter, corresponds to the human condition of plurality."[51] Accordingly, the final adjudicatory event of *The Winter's Tale* imagines judgment not in the narrow institutional terms of judicial decision-making, but in the broader terms of Kant's "enlarged mentality," the notion that led Arendt to observe that judgment, when exercised properly, was "one, if not the most, important activity in which . . . sharing-the-world-with-others comes to pass." To judge – morally or aesthetically, oneself or another – is, in Arendt's words, to "remain in this world of universal interdependence."[52] In *The Winter's Tale*, the conditional judgment passed on Leontes by the oracle of Apollo provides a pathway back to "interdependence" and back to a kind of collaborative justice that takes the form of "sharing-the-world-with-others."

Whereas many of the plays we have looked at in this book explore what judgment *is*, *The Winter's Tale* explores what judgment *ought to be*. The cooperative dynamics that Shakespeare examines in earlier tragedies and comedies become in this play something that is worked towards and finally achieved through suffering, forgiveness, and, of course, Paulina's careful planning. This collaborative, anti-egocentric form of judgment becomes the means through which political community is reconstructed and the bonds of family and service (at least partially) restored.

Consequently, judgment in *The Winter's Tale* carries a unique kind of ethical freight. It works to align communalism and otherness with the good, and egocentrism with a form of violence that tears at the foundation of that good. The treatment of judgment in *The Winter's Tale* is informed by early modern ideas about law: the idea that adjudication is, or should be, a participatory affair, and the idea that bringing personal innovation into the process of arbitration is a form of abuse. But as we have seen throughout this book, Shakespeare frequently uses imaginative resources from one part of his culture to address an idea that we would normally think of as belonging to another. *The Winter's Tale* may speak from within the conceptual realm of early modern legal culture, but judgment in the play ultimately has less to tell us about law *per se* than it does about what I referred to earlier as the hazards of extreme individualism. Judgment, that is, provides a framework for showcasing the social and moral risks we take when we cease to think in, and through, the presence of others. And by the end of the play it provides an equally compelling framework for thinking about how we might manage those risks.

CODA: REIMAGINING JUDGMENT

Feeling, *objects*, *vision*, *making*, *facing*, and *community* comprise a Shakespearean lexicon of judgment, a phenomenological vocabulary marked by both the intellectual culture of early modernity and the transactional dynamics of theater. So, what is it exactly that this lexicon allows us to say, think, or imagine about judgment? And why does it matter? Answers to these questions have been emerging gradually over the course of the preceding chapters, and I have gestured towards them whenever possible. With the end now in sight, let us return to them in a more direct and deliberate manner.

To answer the first question, I invoke three key assertions that have animated this book. First, Shakespeare's theater helps us reimagine judgment as collaborative. Instead of being a purely individual capacity, a cognitive operation of a sole mind assessing the world, judgment in Shakespearean theater is a group effort. It requires an interlocutor – sometimes many. Whether it is the communal reckoning-through-revelation at the end of *Measure for Measure* and *The Winter's Tale* or the behest to the audience in the epilogue of *The Tempest*, judgment belongs to the collective world of shared space, shared experience, and shared futures. Be it cooperative or agonistic, social transaction is the ground zero for judgment in the plays we have looked at.

Second, Shakespeare's theater helps us reimagine judgment as embodied. Though a long tradition of post-Enlightenment philosophy places judgment in the mind and makes it the bedfellow of reason, Shakespearean theater insists on the body as a locus of judgment, anchoring it securely to emotion and perception. The closet scene in *Hamlet* models a version of judgment as sensory experience, reminding us that a person of sound judgment must also be a person of feeling. The end of *Twelfth Night* makes the eyes rather than the mind the privileged site of judgment, and in doing so troubles the conventional frontiers that exist between truth and falsehood. Mark Antony's speech to the plebeians in *Julius Caesar*, meanwhile, demonstrates how embodied judgment – judgment evolving out of visual, aural, and manual assessment – is necessarily material, a process embedded in and dependent on physical experience. The plays considered in the preceding chapters show us the phenomenological origins of judgment, the way it always emerges from spaces of encounter between bodies and objects locked together in mutually animating webs of interdependence.

Third, Shakespeare's theater helps us reimagine judgment as creative. Judgment, in other words, is not the ultimate destination. The point is not simply to settle, to decide, to sentence, or to decree and thereby to end something. Judgment does not look backward, nor does it close its eyes and stand rooted, motionless in a present of resolution. Judgment looks forward. It has a momentum that drives towards the future. The communally shared processes of selection, discernment, categorization, and restructuring that lie at the heart of Shakespearean judgment are not about solving a puzzle and returning it to the shelf. They are about redistributing knowledge and agency among a collective so as to form new conditions of social possibility. The scenes of judgment that conclude plays like *Measure for Measure*, *The Winter's Tale*, and *The Tempest* fundamentally change the relationships among the characters on stage such that a future previously unimaginable can now be conceived by the community. This is never a future we as audience members get to see, and it may not be a future that is uniformly positive. But it is a future, always, that makes the previously impossible possible. It opens the door to forms of partnership, collaboration, redemption, and forgiveness for which no script had existed. It can return people to the community who had left it or bring people in who had never been there before. It can also remove people or allow them to remove themselves. One way or another, for better or for worse, judgment in Shakespeare's plays is the precondition for *change*. It is the grounds on which the possibility of change must stand. If judgment is a reckoning with what has been, it also forms a blueprint for what is to come.

Facing, making, and community are terms which help us articulate the collaborative dimension of judgment; feeling, objects, and vision are terms which help us articulate the embodied dimension of judgment; and almost all of these terms are part of a language of creation since the scenes of acknowledgment, collectivity, and physical encounter they describe link discernment to change, action, and new social and political formations. The lexicon of judgment we have assembled in collaboration with Shakespeare, in other words, reminds us how spaces of social and spiritual possibility can open when we trust what the body knows and take seriously the forms of value ascribed by feeling and perception. It reminds us that there is a social physics to judgment, a way in which evaluation functions as an ensemble choreography of recognition, response, conflict, and consensus.

If this is what Shakespeare's lexicon of judgment affords us conceptually and experientially, the answer to the second question – why does it matter? – lies in the way these affordances invite us to detach judgment from certain strands of the liberal tradition with which it has often been bound up. We are invited to remove judgment from the mind, to uncouple it from reason, and to free it from the individual. We are encouraged to rethink judgment's association with generally negative ideas like condemnation, punishment, normativity, regulation, and reductiveness. I recognize, even as I make this assertation, that "liberalism" is a complex and diverse notion, and perhaps especially confusing in our own time when we find the term being used pejoratively by both the political right and the political left, seemingly to refer to opposite things. The right invokes "liberalism" to indicate the left's investment in issues of social and environmental justice. The left – especially, and more specifically, the academic left – invokes "liberalism" (or sometimes "neo-liberalism") to refer to capitalist ideological formations that animate the policies of the right. Moreover, beyond the world of practical politics, there is also something we might refer to more generally as the liberal ethos or temperament, the features of which include open-mindedness, tolerance, sympathy, communality, and plurality.[1]

When I say that Shakespeare helps us see a version of judgment that stands outside the "liberal tradition," I am referring to specific and well-known *philosophical* ideas about reason, action, knowledge, freedom, and individuality which have been discussed at a number of points in the preceding chapters. These philosophical ideas predate liberalism as a set of distinct political and intellectual movements in the Enlightenment, but they were crucial to shaping them. They also contribute forcefully to the economic, political, and social views that would eventually be entrusted to the modern term "neoliberalism." By contrast, the features of what I have called the liberal ethos – open-mindedness, tolerance, sympathy, communality, and plurality – are, as we have seen, very much part of Shakespearean judgment. The power, uniqueness, and utility of this way into a critique of liberal philosophical ideas stands out in relief when we consider that judgment has typically been viewed as part of those ideas, an expression of reason and the autonomous subject, and therefore as one of the things *to be critiqued*. Michel Foucault, we will recall, viewed judgment as central to the regulatory regime of modernity, not as a way out of it. As discussed in the Introduction, the academic left's resistance to liberal humanism in the 1980s took its highest methodological form in deconstruction, a procedure that was presented as an alternative to judgment, the latter understood to be elitist and categorical, opinion parading as universal truth, bias posturing as cultivation. These objections, of course, have to do mostly with *aesthetic* judgment, and given that literary-canon formation has long been the scene of racial- and gender-based exclusion, they are not unfounded. Indeed, for the academic left of the Reagan and Thatcher era, there seemed to be a problem with the very structure of judgment, something essential about it that undermined basic principles of equality.[2]

Recovering a positive and worldmaking form of judgment, therefore, requires first that we distinguish between different versions of judgment, something that has been central to this book

from the beginning. Enlightenment (and post-Enlightenment) aesthetic judgment – the problem that deconstruction offers a solution to – is not the same as the artisanal, practical judgment within
early modern rhetorical culture, nor is it the same as the collective,
embodied judgment of Shakespeare's theater. In addition to dif-
ferentiating between different versions of judgment, we also need
to differentiate between two different principles of equality, often
confused or conflated, both of which exist within that baggy constellation of ideas and policies that we call the liberal tradition. One
of these two principles of equality, Shakespearean judgment does
not undermine. That is the equality of the liberal ethos: the sort
of equality that toleration aims at, that open-mindedness makes
possible, and that communality gives form to. The other principle
of equality, Shakespearean judgment does undermine. That is the
equality of the marketplace. Within a "free market," nothing has
intrinsic value and therefore there are no grounds for judgment.
Everything, and everyone, is equal in its value-free status. Value is
ascribed by the supposedly neutral force of the marketplace itself,
not by inherently biased individuals. Marketplace equality says
that if people will pay $200 for something, it is worth $200; if
people will pay $1,000 for it, it is worth $1,000. If it has 10,000
likes it is good, whether it is an Ingmar Bergman film or a Coca-
Cola commercial. Marketplace equality says, *let the people decide!*
According to this logic, to ascribe value and form judgments that
are not market driven is to undermine equality.[3] One of the great
powers of neoliberalism lies in the way it often manages to present
marketplace equality as coterminous with the liberal-ethos equality of inclusion, toleration, and open-mindedness, when in fact
they are very different things, the former mobilizing the rhetoric
of fairness to serve the interests of the few, the latter creating the
conditions for the social betterment of the many. Shakespearean
theater models a form of judgment that resists the faux equality of
the marketplace precisely so as to foster the generative equality of
human community.

    In defending judgment as modeled by Shakespearean theater,
then, I most certainly do not seek to redeem bias, exclusion, or the
cynical disavowals of self-interest that so often lie hidden behind

universal standards of taste. Such things, it should go without saying, do not deserve redemption. The key observation to make, it seems to me, is that judgment as a whole has been mistakenly lumped in with these negative forces, and to our own detriment. There are aspects of the history and theory of judgment worth recuperating, not least for the transformative social power they potentially have to counter things like bias, exclusivity, and self-interest. Besides, a culture of decision-making and problem-solving grounded purely in metrics is not sufficient to tackle the complex ethical problems that face the world moving forward. We need scripts and practices for collaboratively assigning value that are not beholden to the market-logic of capitalist equality. Theater, especially Shakespearean theater, offers one place where we can find these scripts, where a re-encounter with the experience of judgment can be fostered.

If this sounds like a roundabout way of saying that theater can save the world, well, it is. Not directly, not immediately, and not on its own; but in its own small yet important way, theater provides us with resources that can make us better world citizens. Judgment is chief among them.

NOTES

Introduction

1. Vivasvan Soni, ed., *The Eighteenth Century: Theory and Interpretation* 51 (2010), Special Issue: "The Crisis of Judgment."
2. Hina Nazar, *Enlightened Sentiments: Judgment and Autonomy in the Age of Sensibility* (New York: Fordham University Press, 2012).
3. Thomas Pfau, *Minding the Modern: Human Agency, Intellectual Traditions, and Responsible Knowledge* (Notre Dame, IN: University of Notre Dame Press, 2013).
4. Richard Strier, *The Unrepentant Renaissance: From Petrarch to Shakespeare to Milton* (Chicago: University of Chicago Press, 2011); "Shakespeare and Legal Systems: The Better the Worse (but Not Vice Versa)," in *Shakespeare and the Law: A Conversation Among Disciplines and Professions*, ed. Bradin Cormack, Martha C. Nussbaum, and Richard Strier (Chicago: University of Chicago Press, 2013), 174–200.
5. Lorna Hutson, *The Invention of Suspicion: Law and Mimesis in Shakespeare and Renaissance Drama* (Oxford: Oxford University Press, 2007).
6. Kathy Eden, *Poetic and Legal Fiction in the Aristotelian Tradition* (Princeton, NJ: Princeton University Press, 1986); Joel B. Altman, *The Improbability of Othello: Rhetorical Anthropology and Shakespearean Selfhood* (Chicago: University of Chicago Press, 2010); and Quentin Skinner, *Forensic Shakespeare* (Oxford: Oxford University Press, 2014).
7. Henry S. Turner, *The English Renaissance Stage: Geometry, Poetics, and the Practical Spatial Arts, 1580–1630* (Oxford: Oxford University Press, 2006).

8. J. G. A. Pocock, *The Machiavellian Moment: Florentine Political Thought and the Atlantic Republican Tradition* (Princeton, NJ: Princeton University Press, 1975); Andras Kisery, *Hamlet's Moment: Drama and Political Knowledge in Early Modern England* (Oxford: Oxford University Press, 2016).

9. Julia Reinhard Lupton, *Thinking with Shakespeare: Essays on Politics and Life* (Chicago: University of Chicago Press, 2011); "Judging Forgiveness: Hannah Arendt, W. H. Auden, and *The Winter's Tale*," *New Literary History* 45 (2014): 641–63.

10. Much of the raw material for this unfinished volume can be found in Hannah Arendt, "Judging: Excerpts from Lectures on Kant's Political Philosophy," an appendix to *The Life of the Mind* (San Diego: Harcourt, 1978), 255–72.

11. *OED*, "judgemental/judgmental, *adj.*," 2.

12. The meme is a slight distortion of the actual quotation from Jung's *Flying Saucers: A Modern Myth of Things Seen in the Sky* (1958), which reads, "Thinking is difficult. Therefore, let the herd pronounce judgment." See C. G. Jung, *Flying Saucers: A Modern Myth of Things Seen in the Sky*, trans. R. F. C. Hull (Princeton, NJ: Princeton University Press, 1978), 38.

13. For commentary on the role of numbers, math, and statistics in the history of knowledge-management and judgment, see Mary Poovey, *A History of the Modern Fact: Problems of Knowledge in the Sciences of Wealth and Society* (Chicago: University of Chicago Press, 1998) and Soni, "Introduction: The Crisis of Judgment."

14. Francis Bacon, *The New Organon* (Cambridge: Cambridge University Press, 2000), Aphorism 42.

15. Michel Foucault, *Discipline and Punish: The Birth of the Prison*, trans. Alan Sheridan (New York: Vintage Books, 1977), 19.

16. Foucault, *Discipline and Punish*, 20–21.

17. Foucault, *Discipline and Punish*, 83.

18. Pierre Bourdieu, *Distinction: A Social Critique of the Judgement of Taste*, trans. Richard Nice (Cambridge, MA: Harvard University Press, 1984), 6, 18.

19. Soni, "Introduction: The Crisis of Judgment," 267.

20. Cleanth Brooks, *The Well-Wrought Urn: Studies in the Structure of Poetry* (New York: Harcourt Brace, 1947), 197.

21. Paul de Man, *Allegories of Reading: Figural Language in Rousseau, Nietzsche, Rilke, and Proust* (New Haven, CT: Yale University Press, 1979), 245.

22. Soni, "Introduction: The Crisis of Judgment."
23. Steven Shapin, *A Social History of Truth: Civility and Science in Seventeenth-Century England* (Chicago: University of Chicago Press, 1994), xxv.
24. Shapin, *Social History of Truth*, 5, 6.
25. Shapin, *Social History of Truth*, xxvi.
26. Cicero, *On Duties*, trans. Walter Miller (Cambridge, MA: Harvard University Press, 1913), 145.
27. Thomas Wilson, *The Arte of Rhetorique* (London, 1553), 123; Robert Ascham, *The Schoolmaster* (London, 1570), 151.
28. See Zachary Lesser and Peter Stallybrass, "The First Literary *Hamlet* and the Commonplacing of Professional Plays," *Shakespeare Quarterly* 59 (2008): 371–420 and Laura Estill, *Dramatic Extracts in Seventeenth-Century English Manuscripts: Watching, Reading, Changing Plays* (Newark, NJ: University of Delaware Press, 2015).
29. John Foxe, *Locorum Communium Tituli* (Basel, 1557). A sign of its long-term popularity, *Locorum Communium Tituli* was reprinted in revised and expanded forms in 1572 and 1585.
30. Seneca the Younger, *Epistles II: Epistles 66–92*, trans. Richard M. Gunmere (Cambridge, MA: Harvard University Press, 1920), 279. For discussion, see Ann Moss, *Printed Commonplace-Books and the Structuring of Renaissance Thought* (Oxford: Clarendon Press, 1996), 10–14.
31. Estill, *Dramatic Extracts*, 4–6.
32. The most recent critical edition of one of these commonplace books, Lukas Erne and Devani Singh, eds., *Bel-vedére or the Garden of the Muses: An Early Modern Printed Commonplace Book* (Cambridge: Cambridge University Press, 2020), includes a detailed scholarly apparatus with copious information about the textual and cultural contexts for collections of this sort.
33. See G. K. Hunter, "The Marking of Sententiae in Elizabethan Printed Plays, Poems, and Romances," *The Library* 5th ser. 6 (1951): 171–88 and Lesser and Stallybrass, "First Literary *Hamlet*."
34. See Peter Stallybrass, Roger Chartier, J. Franklin Mowery, and Heather Wolfe, "Hamlet's Tables and the Technologies of Writing in Renaissance England," *Shakespeare Quarterly* 55 (2004): 379–419 and Andrew Gurr, *Playgoing in Shakespeare's England* (Cambridge: Cambridge University Press, 2004), 240.
35. For a study that explores this in the context of the professionalization of politics, see Kisery, *Hamlet's Moment*, 37–88, 206–42.

36. Stefano Guazzo, *The Civile Conversation* (London, 1581), 4–5.

37. Deborah E. Harkness, *The Jewel House: Elizabethan London and the Scientific Revolution* (New Haven, CT: Yale University Press, 2007), 9.

38. See further Peter Mack, *Elizabethan Rhetoric: Theory and Practice* (Cambridge: Cambridge University Press, 2002), 11–47 and Skinner, *Forensic Shakespeare*, 25–41.

39. Skinner, *Forensic Shakespeare*, 11–25; Turner, *English Renaissance Stage*, 45–55.

40. Julia Reinhard Lupton writes brilliantly on the modern concept of "design" in early modern contexts in *Shakespeare Dwelling: Designs for the Theater of Life* (Chicago: University of Chicago Press, 2018).

41. Jon Hesk, "Types of Oratory," in *The Cambridge Companion to Ancient Rhetoric*, ed. Erik Gunderson (Cambridge: Cambridge University Press, 2009), 145–61 (pp. 150–56).

42. See Denis Kezar, *Solon and Thespis: Law and Theater in the English Renaissance* (Notre Dame, IN: University of Notre Dame Press, 2007).

43. Leo Salinger, "Jacobean Playwrights and 'Judicious' Spectators,'" *Renaissance Drama* 22 (1991): 209–34 (p. 210).

44. John Lyly, *Midas*, "Prologue," in *The Complete Works of John Lyly*, ed. R. Warwick Bond, 3 vols. (Oxford: Clarendon Press, 1902), 3:12 and Christopher Marlowe, *Doctor Faustus*, ed. Paul Menzer (London: Bloomsbury, 2019), Chorus. 9.

45. Ben Jonson, "Induction," in *Every Man Out of His Humour*, ed. Helen Ostovich (Manchester: Manchester University Press, 2001), 56–65.

46. William Shakespeare, *Hamlet*, rev. ed., ed. Ann Thompson and Neil Taylor (London: Bloomsbury, 2016), 3.2.26.

47. Ben Jonson, "To the Reader," in *The Alchemist*, in *Ben Jonson: Five Plays*, ed. G. A. Wilkes (Oxford: Oxford University Press, 1981), 14–16.

48. Thomas Heywood, "Prologue" to *The Silver Age*, in *The Dramatic Works of Thomas Heywood*, ed. R. H. Shepherd, 6 vols. (London: Pearson, 1874), 3:79.

49. Thomas Dekker, *The Gull's Horn-Book* (London, 1609), 27–28.

50. Shapin, *Social History of Truth*, xix.

51. See John Fortescue, *De Laudibus Legum Angliae*, ed. and trans. S. B. Chrimes (Cambridge: Cambridge University Press, 1949), 38–41.

52. Pocock, *Machiavellian Moment*, 16.

53. Pocock, *Machiavellian Moment*, 24.

54. Raymond Williams, *Keywords: A Vocabulary of Culture and Society* (Oxford: Oxford University Press, 1976).

Chapter 1

1. See William Shakespeare, *Hamlet: A New Variorum Edition*, ed. H. H. Furness, 2 vols. (Philadelphia: J. B. Lippincott and Co., 1877), 2:273 (for Goethe) and 2:178 (for MacKenzie).

2. Robin Headlam-Wells, *Shakespeare on Masculinity* (Cambridge: Cambridge University Press, 2000), 81.

3. Harold Bloom, *Shakespeare: The Invention of the Human* (New York: Riverhead Books, 1998), 409. For Coleridge, see "Notes on Hamlet," in *Coleridge's Essays and Lectures on Shakespeare and Some Other Old Poets and Dramatists*, ed. Ernest Rhys (London: J. M. Dent, 1907). See also Jonathan Bate, *The Genius of Shakespeare* (London: Picador, 1997) and Andrew Welsh, *Hamlet in His Modern Guises* (Princeton, NJ: Princeton University Press, 2001).

4. John Lee, *Shakespeare's* Hamlet *and the Controversies of Self* (Oxford: Clarendon Press, 2000), 1; Marjorie Garber, *Shakespeare After All* (New York: Anchor Books, 2004), 4.

5. Margreta de Grazia, Hamlet *without Hamlet* (Cambridge: Cambridge University Press, 2007), 1.

6. Henry MacKenzie, *The Mirror*, no. 99, 18 April 1780, qtd. in Shakespeare, *Hamlet: A New Variorum Edition*, 2:148.

7. David Bevington, *Murder Most Foul: Hamlet through the Ages* (Oxford: Oxford University Press, 2011), 98–99.

8. Quotations and line references are from William Shakespeare, *Hamlet*, rev. ed., ed. Ann Thompson and Neil Taylor (London: Bloomsbury, 2016).

9. Aristotle, *Nicomachean Ethics*, ed. Roger Crisp (Cambridge: Cambridge University Press, 2000), 1109b20.

10. For background, see especially David Summers, *The Judgment of Sense: Renaissance Naturalism and the Rise of Aesthetics* (Cambridge: Cambridge University Press, 1987).

11. Aristotle, *On the Soul*, 432a15, 426b–c, in Aristotle, *On the Soul, Parva Naturalia, On Breath*, trans. W. S. Hett (Cambridge, MA: Harvard University Press, 1936).

12. Abraham Fraunce, *The Lawyers Logike* (London, 1588), 91.

13. There is a fairly vast critical literature on Calvinism, the early modern reception of Stoicism, and the relationship between Christian

and ancient thought within Renaissance humanism more generally. In the context of the present discussion, good places to start are Thomas F. Torrance, *Calvin's Doctrine of Man* (London: Lutterworth, 1952); William J. Bouwsma, "The Two Faces of Humanism: Stoicism and Augustinianism in Renaissance Thought," in *A Usable Past: Essays in European Cultural History* (Berkeley: University of California Press, 1990), 19–73; Malcolm Schofield, *The Stoic Idea of the City* (Cambridge: Cambridge University Press, 1991); Margaret Graver, *Stoicism and Emotion* (Chicago: University of Chicago Press, 2007); and Roberta Kwan, *Shakespeare, the Reformation, and the Interpreting Self* (Edinburgh: Edinburgh University Press, 2023). For two studies that show how early modern writers pushed back against these theological and philosophical orientations, see Christopher Tilmouth, *Passion's Triumph Over Reason: A History of the Moral Imagination from Spenser to Rochester* (Oxford: Oxford University Press, 2007) and Richard Strier, *The Unrepentant Renaissance from Petrarch to Shakespeare to Milton* (Chicago: University of Chicago Press, 2011).

14. Timothy Hampton, "Difficult Engagements: Private Passion and Public Service in Montaigne's *Essais*," in *Politics and the Passions, 1500–1850*, ed. Victoria Kahn, Neil Saccamano, and Daniela Coli (Princeton, NJ: Princeton University Press, 2006), 30–48. See also Graver, *Stoicism and Emotion* and Donovan Sherman, "Stoicism," in *Shakespeare and Virtue: A Handbook*, ed. Julia Reinhard Lupton and Donovan Sherman (Cambridge: Cambridge University Press, 2023), 69–80.

15. Thomas Wright, *The Passions of the Minde in Generall* (London, 1601), 12–14.

16. Philippe de Mornay, *The True Knowledge of a Man's Owne Selfe* (London, 1602), 2.

17. See Boethius, *Tractates/The Consolation of Philosophy*, trans. H. F. Stewart and E. K. Rand (Cambridge, MA: Harvard University Press, 1962), 388–91.

18. Bonaventure, *Opera Omnia*, 10 vols. (Quaracchi: Collegium S. Bonaventure, 1882–1902), 2:221.

19. For the signet ring and wax image, see Aristotle, *On the Soul*, 424a17–24.

20. John Locke, *An Essay Concerning Human Understanding*, ed. Roger Woolhouse (London: Penguin Books, 1997), 577, 143.

21. Locke, *Essay*, 254.

22. Locke, *Essay*, 255.

23. *OED*, "theatre, theater, *n.*," 1; William N. West, *Theaters and Encyclopedias in Early Modern Europe* (Cambridge: Cambridge University Press, 2002), 46.

24. Stephanie Elsky's *Custom, Common Law, and the Constitution of English Renaissance Literature* (Oxford: Oxford University Press, 2020) is especially sensitive to the way collectivity and sociality undergird the formal and imaginative links between English common law and literature in the early modern period.

25. John Fortescue, *De Laudibus Legum Angliae*, ed. and trans. S. B. Chrimes (Cambridge: Cambridge University Press, 1949), 20–23.

26. Fortescue, *De Laudibus*, 39–41.

27. J. G. A. Pocock, *The Machiavellian Moment: Florentine Political Thought and the Atlantic Republican Tradition* (Princeton, NJ: Princeton University Press, 1975), 14.

28. See further Glenn Burgess, *The Politics of the Ancient Constitution: An Introduction to English Political Thought, 1600–42* (Basingstoke: Macmillan, 1992), 1–78.

29. This was later printed in part twelve of Coke's reports. See Edward Coke, *The Twelfth Part of the Reports of Sir Edward Coke* (London, 1656), 58–62. For discussion, see Allen D. Boyer, *Sir Edward Coke and the Elizabethan Age* (Stanford, CA: Stanford University Press, 2003), 83–107.

30. See G. W. F. Hegel, "Dramatic Poetry," in *Aesthetics: Lectures on Fine Art: Volume 2*, ed. T. M. Knox (Oxford: Oxford University Press, 1998), 1158–1238 and Jacob Burckhardt, *The Civilization of the Renaissance in Italy* (Mineola, NY: Dover, 2010). For a series of varied and provocative discussions of different aspects of this critical inheritance, see Hugh Grady, ed., *Shakespeare and Modernity: Early Modern to Millennium* (London: Routledge, 2000).

31. See A. C. Bradley, "The Substance of Shakespearean Tragedy," in *Shakespearean Tragedy* (London: Penguin Books, 1991), 23–51.

32. Stephen Greenblatt, *Renaissance Self-fashioning from More to Shakespeare* (Chicago: University of Chicago Press, 1980), 1.

33. Stephen Greenblatt, *Shakespeare's Freedom* (Chicago: University of Chicago Press, 2010).

34. Peter Holbrook, *Shakespeare's Individualism* (Cambridge: Cambridge University Press, 2010), 1.

35. Søren Kierkegaard, *The Sickness Unto Death*, trans. Alastair Hannay (London: Penguin Books, 1989), 62–63; Martin Heidegger, *Being*

and Time, trans. Joan Stambaugh, rev. Dennis J. Schmidt (Albany: SUNY Press, 1996), 119.

36. Holbrook, *Shakespeare's Individualism*, 12–13.

37. See, for example, R. F. Brissenden, *Virtue in Distress: Studies in the Novel of Sentiment from Richardson to Sade* (New York: Barnes & Noble Press, 1974); John Mullan, *Sentiment and Sociability: The Language of Feeling in the Eighteenth Century* (Oxford: Clarendon Press, 1988); Lynn Festa, *Sentimental Figures of Empire in Eighteenth-Century Britain and France* (Baltimore, MD: Johns Hopkins University Press, 2006); and Hina Nazar, *Enlightened Sentiments: Judgment and Autonomy in the Age of Sensibility* (New York: Fordham University Press, 2012).

38. Nazar, *Enlightened Sentiments*, 2.

39. David Hume, *A Treatise of Human Nature*, ed. L. A. Selby-Bigge, 2nd ed. (Oxford: Clarendon Press, 1978), 471.

40. Immanuel Kant, *Critique of Judgment*, trans. Werner S. Pluhar (Indianapolis, IN: Hackett Publishing Company, 1987), 160.

41. See Hannah Arendt, "The Crisis in Culture: Its Social and Its Political Significance" and "Truth and Politics," in *Between Past and Future: Eight Exercises in Political Thought* (London: Penguin Books, 1993), 197–226, 227–64; "Personal Responsibility Under Dictatorship" and "Some Questions of Moral Philosophy," in *Responsibility and Judgment*, ed. Jerome Kohn (New York: Random House, 2003), 17–48, 49–146; and *The Life of the Mind* (San Diego: Harcourt, 1978), 69, 93–95, 193. In addition to the two completed volumes of *The Life of the Mind* – "Thinking" and "Willing" – Arendt had intended to produce a third, on "Judging." She died before she was able to complete this section but much of the raw material for it can be found in the appendix to the Harcourt edition (255–72), "Judging: Excerpts from Lectures on Kant's Political Philosophy."

42. Adam Smith, *The Theory of Moral Sentiments*, ed. D. D. Raphael and A. L. Macfie (Indianapolis, IN: Liberty Fund, 1982), 110.

43. See further Kevin Curran and James Kearney, "Introduction," *Criticism* 54 (2012): 353–64, Special Issue: "Shakespeare and Phenomenology," ed. Kevin Curran and James Kearney. Seminal phenomenological works within philosophy include Edmund Husserl, *Logical Investigations*, trans. J. N. Findlay (Amherst, NY: Humanity Books, 2000) and *Ideas Pertaining to a Pure Phenomenology and to a Phenomenological Philosophy*, trans. F. Kersten (Dordrecht:

Kluwer Academic Publishers, 1983); Heidegger, *Being and Time*; Maurice Merleau-Ponty, *The Phenomenology of Perception*, trans. Colin Smith (London: Routledge, 2008); and Arendt, *Life of the Mind*. Bruce R. Smith ushered phenomenology into early modern studies with his article "Premodern Sexualities," *PMLA* 115 (2000): 318–29, which paved the way for a number of important books dealing with "historical phenomenology," including Mary Floyd-Wilson, *English Ethnicity and Race in Early Modern Drama* (Cambridge: Cambridge University Press, 2003); Gail Kern Paster, *Humoring the Body: Emotions and the Shakespearean Stage* (Chicago: University of Chicago Press, 2004); and Bruce R. Smith, *The Key of Green: Passion and Perception in Renaissance Culture* (Chicago: University of Chicago Press, 2009) and *Phenomenal Shakespeare* (Malden, MA: Wiley-Blackwell, 2010).

Chapter 2

1   See Graham Harman, *Tool-Being: Heidegger and the Metaphysics of Objects* (Chicago: Open Court Press, 2002) and *Object-Oriented Ontology: A New Theory of Everything* (London: Penguin Books, 2018). Harman does undertake a sustained engagement with phenomenology in *Guerrilla Metaphysics: Phenomenology and the Carpentry of Things* (Chicago: Open Court Press, 2005).

2. Jane Bennett, *Vibrant Matter: A Political Ecology of Things* (Durham, NC: Duke University Press, 2010), vii.

3. Bennett, *Vibrant Matter*, viii. See Bruno Latour, *Politics of Nature: How to Bring the Sciences into Democracy* (Cambridge, MA: Harvard University Press, 2004), 237.

4. See Gilles Deleuze and Félix Guattari, *A Thousand Plateaus: Capitalism and Schizophrenia* (Minneapolis: University of Minnesota Press, 1987), 351–423.

5. On new materialism, see Stacey Alaimo and Susan J. Hekman, "Introduction: Emerging Models of Materiality in Feminist Theory," in *Material Feminisms*, ed. Stacey Alaimo and Susan J. Hekman (Bloomington, IN: Indiana University Press, 2008), 1–19; Diana Coole and Samantha Frost, "Introducing the New Materialisms," in *New Materialisms: Ontology, Agency, and Politics*, ed. Diana Coole and Samantha Frost (Durham, NC: Duke University Press, 2010), 1–43; and Rick Dolphijn and Iris van der Tuin, "The Transversality of New Materialism," in *New Materialism: Interviews and Cartographies*, ed.

Rick Dolphijn and Iris van der Tuin (Ann Arbor, MI: Open Humanities Press, 2012), 93–113.

6. Though she pursues a very particular argument, Victoria Kahn's *Rhetoric, Prudence, and Skepticism in the Renaissance* (Ithaca, NY: Cornell University Press, 1985) remains one of the best, and most intellectually sophisticated, places to begin learning about prudence during the early modern period.

7. For more on this way of approaching virtue, see Kevin Curran, "The Four Cardinal Virtues," in *Shakespeare and Virtue: A Handbook*, ed. Julia Reinhard Lupton and Donovan Sherman (Cambridge: Cambridge University Press, 2023), 113–24 and "Everyday Dramaturgy: Virtue and the Craft of Living," in *Shakespeare's Virtuous Theatre: Power, Capacity, and the Good*, ed. Kent Lenhof, Julia Reinhard Lupton, and Carolyn Sale (Edinburgh: Edinburgh University Press, 2023), 287–94. Anyone writing on virtue in a way that seeks to give the topic contemporary urgency is indebted, directly or indirectly, to the pioneering work of Martha Nussbaum. See, for instance, *Poetic Justice: The Literary Imagination and Public Life* (Boston, MA: Beacon Press, 1995); *Frontiers of Justice: Disability, Nationality, Species Membership* (Cambridge, MA: Harvard University Press, 2006); and *Creating Capabilities: The Human Development Approach* (Cambridge, MA: Harvard University Press, 2011).

8. Istvan P. Bejczy, "Les vertus cardinals dans l'hagiographie latine du Moyen Âge," *Analecta Bollandiana: Revue critique d'hagiographie* 122 (2004): 313–60.

9. See further Charles B. Schmitt, *John Case and Aristotelianism in Renaissance England* (Montreal: McGill-Queen's University Press, 1983); Neal Wood, "Cicero and the Political Thought of the Early English Renaissance," *Modern Language Quarterly* 51 (1990): 185–207; and Christopher Crosbie, *Revenge Tragedy and Classical Philosophy on the Early Modern Stage* (Edinburgh: Edinburgh University Press, 2019), 92–94.

10. See further Norman Muir, "Middle-Class Heroism and the Cardinal Virtue Fortitude in Thomas Dekker's 'Honest Whore' Plays," *Explorations in Renaissance Culture* 15 (1989): 83–97; Reid Barbour, *English Epicureans and Stoics: Ancient Legacies in Early Stuart Culture* (Amherst: University of Massachusetts Press, 1998); and Istvan P. Bejczy, *The Cardinal Virtues in the Middle Ages: A Study in Moral Thought from the Fourth to the Fourteenth Century* (Leiden: Brill, 2011).

11. Lodowyck Bryskett, *A Discourse of Civill Life* (London, 1606), 185.

12. Cicero, *On Duties*, trans. Walter Miller (Cambridge, MA: Harvard University Press, 1913), I.15, I.17.

13. Jacques Taminiaux, *The Thracian Maid and the Professional Thinker: Heidegger and Arendt* (Albany: SUNY Press, 1997), 108; Paul Kottman, *A Politics of the Scene* (Stanford, CA: Stanford University Press, 2008), 4–5, 30–35.

14. Aristotle, *Nicomachean Ethics*, ed. Roger Crisp (Cambridge: Cambridge University Press, 2000), 1141b.

15. See Henry S. Turner, *The English Renaissance Stage: Geometry, Poetics, and the Practical Spatial Arts* (Oxford: Oxford University Press, 2006), 14; Kevin Sharpe, "Virtues, Passions, and Politics in Early Modern England," *History of Political Thought* 32 (2011): 773–98; and Dori Coblentz, *Fencing, Form, and Cognition on the Early Modern Stage: Artful Devices* (Edinburgh: Edinburgh University Press, 2021).

16. Aristotle, *Nicomachean Ethics*, 1140a–b.

17. Aristotle, *Nicomachean Ethics*, 1142a. For discussion, see Lois S. Self, "Rhetoric and Phronesis: The Aristotelian Ideal," *Philosophy & Rhetoric* 12 (1979): 130–45 (p. 135).

18. On temperance and the mean, see Joshua Scodel, *Excess and the Mean in Early Modern English Literature* (Princeton, NJ: Princeton University Press, 2002), and on the relationships among prudence, courage, temperance, and justice, see Unhae Park Langis, *Passion, Prudence, and Virtue in Shakespearean Drama* (London: Bloomsbury, 2011).

19. To date, the most wide-ranging and theoretically nuanced overview of virtue with Shakespeare at its center is Lupton and Sherman, *Shakespeare and Virtue*. Other useful works of scholarship in this vein include Patrick Grey and John D. Cox, eds., *Shakespeare and Renaissance Ethics* (Cambridge: Cambridge University Press, 2014); Holly Crocker, *The Matter of Virtue: Women's Ethical Action from Chaucer to Shakespeare* (Philadelphia: University of Pennsylvania Press, 2019); and, for a slightly broader audience, Scott Newstock, *How to Think Like Shakespeare: Lessons from a Renaissance Education* (Princeton, NJ: Princeton University Press, 2020).

20. Quotations and line references are from William Shakespeare, *Julius Caesar*, ed. David Daniell (London: Bloomsbury, 1998).

21. Perez Zagorin, *Ways of Lying: Dissimulation, Persecution, and Conformity in Early Modern Europe* (Cambridge, MA: Harvard University Press, 1990), 255.

22. See, for example, Francis Bacon, "Of Simulation and Dissimulation," in *The Works of Francis Bacon*, ed. James Spedding, 14 vols. (London: Longman & Co., 1857–74), 12:95–98, and for historical commentary, J. H. M. Salmon, "Seneca and Tacitus in Jacobean England," in *The Mental World of the Jacobean Court*, ed. Linda Levy Peck (Cambridge: Cambridge University Press, 1991), 169–88; Malcolm Smuts, "Court-Centred Politics and the Uses of Roman Historians, c. 1590–1630," in *Culture and Politics in Early Stuart England*, ed. Kevin Sharpe and Peter Lake (Stanford, CA: Stanford University Press, 1993), 21–43; and David Coast, *News and Rumour in Jacobean England: Information, Court Politics, and Diplomacy, 1618–25* (Manchester: Manchester University Press, 2016).

23. The best overview of these cultural developments remains Barbara Shapiro, *A Culture of Fact: England, 1550–1720* (Ithaca, NY: Cornell University Press, 2000).

24. Murray L. Chapman, "A Sixteenth-Century Trial for Felony in the Court of Great Sessions for Montgomeryshire," *Montgomeryshire Collections* 78 (1990): 167–70.

25. I wish to thank Christopher Warren for drawing my attention to *Venetian Ambassador v. Brooke* in a personal correspondence. For an excellent discussion of the widely reported international dimension of this case, see Warren's *Literature and the Law of Nations, 1580–1680* (Oxford: Oxford University Press, 2015), 74. A full account of the case can be found in Alain Wijffels, "Sir Julius Caesar and the Merchants of Venice," in *Geschichte der Zentraljustiz in Mitteleuropa: Festschrift für Bernhard Diestelkamp zum 65. Geburtstag*, ed. Bernhard Diestelkamp, Friedrich Battenberg, and Filippo Ranieri, 195–219 (Weimar: Böhlau, 1994).

26. Aristotle, *Art of Rhetoric*, trans. J. H. Freese (Cambridge, MA: Harvard University Press, 1926). For discussion, see R. W. Serjeantson, "Testimony and Proof in Early Modern England," *Studies in the History and Philosophy of Science* 30 (1999): 195–236 (pp. 202–8).

27. *Calendar of State Papers and Manuscripts, Relating to English Affairs, Existing in the Archives and Collections of Venice, and in Other Libraries of Northern Italy* (London: Her Majesty's Stationery Office, 1864), 9:229.

28. Shapiro, *Culture of Fact*, 9.

29. Aristotle, *Nicomachean Ethics*, 1115a.

30. See further Howard J. Curzer, *Aristotle and the Virtues* (Oxford: Oxford University Press, 2012), 19–64.

31. Jean Fuzier, "Rhetoric versus Rhetoric: A Study of Shakespeare's *Julius Caesar*, Act III, Scene 2," *Cahiers Elisabéthains* 5 (1974): 25–65 (p. 32).

32. John Palmer, *Political Characters of Shakespeare* (London: Macmillan and Company, 1945), 23–27; Milton Crane, *Shakespeare's Prose* (Chicago: University of Chicago Press, 1951), 144–45; M. M. Mahood, *Shakespeare's Wordplay* (London: Methuen, 1969), 180; Ruth Nevo, *Tragic Form in Shakespeare* (Princeton, NJ: Princeton University Press, 1972), 119–20.

33. Gayle Greene, "'The Power of Speech / To Stir Men's Blood': The Language of Tragedy in Shakespeare's *Julius Caesar*," *Renaissance Drama* 11 (1980): 67–93 (p. 69).

34. Greene, "'Power of Speech,'" 88.

35. Lauren Leigh Rollins, "'Republicans' Behaving Badly: Anachronism, Monarchy, and the English Imperial Model in *Julius Caesar* and *Antony and Cleopatra*," *Medieval and Renaissance Drama in England* 30 (2017): 165–80 (p. 175).

36. Rollins, "'Republicans' Behaving Badly," 176.

37. Robert F. Wilson, Jr., "The Populist *Julius Caesar*," *Shakespeare Bulletin* 13 (1995): 37–38 (p. 38; emphasis added).

38. On the effects of Nilüfer Demir's photograph of Alan Kurdi, see Carolyn Pedwell, "Mediated Habits: Images, Networked Affect and Social Change," *Subjectivity* 10 (2017): 147–69. More generally, see Wendy Atkins-Sayre, "Articulating Identity: People for the Ethical Treatment of Animals and the Animal/Human Divide," *Western Journal of Communication* 74 (2010): 309–28; Daniel Yankelovitch, *Coming to Public Judgment: Making Democracy Work in a Complex World* (Syracuse, NY: Syracuse University Press, 1991); and Laura Gries, *Still Life with Rhetoric: A New Materialist Approach for Visual Rhetorics* (Boulder: University Press of Colorado, 2015). I wish to thank Ryan Skinnell for advising me on scholarship dealing with contemporary rhetoric.

39. The fact that none of these conceptual nuances, nor the broader Aristotelian rhetorical tradition, is taken into account is why I disagree fundamentally with Julian C. Rice who argues that in making his orators appeal to the senses, Shakespeare "consciously intended the play to be a commentary on human limitation." See "*Julius Caesar* and the Judgment of the Senses," *Studies in English Literature, 1500–1900* 13 (1973): 238–55 (p. 238).

40. Maksymilian Del Mar, *Artefacts of Legal Inquiry: The Value of Imagination in Adjudication* (London: Hart Publishing, 2020), 1, 78, and

see more generally 78–124. Terence Cave has discussed how similar processes are at work in literary contexts in *Thinking with Literature: Towards a Cognitive Criticism* (Oxford: Oxford University Press, 2016). As ever, there are conceptual and formal links that run through rhetoric, law, and literature and drama.

41. William M. A. Grimaldi, "Studies in the Philosophy of Aristotle's *Rhetoric*," *Hermes* 25 (1972): 1–151 (16–17).

42. Cara Finnegan, "The Naturalistic Enthymeme and Visual Argument: Photographic Representation in the 'Skull Controversy,'" *Argumentation and Advocacy* 37 (2001): 133–50; Valerie J. Smith, "Aristotle's Classical Enthymeme and the Visual Argumentation of the Twenty-First Century," *Argumentation and Advocacy* 43 (2007): 114–23.

43. Brian Massumi, ed., *A Sock to Thought: Expression After Deleuze and Guattari* (London: Routledge, 2002); Jill Bennett, *Empathic Vision: Affect, Trauma, and Contemporary Art* (Stanford, CA: Stanford University Press, 2005), 11.

44. Deleuze and Guattari, *Thousand Plateaus*, 39–110 and 404–23. And see further Bruno Latour, *Reassembling the Social: An Introduction to Actor-Network Theory* (Oxford: Open University Press, 2005); Manuel Delanda, *A New Philosophy of Society: Assemblage Theory and Social Complexity* (London: Continuum, 2006); and Ian Buchanan, *Assemblage Theory and Method* (London: Bloomsbury, 2020).

45. Deleuze and Guattari, *Thousand Plateaus*, 88.

Chapter 3

1. Stuart Clark, *Vanities of the Eye: Vision in Early Modern Culture* (Oxford: Oxford University Press, 2006), 1.

2. An excellent overview of these kinds of issues can be found in the essays gathered in *SPELL: Swiss Papers in English Language and Literature* 34 (2017), Special Issue: "What is an Image in Medieval and Early Modern England?," ed. Antoinina Bevan Zlatar and Olga Timofeeva.

3. Lorraine Daston and Peter Galison, *Objectivity* (New York: Zone Books, 2007), 23.

4. Thomas Wilson, *The Arte of Rhetorique* (London, 1553), 116.

5. Helkiah Crooke, *Mikrokosmographia* (London, 1615), 530.

6. Ambroise Paré, *The Workes*, trans T. Johnson (London, 1634), 181–82.

7. Jeremy Bentham, *Panopticon; or, the Inspection House* (London, 1791); Proverbs 20:8.

8. Quotations and line references are from William Shakespeare, *Othello*, rev. ed., ed. E. A. J. Honigmann (London: Bloomsbury, 2016).

9. Martin Heidegger, *Being and Time*, trans. Joan Stambaugh, rev. Dennis J. Schmidt (Albany: SUNY Press, 1996), 142.

10. Three good sources for discussions of various aspects of the ideas presented thus far are Stanley Cavell, *Disowning Knowledge: In Seven Plays of Shakespeare* (Cambridge: Cambridge University Press, 1987), 125–42; Katharine Eisaman Maus, *Inwardness and Theater in the English Renaissance* (Chicago: University of Chicago Press, 1995), 104–27; and James A. Knapp, "'Ocular Proof': Archival Revelations and Aesthetic Response," *Poetics Today* 24 (2003): 695–727.

11. René Descartes, *Discourse on Method and Meditations on First Philosophy*, trans. Donald Kress (Indianapolis, IN: Hackett Publishing Company, 1998), 21. For a smart discussion of this passage, see David Michael Levin, *The Opening of Vision: Nihilism and the Postmodern Situation* (London: Routledge, 1988), 95–96.

12. See Charles Taylor, *Sources of the Self: The Making of the Modern Identity* (Cambridge, MA: Harvard University Press, 1989). Donna Haraway's influential feminist critique of the disembodied epistemologies of science can be found in "Situated Knowledges: The Science Question in Feminism and the Privilege of Partial Perspective," *Feminist Studies* 14 (1988): 524–83. Descartes's description of the relationship between seeing and knowing in *Meditations* sets the scene for early eighteenth-century works like Isaac Newton, *Opticks* (London, 1704) and George Berkeley, *An Essay towards a New Theory of Vision* (Dublin, 1709).

13. Clark, *Vanities of the Eye*, 9–12.

14. See Aristotle, *On the Soul*, in *On the Soul, Parva Naturalia, On Breath*, trans. W. S. Hett (Cambridge, MA: Harvard University Press, 1936) and, for discussion, Erica Fudge, *Brutal Reasoning: Animals, Rationality, and Humanity in Early Modern England* (Ithaca, NY: Cornell University Press, 2006), 7–38.

15. See Ted Schmaltz, "The Science of Mind," in *The Cambridge Companion to Early Modern Philosophy*, ed. Donald Rutherford (Cambridge: Cambridge University Press, 2006), 136–69 (p. 157). On neo-scholasticism, see M. W. F. Stone, "Aristotelianism and Scholasticism in Early Modern Philosophy," in *The Blackwell Companion to*

Early Modern Philosophy, ed. Stephen Nadler (Malden, MA: Wiley-Blackwell, 2002), 7–25 and "Scrupolosity, Probabilism, and Conscience: The Origins of the Debate in Early Modern Scholasticism," in *Contexts of Conscience in Early Modern Europe, 1500–1700*, ed. Harald Braun and Edward Vallance (Basingstoke: Palgrave Macmillan, 2004), 507–50.

16. Aristotle, *On the Soul*, 432a 1.5–8.

17. Crooke, *Mikrokosmographia*, 502.

18. Debora Shuger, "The 'I' of the Beholder: Renaissance Mirrors and the Reflexive Mind," in *Renaissance Culture and the Everyday*, ed. Patricia Fumerton and Simon Hunt (Philadelphia: University of Pennsylvania Press, 1999), 21–41 (p. 33).

19. Maurice Merleau-Ponty, *The Phenomenology of Perception*, trans. Colin Smith (London: Routledge, 2008), 373.

20. Merleau-Ponty, *Phenomenology*, 241.

21. Merleau-Ponty, *Phenomenology*, vii (emphasis added).

22. Robert Sokolowski, *Introduction to Phenomenology* (Cambridge: Cambridge University Press, 2000), 206, 202.

23. William Fulke, *A Goodly Gallerye with a most Pleasant Prospect* (London, 1563), 41r–41v.

24. John Dee, "Mathematicall Preface" to *The Elements of Geometrie of Euclid of Megara* (London, 1570), A1v. For further discussion, see Wendy Beth Hyman, "The Inner Lives of Renaissance Machines," in *Renaissance Personhood: Materiality, Taxonomy, Process*, ed. Kevin Curran (Edinburgh: Edinburgh University Press, 2020), 44–61.

25. George Hakewill, *The Vanitie of the Eie* (Oxford, 1608), 1.

26. William Rankins, *A Mirror of Monsters* (London, 1571), 85–86.

27. See Benjamin Bertram, *The Time is Out of Joint: Skepticism in Shakespeare's England* (Newark: University of Delaware Press, 2004), chap. 4 and Robert B. Pierce, "'I stumbled when I saw': Interpreting Gloucester's Blindness in *King Lear*," *Philosophy and Literature* 36 (2012): 153–65.

28. Quotations and line references are from William Shakespeare, *King Lear*, ed. Stanley Wells (Oxford: Oxford University Press, 2000).

29. See Jacques Taminiaux, *The Thracian Maid and the Professional Thinker: Heidegger and Arendt* (Albany: SUNY Press, 1997), 108 and Levin, *Opening of Vision*, 100.

30. Quotations and line references are from William Shakespeare, *Macbeth*, updated ed., ed. A. R. Braunmuller (Cambridge: Cambridge University Press, 2008).

31. Quotations and line references are from William Shakespeare, *Measure for Measure*, ed. N. W. Bawcutt (Oxford: Oxford University Press, 1991).

32. Quotations and line references are from William Shakespeare, *Twelfth Night*, ed. Roger Warren and Stanley Wells (Oxford: Oxford University Press, 1994).

33. See further Lorna Hutson, *Circumstantial Shakespeare* (Oxford: Oxford University Press, 2015).

34. Michael Witmore, *Culture of Accidents: Unexpected Knowledges in Early Modern England* (Stanford, CA: Stanford University Press, 2002), 134.

35. T. G. Bishop, *Shakespeare and the Theater of Wonder* (Cambridge: Cambridge University Press, 1996), 3. See also Stephen Greenblatt, *Marvelous Possessions: The Wonder of the New World* (Chicago: University of Chicago Press, 1991). I am grateful to Rocco Coronato for sharing helpful forthcoming work on the Neoplatonic contexts of wonder and sensation in *Twelfth Night*.

36. Daston and Galison, *Objectivity*, 23.

37. *OED*, "theatre, theater, *n*.," 1; William N. West, *Theaters and Encyclopedias in Early Modern Europe* (Cambridge: Cambridge University Press, 2002), 46.

38. *OED*, "theory," 1; F. E. Peters, *Greek Philosophical Terms: A Historical Lexicon* (New York: New York University Press, 1967), 194. The link between theater and theory (conceptual and etymological) has been noted by Nikolas Lobkowicz, *Theory and Practice: History of a Concept from Aristotle to Marx* (Notre Dame, IN: University of Notre Dame Press, 1967), 7 n.9; Martin Heidegger, "Science and Reflection," in *The Question Concerning Technology and Other Essays*, trans. W. Lovitt (New York: Harper and Row, 1977), 155–82 (pp. 163–66); Levin, *Opening of Vision*, 100, 164; West, *Theaters and Encyclopedias*, 47; Paul Kottman, *A Politics of the Scene* (Stanford, CA: Stanford University Press, 2008), 30–35; and Kevin Curran, *Shakespeare's Legal Ecologies: Law and Distributed Selfhood* (Evanston, IL: Northwestern University Press, 2017), 96–100.

39. West, *Theaters and Encyclopedias*, 1, 45.

40. Thomas Elyot, *The Image of Governance* (London, 1541), 42v.

41. West, *Theaters and Encyclopedias*, 3 (emphasis added).

42. Katherine Eggert, *Disknowledge: Literature, Alchemy, and the End of Humanism in Renaissance England* (Philadelphia: University of Pennsylvania Press, 2015), 5, 7.

43. I am grateful to Antoinina Bevan Zlatar for pointing out this link.
44. Daston and Galison, *Objectivity*, 39–42.
45. James A. Knapp, "Visual and Ethical Truth in *The Winter's Tale*," *Shakespeare Quarterly* 55 (2004): 253–78 (pp. 59, 253).
46. Knapp, "Visual and Ethical Truth," 254. In a related vein, see Bishop, *Shakespeare and the Theater of Wonder*, 125–75.

Chapter 4

1. G. Bury, *The narrovv vvay, and the last iudgement deliuered in two sermons* (London, 1607), 76.
2. R. Horne, *Life and death foure sermons. the first two, of our preparation to death; and expectation of death. the last two, of place, and the iudgement after death* (London, 1613), 265, 270.
3. R. Bolton, *Mr. Boltons last and learned worke of the foure last things death, iudgement, hell, and heauen* (London, 1632), 145.
4. John Langbein, *Prosecuting Crime in the Renaissance: England, Germany, France* (Cambridge, MA: Harvard University Press, 1974), 104–28; "The Criminal Trial Before the Lawyers," *University of Chicago Law Review* 45 (1978): 263–316; J. S. Cockburn, *Calendar of Assize Records: Introduction* (London: Her Majesty's Stationery Office, 1985), chaps. 6, 8, and Conclusion; J. H. Baker, *The Legal Profession and the Common Law: Historical Essays* (London: The Hambledon Press, 1986), 474–76.
5. Baker, *Legal Profession*, 474.
6. See, for example, Edmund Plowden, *Les commentaries, ou les reportes de Edmunde Plowden* (London, 1571) and *Cy ensuont certeyne cases reportes per Edmunde Plowden* (London, 1579).
7. J. H. Baker, *Legal Profession*, 461–76; *An Introduction to English Legal History* (Oxford: Oxford University Press, 2002), 195–99; Cynthia Herrup, *The Common Peace: Participation and the Criminal Law in Seventeenth-Century England* (Cambridge: Cambridge University Press, 1987), 158–59.
8. Quotations and line references are from William Shakespeare, *The Tempest*, ed. Stephen Orgel (Oxford: Oxford University Press, 1987).
9. Robert Weimann, *Author's Pen and Actor's Voice: Playing and Writing in Shakespeare's Theatre* (Cambridge: Cambridge University Press, 2000), 241.
10. Dudley North, *A Forest of Varieties* (London, 1645), A2a, quoted in Tiffany Stern, *Documents of Performance in Early Modern England*

(Cambridge: Cambridge University Press, 2009), 88. See also Stern's larger discussion, 88–89.

11. John Marston, *The Dutch Courtezan* (London, 1605), A2r.

12. Ben Jonson, *The Alchemist* (London, 1612), A3r.

13. Richard Brome, *The Novella*, in *Five New Playes* (London, 1653), H4b.

14. Thomas Dekker, *The Wonder of a Kingdome* (London, 1636), A2a.

15. Francis Beaumont, John Fletcher, and Philip Massinger, *The Coxcomb*, in Francis Beaumont and John Fletcher, *Comedies and Tragedies* (London, 1647), 2P3b.

16. See Denis Kezar, *Solon and Thespis: Law and Theater in the English Renaissance* (Notre Dame, IN: University of Notre Dame Press, 2007).

17. Stern, *Documents of Performance*, 89.

18. John Marston, *The History of Antonio and Mellida* (London, 1602), B1b.

19. Thomas Heywood, *A Pleasant Comedy, called A Mayden-Head Well Lost* (London, 1634), 13a.

20. Stern, *Documents of Performance*, 92.

21. Thomas Blundeville, *The Arte of Logicke* (London, 1599).

22. Quentin Skinner, *Forensic Shakespeare* (Oxford: Oxford University Press, 2015), 11–25; Henry S. Turner, *The English Renaissance Stage: Geometry, Poetics, and the Practical Spatial Arts* (Oxford: Oxford University Press, 2006), 45–55.

23. Peter Mack, *Elizabethan Rhetoric: Theory and Practice* (Cambridge: Cambridge University Press, 2002), 11–47; Skinner, *Forensic Shakespeare*, 25–41.

24. See further T. W. Baldwin, *William Shakespeare's "Small Latine & Lesse Greeke,"* 2 vols. (Urbana: University of Illinois Press, 1944); Emrys Jones, *The Origins of Shakespeare* (Oxford: Oxford University Press, 1977); and Joel B. Altman, *The Tudor Play of Mind: Rhetorical Inquiry and the Development of Elizabethan Drama* (Berkeley: University of California Press, 1978); and for studies that show how Shakespeare and other playwrights made use of their training in rhetoric and dialectic when crafting speeches and plots having to do with evidence, proof, or doubt, see Kathy Eden, *Poetic and Legal Fiction in the Aristotelian Tradition* (Princeton, NJ: Princeton University Press, 1986), 176–84; Lorna Hutson, *The Invention of Suspicion: Law and Mimesis in Shakespeare and Renaissance Drama* (Oxford: Oxford University Press, 2007); Hutson, *Circumstantial Shakespeare* (Oxford: Oxford University

Press, 2015); Joel B. Altman, *The Improbability of* Othello: *Rhetorical Anthropology and Shakespearean Selfhood* (Chicago: University of Chicago Press, 2010); and Skinner, *Forensic Shakespeare.*

25. Discussions of *decorum* can be found in Michael Moriarty, "Principles of Judgement: Probability, Decorum, Taste, and the *je ne sais quoi*," in *The Cambridge History of Literary Criticism, Volume 3: The Renaissance*, ed. Glyn P. Norton (Cambridge: Cambridge University Press, 1999), 522–28 and Brian Vickers, ed., *English Renaissance Literary Criticism* (Oxford: Oxford University Press, 1999), 44–55.

26. Madeleine Doran, *Endeavors of Art: A Study of Form in Elizabethan Drama* (Madison: University of Wisconsin Press, 1954), 16–17, 33–34, 148–71, 174–75, 234–35.

27. Thomas Wilson, *The Arte of Rhetorique* (London, 1553), 123.

28. Robert Ascham, *The Schoolmaster* (London, 1570), 151.

29. Sir John Harrington, *Apology for Ariosto* (London, 1591), 318.

30. Philip Sidney, *The Defense of Poesy* (London, 1595), 17.

31. Sidney, *Defense of Poesy*, 18 (emphasis added).

32. Samuel Daniel, *A Defense of Rhyme* (London, 1603), 213.

33. Sir William Alexander, *Anacrisis. Or a Censure of some Poets Ancient and Modern* (London, 1634), 298.

34. Henry Peacham, *The Garden of Eloquence* (London, 1577), 250.

35. Hannah Arendt, *Eichmann in Jerusalem: A Report on the Banality of Evil* (London: Penguin Books, 2006), 294–95.

36. Arendt, *Eichmann in Jerusalem*, 297.

37. Arendt, *Eichmann in Jerusalem*, 297.

38. Hannah Arendt, "Personal Responsibility Under Dictatorship," in *Responsibility and Judgment*, ed. Jerome Kohn (New York: Random House, 2003), 17–48 (p. 18).

39. Arendt, "Personal Responsibility," 19.

40. Arendt, "Personal Responsibility," 18.

41. There are, however, no shortage of arguments linking the play as a whole to particular political situations and events in Jacobean England. These range from general to highly specific and include colonial endeavours in the New World and Ireland, the exploration of Africa, the Cleves-Jülich crisis, and the marriage of Princess Elizabeth to Frederick the Elector Palatine. See the following examples of criticism on these topics: Francis Barker and Peter Hulme, "Nymphs and Reapers Heavily Vanish: The Discursive Con-texts of *The Tempest*," in *Alternative Shakespeares*, ed. John Drakakis (London: Methuen, 1985), 206–27; Barbara Fuchs, "Conquering Islands: Contextualizing

The Tempest," *Shakespeare Quarterly* 48 (1997): 45–62; Hans Werner, "*The Hector of Germany or the Palsgrave Prime Elector* and Anglo-German Relations in Early Stuart England: The View from the Popular Stage," in *The Stuart Court and Europe: Essays in Politics and Political Culture*, ed. Malcolm Smuts (Cambridge: Cambridge University Press, 1996), 113–32; Tristan Marshall, "'That's the Misery of Peace': Representations of Martialism in the Jacobean Public Theatre, 1608–13," *The Seventeenth Century* 13 (1998): 1–21; and Rachana Sachdev, "Sycorax in Algiers: Cultural Politics and Gynaecology in Early Modern England," in *A Feminist Companion to Shakespeare*, ed. Dympna Callaghan (Malden, MA: Wiley Blackwell, 2016), 226–43.

42. Jacques Rancière, *The Politics of Literature*, trans. Julie Rose (Cambridge: Polity Press, 2011), 3.

43. Jacques Rancière, *The Emancipated Spectator*, trans. Gregory Elliott (London: Verso, 2011), 19.

44. Christopher Pye, *The Storm at Sea: Political Aesthetics in the Time of Shakespeare* (New York: Fordham University Press, 2015), 8. See also the Introduction to Christopher Pye, ed., *Political Aesthetics in the Era of Shakespeare* (Evanston, IL: Northwestern University Press, 2020). Pye's dense but intellectually rewarding work responds, it seems to me, at least in part, to Graham Hammill's call in *Sexuality and Form: Caravaggio, Marlowe, and Bacon* (Chicago: University of Chicago Press, 2000) for "a shift from the modes of critical analysis that conceive of the aesthetic as a reflection of the social towards modes that reconceive the social and its relation to history through the aesthetic" (2).

45. Hannah Arendt, "Judging: Excerpts from Lectures on Kant's Political Philosophy," in *The Life of the Mind* (San Diego: Harcourt, 1978), 255–72 (pp. 270, 262). These excerpts represent work intended to culminate in a third volume of *The Life of the Mind* on "Judgment," which would complement the two finished volumes, "Thinking" and "Willing." Arendt died before she was able to bring this project to completion.

46. Michel Foucault, *Discipline and Punish: The Birth of the Prison*, trans. Alan Sheridan (New York: Vintage Books, 1977), 83.

Chapter 5

1. Jane Bennett did not coin the term "vital ecologies," but as discussed in Chapter 2, she is one of the most influential contemporary thinkers to have written on the idea evoked by the term. See *Vibrant Matter:*

A Political Ecology of Things (Durham, NC: Duke University Press, 2010). I engage closely with the "ecological" implications of Bennett's work in a Shakespearean context in *Shakespeare's Legal Ecologies: Law and Distributed Selfhood* (Evanston, IL: Northwestern University Press, 2017).

2. Bruce R. Smith, "Outface and Interface," in *Face-to-Face in Shakespearean Drama: Ethics, Performance, Philosophy*, ed. Matthew James Smith and Julia Reinhard Lupton (Edinburgh: Edinburgh University Press, 2019), 27–51.

3. The other two aspects were *vox/sonus* (voice/sound) and *gestus/ motus* (gesture/movement). See Cicero, *On the Orator: Book 3. On Fate. Stoic Paradoxes. Divisions of Oratory*, trans. H. Rackham (Cambridge, MA: Harvard University Press, 1942), 216.

4. I am grateful to Kathy Eden for drawing my attention to the etymology of *facere* and to the notion of *actio*. For the former, see *OED*, "face, *n.*," "Etymology." On the latter, see Andrea Balbo, "Traces of *Actio* in Fragmentary Roman Orators," in *Reading Republican Oratory: Reconstructions, Contexts, Receptions*, ed. Christa Gray, Andrea Balbo, Richard M. A. Marshall, and Catherine E. W. Steel (Oxford: Oxford University Press, 2018), 227–46.

5. See James Thompson, *Performance Affects: Applied Theatre and the End of Effect* (Basingstoke: Palgrave Macmillan, 2009) and Hans Ulrich Gumbrecht, *Production of Presence: What Meaning Cannot Convey* (Stanford, CA: Stanford University Press, 2003).

6. Matthew James Smith and Julia Reinhard Lupton, "Introduction," in *Face-to-Face in Shakespearean Drama*, 6, 16.

7. Harriett Hawkins, *Likeness of Truth in Elizabethan and Restoration Drama* (Oxford: Clarendon Press, 1972), 76, 73. See also Janet Adelman, "Bed Tricks: On Marriage and the End of Comedy in *All's Well That Ends Well* and *Measure for Measure*," in *Shakespeare's Personality*, ed. Norman H. Holland, Sidney Homan, and Bernard J. Paris (Berkeley: University of California Press, 1989), 151–74.

8. Michael D. Friedman, "'O, Let Him Marry Her!': Matrimony and Recompense in *Measure for Measure*," *Shakespeare Quarterly* 46 (1995): 454–64 (p. 454).

9. Pascale Aebischer, "Rape and Politics in *Measure for Measure*: Close Readings in Theatre History," *Shakespeare Bulletin* 26 (2008): 1–23 (p. 7).

10. Aebischer, "Rape and Politics in *Measure for Measure*," 8.

11. Friedman, "'O, Let Him Marry Her!'"

12. In these two respects, Hawkins's reading of the conclusion of *Measure for Measure* is part of a (roughly) mid-century critical tradition that includes, most prominently, M. C. Bradbrook, "Authority, Truth, and Justice in *Measure for Measure*," *Review of English Studies* 17 (1941): 385–99 and Daryl J. Gless, Measure for Measure, *The Law and the Convent* (Princeton, NJ: Princeton University Press, 1979).

13. Quotations and line references are from William Shakespeare, *Measure for Measure*, ed. N. W. Bawcutt (Oxford: Oxford University Press, 1991).

14. Key readings of *Measure for Measure* from the perspective of legal procedure include Andrew Majeske, "Equity's Absence: The Extremity of Claudio's Prosecution and Barnardine's Pardon in Shakespeare's *Measure for Measure*," *Law and Literature* 21 (2009): 169–84; Bernadette Meyler, "'Our Cities Institutions' and the Institution of the Common Law," *Yale Journal of Law and the Humanities* 22 (2010): 441–66; Constance Jordan, "Interpreting Statute in *Measure for Measure*," in *Shakespeare and the Law: A Conversation Among Disciplines and Professions*, ed. Bradin Cormack, Martha C. Nussbaum, and Richard Strier (Chicago: University of Chicago Press, 2013), 101–20; and Virginia Lee Strain, "Preventive Justice in *Measure for Measure*," in *Shakespeare and Judgment*, ed. Kevin Curran (Edinburgh: Edinburgh University Press, 2016), 21–44.

15. Though I am not working in a specifically Levinasian vein in this chapter, any ethically oriented invocation of the "face-to-face encounter" owes something, consciously or unconsciously, to the pioneering work of Emmanuel Levinas. Levinas viewed the face-to-face encounter as a form of micro-sociality, and more profoundly as the most fundamental unit of social existence *per se*. See especially *Totality and Infinity: An Essay on Exteriority*, trans. Alphonso Lingis (Pittsburgh, PA: Duquesne University Press, 1969). I engage more substantially with Levinasian ethics in Chapter 6.

16. There is a great deal written on this topic, but good starting points are John Lyons, "Deixis, Space, and Time," *Semantics* 2 (1977): 636–724 and Geoffrey Nunberg, "Indexality and Deixis," *Linguistics and Philosophy* 19 (1993): 1–43.

17. See further Keir Elam, *The Semiotics of Theatre and Drama*, 2nd ed. (London: Routledge, 2002); Erika Fischer-Lichte, *The Semiotics of Theater*, trans. Jeremy Gaines and Doris L. Jones (Bloomington, IN: Indiana University Press, 1992); Patrice Pavis, *Languages*

of the Stage: Essays in the Semiology of the Theatre (New York: Performing Arts Journal Publications, 1982) and "Performance Analysis: Space, Time, Action," trans. Sinéad Rushe, *Gestos* 22 (1996): 11–32.

18. Edward T. Hall, "A System for the Notation of Proxemic Behavior," *American Anthropologist* 65 (1963): 1003–1026 (p. 1003).

19. Hall, "System for the Notation of Proxemic Behavior," 1008.

20. T. Matthew Ciolek, "The Proxemics Lexicon: A First Approximation," *Journal of Nonverbal Behavior* 8 (1983): 55–80 (p. 62).

21. Kevin Curran, "Shakespearean Comedy and the Senses," in *The Oxford Handbook of Shakespearean Comedy*, ed. Heather Hirschfeld (Oxford: Oxford University Press, 2018), 236–49.

22. Though not specifically concerned with England, Joseph S. Freedman's "Aristotle and the Content of Philosophy Instruction at Central European Schools and Universities during the Reformation Era (1500–1650)," *Proceedings of the American Philosophical Society* 137 (1993): 213–53 provides a helpful anatomy of the way concepts from the rhetorical and virtue traditions figured within European education during the early modern period.

23. Cicero, *On Duties*, trans. Walter Miller (Cambridge, MA: Harvard University Press, 1913), 145. This paragraph draws on Henry S. Turner, *The English Renaissance Stage: Geometry, Poetics, and the Practical Spatial Arts, 1580–1630* (Oxford: Oxford University Press, 2006), 230–31 and Neal Wood, "Cicero and the Political Thought of the Early English Renaissance," *Modern Language Quarterly* 51 (1990): 185–207.

24. Stephen Pender, "The Open Use of Living: Prudence, Decorum, and the 'Square Man,'" *Rhetorica: A Journal of the History of Rhetoric* 23 (2005): 363–400 (p. 368). See also, more generally, Eugene Garver, *Machiavelli and the History of Prudence* (Madison: University of Wisconsin Press, 1987) and Timothy Reiss, *Knowledge, Discovery, and Imagination in Early Modern Europe* (Cambridge: Cambridge University Press, 1997).

25. Hannah H. Gray, "Renaissance Humanism: The Pursuit of Eloquence," *Journal of the History of Ideas* 24 (1963): 497–514 (p. 506).

26. James S. Baumlin, "Ciceronian Decorum and the Temporalities of Renaissance Rhetoric," in *Rhetoric and Kairos: Essays in History, Theory, and Praxis*, ed. Philip Sipiora and James S. Baumlin (Albany: SUNY Press, 2003), 138–63.

27. See Cicero, *On Duties*, 1.35.126–28.

28. Rebecca Wiseman, "A Poetics of the Natural: Sensation, Decorum, and Bodily Appeal in Puttenham's *Art of English Poesy*," *Renaissance Studies* 28 (2014): 33–49 (p. 46).
29. Thomas Elyot, *The Boke Named the Governor*, ed. S. E. Lehmberg (New York: Dutton Press, 1962), 80.
30. Cicero, *On Duties*, 147.
31. See Georg Simmel, "The Problem of Sociology," *The American Journal of Sociology* 15 (1909): 289–320 (esp. 296–98).
32. Simmel is frequently credited with starting the "relational turn" within sociology, now associated with famous theorists like Norbert Elias and Pierre Bourdieu. See Pierpaolo Donati, *Teoria relazionale della società: i concetti di base* (Milan: FrancoAngeli, 2009) and Davide Ruggieri, "Georg Simmel and the 'Relational Turn': Contributions to the Foundation of the Lebenssoziologie Since Simmel," *Simmel Studies* 21 (2017): 43–71. For an example of the way these ideas have influenced early modern studies, see Paul Yachnin and Marlene Eberhart, eds., *Forms of Association: Making Publics in Early Modern England* (Amherst: University of Massachusetts Press, 2015).
33. Related to this sense of judgment are the techniques of probabilistic reasoning. There is a wide-ranging, interdisciplinary critical literature on the topic, but in terms of the present discussion, important studies include J. G. A. Pocock, *The Machiavellian Moment: Florentine Political Thought and the Atlantic Republican Tradition* (Princeton, NJ: Princeton University Press, 1975), 83–85; Anthony Grafton and Lisa Jardine, "Studies for Action: How Gabriel Harvey Read His Livy," *Past and Present* 129 (1990): 30–78; Victoria Kahn, *Machiavellian Rhetoric: From the Counter-Reformation to Milton* (Princeton, NJ: Princeton University Press, 1994), 61–131; and Turner on "projective intelligence" in *English Renaissance Stage*, 216–43.
34. Aristotle, *Rhetoric*, trans Rhys Roberts, in *The Basic Works of Aristotle*, ed. Richard McKeon (New York: Random House, 1941), 1358b 1–3.
35. See further Edward D. Steele, "The Role of the Concept of Choice in Aristotle's *Rhetoric*," *Western Speech* 27 (1963): 77–83 and Lois S. Self, "Rhetoric and Phronesis: The Aristotelian Ideal," *Philosophy & Rhetoric* 12 (1979): 130–45 (pp. 137–38).
36. See Pocock, *Machiavellian Moment*, 24–28. Charles Howard McIlwain distinguished sharply between the two temporal thrusts of early modern governance, with the term *jurisdiction* denoting

backward-looking deliberation and the term *gubernaculum* denoting forward-looking deliberation. See *Constitutionalism: Ancient and Modern* (Ithaca, NY: Cornell University Press, 1940). Though seminal, McIlwain's model has also been critiqued by revisionist historians as overly schematic. See, for example, Donald W. Hanson, *From Kingdom to Commonwealth: The Development of Civic Consciousness in English Political Thought* (Cambridge, MA: Harvard University Press, 1970).

37. Rooted in key phenomenological notions like Heidegger's *In-der-Welt-sein* (Being-in-the-world), Edmund Husserl developed the notion of *Lebenswelt* in *The Crisis of European Sciences and Transcendental Phenomenology* (1936). It would provide a jumping-off point for the phenomenologically influenced sociology of Alfred Schütz and, later, Jürgen Habermas. See Martin Heidegger, *Being and Time*, trans. Joan Stambaugh, rev. Dennis J. Schmidt (Albany: SUNY Press, 1996), 78–90; Edmund Husserl, *The Crisis of European Sciences and Transcendental Phenomenology: An Introduction to Phenomenological Philosophy* (Evanston, IL: Northwestern University Press, 1970); Alfred Schütz, *The Phenomenology of the Social World* (Evanston, IL: Northwestern University Press, 1967); and Jürgen Habermas, *The Theory of Communicative Action, Volume 2: Lifeworld and System: A Critique of Functionalist Reason*, trans. Thomas McCarthy (Boston, MA: Beacon Press, 1985).

38. These are critical commonplaces that can be found in one form or another in many pieces of scholarship dealing with literature and law. The following list offers some examples that span different historical periods and critical styles. Each of these studies, I wish to insist, is rigorous and persuasive, and if they all at some point or other invoke the ideas I am pushing back against, they do so in a way, and with a level of complexity, that appropriately serves their respective arguments. See Richard H. Weisberg, *Poethics, and Other Strategies of Law and Literature* (New York: Columbia University Press, 1992); Christian Biet, "Law, Literature, Theatre: The Fiction of Common Judgment," *Law and Humanities* 5 (2011): 281–92; Alan Read, *Theatre and Law* (London: Bloomsbury, 2015); Minou Arjomand, *Staged: Show Trials, Political Theater, and the Aesthetics of Judgment* (New York: Columbia University Press, 2018); and Julie Stone Peters, *Law as Performance: Theatricality, Spectatorship, and the Making of Law in Ancient, Medieval, and Early Modern Europe* (Oxford: Oxford University Press, 2022).

Chapter 6

1. Modern use of the term "restorative justice" is usually dated to the 1970s, with Albert Eglash's "Beyond Restitution: Creative Restitution," in *Restitution in Criminal Justice: A Critical Assessment of Sanctions*, ed. Joe Hudson and Burt Gallaway (Lexington, MA: Lexington Books, 1977), 90–101 taken as a frequent point of origin. For a genealogy of the term that traces it back much further, to the nineteenth century, see Christian B. N. Gade, "'Restorative Justice': History of the Term's International and Danish Use," in *Nordic Mediation Research*, ed. Anna Nylund, Kaijus Ervasti, and Lin Adrian (New York: Springer, 2018), 27–40.
2. See further Nigel Biggar, "Forgiving Enemies in Northern Ireland," *Journal of Religious Ethics* 36 (2008): 559–79; Roy L. Brooks, *Atonement and Forgiveness: A New Model for Black Reparations* (Berkeley: University of California Press, 2004); and Linda Radzik, *Making Amends: Atonement in Morality, Law, and Politics* (Oxford: Oxford University Press, 2009).
3. Quotations and line references are from William Shakespeare, *The Winter's Tale*, ed. Stephen Orgel (Oxford: Oxford University Press, 1996).
4. Julia Reinhard Lupton, *Thinking with Shakespeare: Essays on Politics and Life* (Chicago: University of Chicago Press, 2011), 169. For Freud and Lacan's work on Judge Schreber, see Sigmund Freud, *The Schreber Case* (London: Penguin Books, 2003) and Jacques Lacan, *The Seminars of Jacques Lacan, Book III: The Psychoses, 1955–56*, trans. Jacques-Alain Miller and Russell Grigg (New York: W. W. Norton & Co., 1997); and "On a Question Prior to Any Possible Treatment of Psychosis," in *Écrits*, trans. Bruce Fink (New York: W. W. Norton & Co., 2006), 445–88.
5. Lupton, *Thinking with Shakespeare*, 168–69. See also Eric Santner's discussion of what he calls "the pure force of law" in *The Royal Remains: The People's Two Bodies and the Endgames of Sovereignty* (Chicago: University of Chicago Press, 2011).
6. The best primary sources for the Quarter Sessions are William Lambarde, *Eirenarcha: or the office of the justices of the peace* (London, 1581) and Michael Dalton, *The Countrey Justice* (London, 1618). For the Assizes, see J. S. Cockburn, ed., *Calendar of Assize Records*, 11 vols. (London: Her Majesty's Stationery Office, 1975–85); *A History of English Assizes, 1558–1714* (Cambridge: Cambridge

University Press, 1972); and "Early Modern Assize Records as Historical Evidence," *Journal of the Society of Archivists* 5 (1975): 215–31.

7. Lambarde, *Eirenarcha*, 57–58, 455.
8. Lambarde, *Eirenarcha*, 286.
9. Lambarde, *Eirenarcha*, 294–95.
10. Lambarde, *Eirenarcha*, 304, 308.
11. Dalton, *Countrey Justice*, 4–6, 13–17, 23–27.
12. Richard Bernard, *The Isle of Man, or, The legall proceedings in Man-shire against sinne* (London, 1627), 129–30.
13. Lorna Hutson, *The Invention of Suspicion: Law and Mimesis in Shakespeare and Renaissance Drama* (Oxford: Oxford University Press, 2007), 30–37.
14. Sister Mary Coogan, *An Interpretation of the Moral Play* (Washington, DC: Catholic University of America Press, 1947); Leo Caruthers, "The Liturgical Setting of *Jacob's Well*," *English Language Notes* 24 (1987): 11–24.
15. Arthur Brandeis, ed., *Jacob's Well, an English treatise on the cleansing of man's conscience*, Early English Texts Society 115 (Oxford: Oxford University Press, 1900), 256–57.
16. Hutson, *Invention of Suspicion*, 37–38.
17. Thomas Garter, *The Commody of the most virtuous and Godlye Susanna* (London, 1578), E1v, E2r.
18. It is not clear if the interlude was actually performed. For David Bevington, the untheatrical stage directions in the printed text are an indication that it was not. See *From Mankind to Marlowe: Growth of Structure in the Popular Drama of Tudor England* (Cambridge, MA: Harvard University Press, 1962), 63. On the other hand, Lorna Hutson points out that there are suggestions for doubling actors on the title-page. See *Invention of Suspicion*, 199.
19. Garter, *Susanna*, E1v.
20. Edward Coke, *Le Quart Part des Reportes del Edward Coke* (London, 1604), B2v.
21. Edward Coke, *The First Part of the Institutes of the Laws of England* (London, 1628), 379.
22. Francis Bacon, *The Major Works*, ed. Brian Vickers (Oxford: Oxford University Press, 2002), 446.
23. James F. Larkin and Paul L. Hughes, eds., *Stuart Royal Proclamations: Volume 1: Proclamations of James I* (Oxford: Clarendon Press, 1973), 169 n.2.

24. Larkin and Hughes, *Stuart Royal Proclamations*, 169–70.

25. Thomas Andrew Green, *Verdict According to Conscience: Perspectives on the English Criminal Trial Jury, 1200–1800* (Chicago: University of Chicago Press, 1985), 105–52; Cynthia Herrup, *The Common Peace: Participation and the Criminal Law in Seventeenth-Century England* (Cambridge: Cambridge University Press, 1987), 158–64.

26. Herrup, *Common Peace*, 166.

27. Hannah Arendt, "The Crisis in Culture: Its Social and Its Political Significance," in *Between Past and Future: Eight Exercises in Political Thought* (London: Penguin Books, 1993), 197–226 (p. 222).

28. On the oracle in the context of early modern legal practice, see Virginia Lee Strain, "*The Winter's Tale* and the Oracle of the Law," *English Literary History* 78 (2011): 557–84.

29. Lambarde, *Eirenarcha*, 57–58.

30. See further Kevin Curran, *Shakespeare's Legal Ecologies: Law and Distributed Selfhood* (Evanston, IL: Northwestern University Press, 2017), 49–77.

31. Emmanuel Levinas, *Totality and Infinity: An Essay on Exteriority*, trans. Alphonso Lingis (Pittsburgh, PA: Duquesne University Press, 1969) and *Otherwise than Being, or Beyond Essence*, trans. Alphonso Lingis (Pittsburgh, PA: Duquesne University Press, 1998).

32. Levinas, *Totality and Infinity*, 37.

33. René Descartes, *Discourse on Method and Meditations on First Philosophy* (Indianapolis, IN: Hackett Publishing Company, 1998), 18.

34. Levinas, *Totality and Infinity*, 44.

35. Levinas, *Totality and Infinity*, 43.

36. Levinas, *Totality and Infinity*, 39–43; *Otherwise than Being*, 85.

37. Simon Critchley, *Infinitely Demanding: Ethics of Commitment, Politics of Resistance* (London: Verso, 2007), 10–11.

38. See, for example, Stewart Motha, "Mabo: Encountering the Epistemic Limit of the Recognition of 'Difference,'" *Griffith Law Review* 7 (1998): 79–96; Costas Douzinas, *The End of Human Rights: Critical Legal Thought at the Turn of the Century* (Oxford: Hart Publishing, 2000); Peter Fitzpatrick, *Modernism and the Grounds of Law* (Cambridge: Cambridge University Press, 2001); and Marinos Diamantides, *The Ethics of Suffering: Modern Law, Philosophy, and Medicine* (Aldershot: Ashgate, 2000) and "In the Company of Priests: Meaninglessness, Suffering, and Compassion in the Thoughts of Nietzsche and Levinas," *Cardozo Law Review* 24 (2003): 1275–1307.

39. Desmond Manderson, *Proximity, Levinas, and the Soul of Law* (Montreal: McGill-Queen's University Press, 2006).

40. For a sustained Levinasian reading of *The Winter's Tale*, though one with a different set of concerns than this chapter, see James A. Knapp, "Visual and Ethical Truth in *The Winter's Tale*," *Shakespeare Quarterly* 55 (2004): 253–78.

41. See, for example, Northrop Frye, *A Natural Perspective: The Development of Shakespearean Comedy and Romance* (New York: Columbia University Press, 1965), 72–117, as well as the introductions to standard critical editions of the play, such as *The Winter's Tale*, ed. Stephen Orgel (Oxford: Oxford University Press, 1996), 39–41, and *The Winter's Tale*, ed. John Pitcher (London: Bloomsbury, 2010), 117–18.

42. In a perceptive analysis of *The Winter's Tale*, Julia Reinhard Lupton distinguishes between forgiveness and blessing, arguing that it is the latter rather than the former that we see at the end of the play. See "Judging Forgiveness: Hannah Arendt, W. H. Auden, and *The Winter's Tale*," *New Literary History* 45 (2014): 641–63.

43. Desmond Tutu, *No Future Without Forgiveness* (New York: Doubleday, 1999).

44. Tutu, *No Future*, 19.

45. I am not aware of any sources that demonstrate indisputably that Tutu had read Arendt or that he had Arendt in mind when he was formulating his approach to a post-apartheid South Africa, but the similarities between their ideas is often remarked in both scholarly and public writing on restorative justice and the politics of forgiveness.

46. Tutu, *No Future*, 21.

47. See, for example, Marilyn McCord Adams, "Forgiveness: A Christian Model," *Faith and Philosophy* 8 (1991): 277–304; P. E. Digeser, *Political Forgiveness* (Ithaca, NY: Cornell University Press, 2001); and Leo Zaibert, "The Paradox of Forgiveness," *Journal of Moral Philosophy* 6 (2009): 365–93.

48. Tutu, *No Future*, 32.

49. Sarah Beckwith, *Shakespeare and the Grammar of Forgiveness* (Ithaca, NY: Cornell University Press, 2011), 133.

50. Stanley Cavell, "Recounting Gains, Showing Losses: Reading *The Winter's Tale*," in *Disowning Knowledge: In Seven Plays of Shakespeare* (Cambridge: Cambridge University Press, 1987), 193–222.

51. Hannah Arendt, *The Human Condition* (Chicago: University of Chicago Press, 1998), 7.

52. Arendt, "Truth and Politics," in *Between Past and Future*, 197–226 (pp. 221, 242).

Coda

1. Amanda Anderson writes compellingly on this topic in *Bleak Liberalism* (Chicago: University of Chicago Press, 2016).
2. For a defense of aesthetic judgment from within the academic left (which was rare in its era), see John Guillory, *Cultural Capital: The Problem of Literary Canon Formation* (Chicago: University of Chicago Press, 1993).
3. On judgment and equality, I have learned from Michael W. Clune, *A Defense of Judgment* (Chicago: University of Chicago Press, 2021).

BIBLIOGRAPHY

Primary

Alexander, Sir William. *Anacrisis. Or a Censure of Some Poets Ancient and Modern*. London, 1634.

Aristotle. *Art of Rhetoric*, trans. J. H. Freese. Cambridge, MA: Harvard University Press, 1926.

———. *The Basic Works of Aristotle*, ed. Richard McKeon. New York: Random House, 1941.

———. *The Complete Works of Aristotle: The Revised Oxford Translation*, ed. Jonathan Barnes, 2 vols., Bollingen Series LXXI 2. Princeton, NJ: Princeton University Press, 1984.

———. *Nicomachean Ethics*, ed. Roger Crisp. Cambridge: Cambridge University Press, 2000.

———. *On the Soul, Parva Naturalia, On Breath*, trans. W. S. Hett. Cambridge, MA: Harvard University Press, 1936.

Ascham, Robert. *The Schoolmaster*. London, 1570.

Bacon, Francis. *The Major Works*, ed. Brian Vickers. Oxford: Oxford University Press, 2002.

———. *The New Organon*. Cambridge: Cambridge University Press, 2000.

———. *The Works of Francis Bacon*, ed. James Spedding, 14 vols. London: Longman & Co., 1857–74.

Beaumont, Francis, and John Fletcher, *Comedies and Tragedies*. London, 1647.

Bentham, Jeremy. *Panopticon; or, the Inspection House*. London, 1791.

Berkeley, George. *An Essay towards a New Theory of Vision*. Dublin, 1709.

Bernard, Richard. *The Isle of Man, or, The legall proceedings in Manshire against sinne*. London, 1627.

Blundeville, Thomas. *The Arte of Logicke*. London, 1599.

Boethius, *Tractates/The Consolation of Philosophy*, trans. H. F. Stewart and E. K. Rand. Cambridge, MA: Harvard University Press, 1962.

Bolton, R. *Mr. Boltons last and learned worke of the foure last things death, iudgement, hell, and heauen*. London, 1632.

Bonaventure. *Opera Omnia*, 10 vols. Quaracchi: Collegium S. Bonaventure, 1882–1902.

Brandeis, Arthur, ed. *Jacob's Well, an English treatise on the cleansing of man's conscience*, Early English Texts Society 115. Oxford: Oxford University Press, 1900.

Brome, Richard. *The Novella*, in *Five New Playes*. London, 1653.

Bryskett, Lodowyck. *A Discourse of Civill Life*. London, 1606.

Bury, G. *The narrovv vvay, and the last iudgement deliuered in two sermons*. London, 1607.

Calendar of State Papers and Manuscripts, Relating to English Affairs, Existing in the Archives and Collections of Venice, and in Other Libraries of Northern Italy. London: Her Majesty's Stationery Office, 1864.

Cicero. *On Duties*, trans. Walter Miller. Cambridge, MA: Harvard University Press, 1913.

——. *On the Orator: Book 3. On Fate. Stoic Paradoxes. Divisions of Oratory*, trans. H. Rackham. Cambridge, MA: Harvard University Press, 1942.

Cockburn, J. S., ed. *Calendar of Assize Records*, 11 vols. London: Her Majesty's Stationery Office, 1975–85.

Coke, Edward. *Le Quart Part des Reportes del Edward Coke*. London, 1604.

——. *The First Part of the Institutes of the Laws of England*. London, 1628.

——. *The Twelfth Part of the Reports of Sir Edward Coke*. London, 1656.

Crooke, Helkiah. *Mikrokosmographia*. London, 1615.

Dalton, Michael. *The Countrey Justice*. London, 1618.

Daniel, Samuel. *A Defense of Rhyme*. London, 1603.

Dee, John. "Mathematicall Preface" to *The Elements of Geometrie of Euclid of Megara*. London, 1570.

Dekker, Thomas. *The Gull's Horn-Book*. London, 1609.

——. *The Wonder of a Kingdome*. London, 1636.

Descartes, René. *Discourse on Method and Meditations on First Philosophy*, trans. Donald Kress. Indianapolis, IN: Hackett Publishing Company, 1998.

Elyot, Thomas. *The Boke Named the Governor*, ed. S. E. Lehmberg. New York: Dutton Press, 1962.

——. *The Image of Governance*. London, 1541.

Fortescue, John. *De Laudibus Legum Angliae*, ed. and trans. S. B. Chrimes. Cambridge: Cambridge University Press, 1949.

Foxe, John. *Locorum Communium Tituli*. Basel, 1557.

Fraunce, Abraham. *The Lawyers Logike*. London, 1588.

Fulke, William. *A Goodly Gallerye with a most Pleasant Prospect*. London, 1563.

Garter, Thomas. *The Commody of the most virtuous and Godlye Susanna*. London, 1578.

Guazzo, Stefano. *The Civile Conversation*. London, 1581.

Hakewill, George. *The Vanitie of the Eie*. Oxford, 1608.

Harrington, Sir John. *Apology for Ariosto*. London, 1591.

Heywood, Thomas. *The Dramatic Works of Thomas Heywood*, ed. R. H. Shepherd, 6 vols. London: Pearson, 1874.

——. *A Pleasant Comedy, called A Mayden-Head Well Lost*. London, 1634.

Horne, R. *Life and death foure sermons. the first two, of our preparation to death; and expectation of death. the last two, of place, and the iudgement after death*. London, 1613.

Hume, David. *A Treatise of Human Nature*, ed. L. A. Selby-Bigge, 2nd ed. Oxford: Clarendon Press, 1978.

Jonson, Ben. *The Alchemist*. London, 1612.

——. *Ben Jonson: Five Plays*, ed. G. A. Wilkes. Oxford: Oxford University Press, 1981.

——. *Every Man Out of His Humour*, ed. Helen Ostovich. Manchester: Manchester University Press, 2001.

Lambarde, William. *Eirenarcha: or the office of the justices of the peace*. London, 1581.

Larkin, James F., and Paul L. Hughes, eds., *Stuart Royal Proclamations: Volume 1: Proclamations of James I*. Oxford: Clarendon Press, 1973.

Leighton, William. *Vertue Triumphant, or A lively description of the foure vertues cardinall dedicated to the Kings majesty*. London, 1603.

Locke, John. *An Essay Concerning Human Understanding*, ed. Roger Woolhouse. London: Penguin Books, 1997.

Lyly, John. *The Complete Works of John Lyly*, ed. R. Warwick Bond, 3 vols. Oxford: Clarendon Press, 1902.

Mancyn, Dominic. *The Myrrour of Good Maners, conteyning the iiii vertues callyd cardynall*. London, 1520.

Marlowe, Christopher. *Doctor Faustus*, ed. Paul Menzer. London: Bloomsbury, 2019.

Marston, John. *The Dutch Courtezan*. London, 1605.

——. *The History of Antonio and Mellida*. London, 1602.

Mornay, Philippe de. *The True Knowledge of a Man's Owne Selfe*. London, 1602.

Newton, Isaac. *Opticks*. London, 1704.

North, Dudley. *A Forest of Varieties*. London, 1645.

Oxford English Dictionary Online. Oxford: Oxford University Press. http://www.oed.com

Paré, Ambroise. *The Workes*, trans T. Johnson. London, 1634.

Peacham, Henry. *The Garden of Eloquence*. London, 1577.

Plowden, Edmund. *Cy ensuont certeyne cases reportes per Edmunde Plowden*. London, 1579.

——. *Les commentaries, ou les reportes de Edmunde Plowden*. London, 1571.

Rankins, William. *A Mirror of Monsters*. London, 1571.

Seneca the Younger. *Epistles II: Epistles 66–92*, trans. Richard M. Gunmere. Cambridge, MA: Harvard University Press, 1920.

Shakespeare, William. *Hamlet*, rev. ed., ed. Ann Thompson and Neil Taylor. London: Bloomsbury, 2016.

——. *Hamlet: A New Variorum Edition*, ed. H. H. Furness, 2 vols. 2:148. Philadelphia: J. B. Lippincott and Co., 1877.

——. *Julius Caesar*, ed. David Daniell. London: Bloomsbury, 1998.

——. *King Lear*, ed. Stanley Wells. Oxford: Oxford University Press, 2000.

——. *Macbeth*, updated ed., ed. A. R. Braunmuller. Cambridge: Cambridge University Press, 2008.

——. *Measure for Measure*, ed. N. W. Bawcutt. Oxford: Oxford University Press, 1991.

——. *Othello*, rev. ed., ed. E. A. J. Honigmann. London: Bloomsbury, 2016.

——. *The Tempest*, ed. Stephen Orgel. Oxford: Oxford University Press, 1987.

——. *Twelfth Night*, ed. Roger Warren and Stanley Wells. Oxford: Oxford University Press, 1994.

——. *The Winter's Tale*, ed. Stephen Orgel. Oxford: Oxford University Press, 1996.

——. *The Winter's Tale*, ed. John Pitcher. London: Bloomsbury, 2010.

Sidney, Philip. *The Defense of Poesy*. London, 1595.

Spinoza, Baruch. *The Ethics, Treatise on the Emendation of the Intellect, and Selected Letters*, trans. Samuel Shirley, ed. Seymour Feldman. Indianapolis, IN: Hackett Publishing Company, 1992.

Wilson, Thomas. *The Arte of Rhetorique*. London, 1553.

Wright, Thomas. *The Passions of the Minde in Generall*. London, 1601.

Secondary

Adams, Marilyn McCord. "Forgiveness: A Christian Model." *Faith and Philosophy* 8 (1991): 277–304.

Adelman, Janet. "Bed Tricks: On Marriage and the End of Comedy in *All's Well That Ends Well* and *Measure for Measure*," in *Shakespeare's Personality*, ed. Norman H. Holland, Sidney Homan, and Bernard J. Paris. 151–74. Berkeley: University of California Press, 1989.

Aebischer, Pascale. "Rape and Politics in *Measure for Measure*: Close Readings in Theatre History." *Shakespeare Bulletin* 26 (2008): 1–23.

Alaimo, Stacey, and Susan J. Hekman. "Introduction: Emerging Models of Materiality in Feminist Theory," in *Material Feminisms*, ed. Stacey Alaimo and Susan J. Hekman. 1–19. Bloomington, IN: Indiana University Press, 2008.

——, ed. *Material Feminisms*. Bloomington, IN: Indiana University Press, 2008.

Altman, Joel B. *The Improbability of Othello: Rhetorical Anthropology and Shakespearean Selfhood*. Chicago: University of Chicago Press, 2010.

——. *The Tudor Play of Mind: Rhetorical Inquiry and the Development of Elizabethan Drama*. Berkeley: University of California Press, 1978.

Anderson, Amanda. *Bleak Liberalism*. Chicago: University of Chicago Press, 2016.

Arendt, Hannah. *Between Past and Future: Eight Exercises in Political Thought*. London: Penguin Books, 1993.

——. *Eichmann in Jerusalem: A Report on the Banality of Evil*. London: Penguin Books, 2006.

——. *The Human Condition*. Chicago: University of Chicago Press, 1998.

——. *The Life of the Mind*. San Diego: Harcourt, 1978.

——. *Responsibility and Judgment*, ed. Jerome Kohn. New York: Random House, 2003.

Arjomand, Minou. *Staged: Show Trials, Political Theater, and the Aesthetics of Judgment*. New York: Columbia University Press, 2018.

Atkins-Sayre, Wendy. "Articulating Identity: People for the Ethical Treatment of Animals and the Animal/Human Divide." *Western Journal of Communication* 74 (2010): 309–28.

Baker, J. H. *An Introduction to English Legal History*. Oxford: Oxford University Press, 2002.

———. *The Legal Profession and the Common Law: Historical Essays*. London: The Hambledon Press, 1986.

Balbo, Andrea. "Traces of *Actio* in Fragmentary Roman Orators," in *Reading Republican Oratory: Reconstructions, Contexts, Receptions*, ed. Christa Gray, Andrea Balbo, Richard M. A. Marshall, and Catherine E. W. Steel. 227–46. Oxford: Oxford University Press, 2018.

Baldwin, T. W. *William Shakespeare's "Small Latine & Lesse Greeke,"* 2 vols. Urbana: University of Illinois Press, 1944.

Barbour, Reid. *English Epicureans and Stoics: Ancient Legacies in Early Stuart Culture*. Amherst: University of Massachusetts Press, 1998.

Barker, Francis, and Peter Hulme. "Nymphs and Reapers Heavily Vanish: The Discursive Con-texts of *The Tempest*," in *Alternative Shakespeares*, ed. John Drakakis. 206–27. London: Methuen, 1985.

Bate, Jonathan. *The Genius of Shakespeare*. London: Picador, 1997.

Baumlin, James S. "Ciceronian Decorum and the Temporalities of Renaissance Rhetoric," in *Rhetoric and Kairos: Essays in History, Theory, and Praxis*, ed. Philip Sipiora and James S. Baumlin. 138–63. Albany: SUNY Press, 2003.

Beckwith, Sarah. *Shakespeare and the Grammar of Forgiveness*. Ithaca, NY: Cornell University Press, 2011.

Bejczy, Istvan P. *The Cardinal Virtues in the Middle Ages: A Study in Moral Thought from the Fourth to the Fourteenth Century*. Leiden: Brill, 2011.

———. "Les vertus cardinals dans l'hagiographie latine du Moyen Âge." *Analecta Bollandiana: Revue critique d'hagiographie* 122 (2004): 313–60.

Bennett, Jane. *Vibrant Matter: A Political Ecology of Things*. Durham, NC: Duke University Press, 2010.

Bennett, Jill. *Empathic Vision: Affect, Trauma, and Contemporary Art*. Stanford, CA: Stanford University Press, 2005.

Bergson, Henri. *Creative Evolution*. New York: Barnes & Noble Books, 2005.

Bertram, Benjamin. *The Time is Out of Joint: Skepticism in Shakespeare's England*. Newark: University of Delaware Press, 2004.

Bevan Zlatar, Antoinina, and Olga Timofeeva, eds. *SPELL: Swiss Papers in English Language and Literature* 34 (2017). Special Issue: "What is an Image in Medieval and Early Modern England?"

Bevington, David. *From Mankind to Marlowe: Growth of Structure in the Popular Drama of Tudor England*. Cambridge, MA: Harvard University Press, 1962.

———. *Murder Most Foul: Hamlet through the Ages*. Oxford: Oxford University Press, 2011.

Biet, Christian. "Law, Literature, Theatre: The Fiction of Common Judgment." *Law and Humanities* 5 (2011): 281–92.

Biggar, Nigel. "Forgiving Enemies in Northern Ireland." *Journal of Religious Ethics* 36 (2008): 559–79.

Bishop, T. G. *Shakespeare and the Theater of Wonder*. Cambridge: Cambridge University Press, 1996.

Bloom, Harold. *Shakespeare: The Invention of the Human*. New York: Riverhead Books, 1998.

Bourdieu, Pierre. *Distinction: A Social Critique of the Judgement of Taste*, trans. Richard Nice. Cambridge, MA: Harvard University Press, 1984.

Bouwsma, William J. *A Usable Past: Essays in European Cultural History*. Berkeley: University of California Press, 1990.

Boyer, Allen D. *Sir Edward Coke and the Elizabethan Age*. Stanford, CA: Stanford University Press, 2003.

Bracton, Henri de. *On the Laws and Customs of England*, ed. Samuel E. Thorne, 4 vols. Cambridge, MA: Belknap Press, 1968.

Bradbrook, M. C. "Authority, Truth, and Justice in *Measure for Measure*." *Review of English Studies* 17 (1941): 385–99.

Bradley, A. C. "The Substance of Shakespearean Tragedy," in *Shakespearean Tragedy*. 23–51. London: Penguin Books, 1991.

Braun, Harald, and Edward Vallance, eds. *Contexts of Conscience in Early Modern Europe, 1500–1700*. Basingstoke: Palgrave Macmillan, 2004.

Brewer, John, and Susan Staves, eds. *Early Modern Conceptions of Property*. London: Routledge, 1995.

Brissenden, R. F. *Virtue in Distress: Studies in the Novel of Sentiment from Richardson to Sade*. New York: Barnes & Noble Press, 1974.

Brooks, Cleanth. *The Well-Wrought Urn: Studies in the Structure of Poetry*. New York: Harcourt Brace, 1947.

Brooks, C. W. *Pettyfoggers and Vipers of the Commonwealth: The "Lower Branch" of the Legal Profession in Early Modern England*. Cambridge: Cambridge University Press, 1986.

Brooks, Peter, and Paul Gewirtz, eds. *Law's Stories: Narrative and Rhetoric in the Law.* New Haven, CT: Yale University Press, 1996.

Brooks, Roy L. *Atonement and Forgiveness: A New Model for Black Reparations.* Berkeley: University of California Press, 2004.

Buchanan, Ian. *Assemblage Theory and Method.* London: Bloomsbury, 2020.

Buckle, Stephen. *Natural Law and the Theory of Property.* Oxford: Clarendon Press, 1991.

Burckhardt, Jacob. *The Civilization of the Renaissance in Italy.* Mineola, NY: Dover, 2010.

Burgess, Glenn. *The Politics of the Ancient Constitution: An Introduction to English Political Thought, 1600–42.* Basingstoke: Macmillan, 1992.

Butler, Judith. *Parting Ways: Jewishness and the Critique of Zionism.* New York: Columbia University Press, 2012.

Cardozo, Benjamin N. *Law and Literature and Other Essays and Addresses.* New York: Harcourt, Brace, and Co., 1931.

Caruthers, Leo. "The Liturgical Setting of *Jacob's Well.*" *English Language Notes* 24 (1987): 11–24.

Cave, Terence. *Thinking with Literature: Towards a Cognitive Criticism.* Oxford: Oxford University Press, 2016.

Cavell, Stanley. *Disowning Knowledge: In Seven Plays of Shakespeare.* Cambridge: Cambridge University Press, 1987.

Chanter, Tina. "Hands That Give and Take," in *Levinas, Law, and Politics*, ed. Marinos Diamantides. 71–80. London: Routledge, 2007.

Chapman, Murray L. "A Sixteenth-Century Trial for Felony in the Court of Great Sessions for Montgomeryshire." *Montgomeryshire Collections* 78 (1990): 167–70.

Ciolek, T. Matthew. "The Proxemics Lexicon: A First Approximation." *Journal of Nonverbal Behavior* 8 (1983): 55–80.

Clark, Stuart. *Vanities of the Eye: Vision in Early Modern Culture.* Oxford: Oxford University Press, 2006.

Clune, Michael W. *A Defense of Judgment.* Chicago: University of Chicago Press, 2021.

Coast, David. *News and Rumour in Jacobean England: Information, Court Politics, and Diplomacy, 1618–25.* Manchester: Manchester University Press, 2016.

Coblentz, Dori. *Fencing, Form, and Cognition on the Early Modern Stage: Artful Devices.* Edinburgh: Edinburgh University Press, 2021.

Cockburn, J. S. *Calendar of Assize Records: Introduction.* London: Her Majesty's Stationery Office, 1985.

———. "Early Modern Assize Records as Historical Evidence." *Journal of the Society of Archivists* 5 (1975): 215–31.

———. *A History of English Assizes, 1558–1714*. Cambridge: Cambridge University Press, 1972.

Coleridge, Samuel Taylor. "Notes on Hamlet," in *Coleridge's Essays and Lectures on Shakespeare and Some Other Old Poets and Dramatists*, ed. Ernest Rhys. London: J. M. Dent, 1907.

Coogan, Sister Mary. *An Interpretation of the Moral Play*. Washington, DC: Catholic University of America Press, 1947.

Cook, Harold J. *The Decline of the Old Medical Regime in Stuart London*. Ithaca, NY: Cornell University Press, 1986.

Coole, Diana, and Samantha Frost. "Introducing the New Materialisms," in *New Materialisms: Ontology, Agency, and Politics*, ed. Diana Coole and Samantha Frost. 1–43. Durham, NC: Duke University Press, 2010.

———, eds. *New Materialisms: Ontology, Agency, and Politics*. Durham, NC: Duke University Press, 2010.

Cormack, Bradin. *"A Power to Do Justice": Jurisdiction, English Literature, and the Rise of Common Law*. Chicago: University of Chicago Press, 2008.

———. "Shakespeare Possessed: Legal Affect and the Time of Holding," in *Shakespeare and the Law*, ed. Paul Raffield and Gary Watt. 83–100. Oxford: Hart Publishing, 2008.

Cormack, Bradin, Martha C. Nussbaum, and Richard Strier, eds. *Shakespeare and the Law: A Conversation Among Disciplines and Professions*. Chicago: University of Chicago Press, 2013.

Crane, Milton. *Shakespeare's Prose*. Chicago: University of Chicago Press, 1951.

Critchley, Simon. *Infinitely Demanding: Ethics of Commitment, Politics of Resistance*. London: Verso, 2007.

Crocker, Holly. *The Matter of Virtue: Women's Ethical Action from Chaucer to Shakespeare*. Philadelphia: University of Pennsylvania Press, 2019.

Crosbie, Christopher. *Revenge Tragedy and Classical Philosophy on the Early Modern Stage*. Edinburgh: Edinburgh University Press, 2019.

Curran, Kevin. "Everyday Dramaturgy: Virtue and the Craft of Living," in *Shakespeare's Virtuous Theatre: Power, Capacity, and the Good*, ed. Kent Lenhof, Julia Reinhard Lupton, and Carolyn Sale. 287–94. Edinburgh: Edinburgh University Press, 2023.

———. "The Four Cardinal Virtues," in *Shakespeare and Virtue: A Handbook*, ed. Julia Reinhard Lupton and Donovan Sherman. 113–24. Cambridge: Cambridge University Press, 2023.

———, ed. *Renaissance Personhood: Materiality, Taxonomy, Process.* Edinburgh: Edinburgh University Press, 2020.

———, ed. *Shakespeare and Judgment.* Edinburgh: Edinburgh University Press, 2016.

———. "Shakespearean Comedy and the Senses," in *The Oxford Handbook of Shakespearean Comedy*, ed. Heather Hirschfeld. 236–49. Oxford: Oxford University Press, 2018.

———. *Shakespeare's Legal Ecologies: Law and Distributed Selfhood.* Evanston, IL: Northwestern University Press, 2017.

Curran, Kevin, and James Kearney. "Introduction." *Criticism* 54 (2012): 353–64. Special Issue: "Shakespeare and Phenomenology," ed. Kevin Curran and James Kearney.

Curzer, Howard J. *Aristotle and the Virtues.* Oxford: Oxford University Press, 2012.

Daston, Lorraine, and Peter Galison. *Objectivity.* New York: Zone Books, 2007.

Delanda, Manuel. *A New Philosophy of Society: Assemblage Theory and Social Complexity.* London: Continuum, 2006.

Deleuze, Gilles, and Félix Guattari. *A Thousand Plateaus: Capitalism and Schizophrenia.* Minneapolis: University of Minnesota Press, 1987.

Del Mar, Maksymilian. *Artefacts of Legal Inquiry: The Value of Imagination in Adjudication.* London: Hart Publishing, 2020.

de Man, Paul. *Allegories of Reading: Figural Language in Rousseau, Nietzsche, Rilke, and Proust.* New Haven, CT: Yale University Press, 1979.

Diamantides, Marinos. *The Ethics of Suffering: Modern Law, Philosophy, and Medicine.* Aldershot: Ashgate, 2000.

———. "In the Company of Priests: Meaninglessness, Suffering, and Compassion in the Thoughts of Nietzsche and Levinas." *Cardozo Law Review* 24 (2003): 1275–1307.

Digeser, P. E. *Political Forgiveness.* Ithaca, NY: Cornell University Press, 2001.

Dolphijn, Rick, and Iris van der Tuin, eds. *New Materialism: Interviews and Cartographies.* Ann Arbor, MI: Open Humanities Press, 2012.

———. "The Transversality of New Materialism," in *New Materialism: Interviews and Cartographies*, ed. Rick Dolphijn and Iris van der Tuin. 93–113. Ann Arbor, MI: Open Humanities Press, 2012.

Donati, Pierpaolo. *Teoria relazionale della società: i concetti di base.* Milan: FrancoAngeli, 2009.

Doran, Madeleine. *Endeavors of Art: A Study of Form in Elizabethan Drama.* Madison: University of Wisconsin Press, 1954.

Douzinas, Costas. *The End of Human Rights: Critical Legal Thought at the Turn of the Century.* Oxford: Hart Publishing, 2000.

Eden, Kathy. *Poetic and Legal Fiction in the Aristotelian Tradition.* Princeton, NJ: Princeton University Press, 1986.

Eggert, Katherine. *Disknowledge: Literature, Alchemy, and the End of Humanism in Renaissance England.* Philadelphia: University of Pennsylvania Press, 2015.

Eglash, Albert. "Beyond Restitution: Creative Restitution," in *Restitution in Criminal Justice: A Critical Assessment of Sanctions*, ed. Joe Hudson and Burt Gallaway. 90–101. Lexington, MA: Lexington Books, 1977.

Elam, Keir. *The Semiotics of Theatre and Drama*, 2nd ed. London: Routledge, 2002.

Elsky, Stephanie. *Custom, Common Law, and the Constitution of English Renaissance Literature.* Oxford: Oxford University Press, 2020.

Erne, Lukas, and Devani Singh, eds. *Bel-vedére or the Garden of the Muses: An Early Modern Printed Commonplace Book.* Cambridge: Cambridge University Press, 2020.

Estill, Laura. *Dramatic Extracts in Seventeenth-Century English Manuscripts: Watching, Reading, Changing Plays.* Newark, NJ: University of Delaware Press, 2015.

Farley-Hill, David, ed. *Critical Responses to Hamlet, 1600–1900*, 4 vols. New York: AMS Press, 1995.

Festa, Lynn. *Sentimental Figures of Empire in Eighteenth-Century Britain and France.* Baltimore, MD: Johns Hopkins University Press, 2006.

Finnegan, Cara. "The Naturalistic Enthymeme and Visual Argument: Photographic Representation in the 'Skull Controversy.'" *Argumentation and Advocacy* 37 (2001): 133–50.

Fischer-Lichte, Erika. *The Semiotics of Theater*, trans. Jeremy Gaines and Doris L. Jones. Bloomington, IN: Indiana University Press, 1992.

Fitzpatrick, Peter. *Modernism and the Grounds of Law.* Cambridge: Cambridge University Press, 2001.

Floyd-Wilson, Mary. *English Ethnicity and Race in Early Modern Drama.* Cambridge: Cambridge University Press, 2003.

Foucault, Michel. *Discipline and Punish: The Birth of the Prison*, trans. Alan Sheridan. New York: Vintage Books, 1977.

Freedman, Joseph S. "Aristotle and the Content of Philosophy Instruction at Central European Schools and Universities during the Reformation Era (1500–1650)." *Proceedings of the American Philosophical Society* 137 (1993): 213–53.

Freud, Sigmund. *The Schreber Case.* London: Penguin Books, 2003.

Friedman, Michael D. "'O, Let Him Marry Her!': Matrimony and Recompense in *Measure for Measure.*" *Shakespeare Quarterly* 46 (1995): 454–64.

Frye, Northrop. *A Natural Perspective: The Development of Shakespearean Comedy and Romance.* New York: Columbia University Press, 1965.

Fuchs, Barbara. "Conquering Islands: Contextualizing *The Tempest.*" *Shakespeare Quarterly* 48 (1997): 45–62.

Fudge, Erica. *Brutal Reasoning: Animals, Rationality, and Humanity in Early Modern England.* Ithaca, NY: Cornell University Press, 2006.

Furness, H. H., ed. *Hamlet: A New Variorum Edition,* 2 vols. Philadelphia: J. B. Lippincott and Co., 1877.

Fuzier, Jean. "Rhetoric versus Rhetoric: A Study of Shakespeare's *Julius Caesar,* Act III, Scene 2." *Cahiers Elisabéthains* 5 (1974): 25–65.

Gade, Christian B. N. "'Restorative Justice': History of the Term's International and Danish Use," in *Nordic Mediation Research,* ed. Anna Nylund, Kaijus Ervasti, and Lin Adrian. 27–40. New York: Springer, 2018.

Garber, Marjorie. *Shakespeare After All.* New York: Anchor Books, 2004.

Garver, Eugene. *Machiavelli and the History of Prudence.* Madison: University of Wisconsin Press, 1987.

Gless, Daryl J. Measure for Measure, *The Law and the Convent.* Princeton, NJ: Princeton University Press, 1979.

Grady, Hugh, ed. *Shakespeare and Modernity: Early Modern to Millennium.* London: Routledge, 2000.

Grafton, Anthony, and Lisa Jardine. "Studies for Action: How Gabriel Harvey Read His Livy." *Past and Present* 129 (1990): 30–78.

Graver, Margaret. *Stoicism and Emotion.* Chicago: University of Chicago Press, 2007.

Gray, Christa, Andrea Balbo, Richard M. A. Marshall, and Catherine E. W. Steel, eds. *Reading Republican Oratory: Reconstructions, Contexts, Receptions.* Oxford: Oxford University Press, 2018.

Gray, Hannah H. "Renaissance Humanism: The Pursuit of Eloquence." *Journal of the History of Ideas* 24 (1963): 497–514.

Grazia, Margreta de. Hamlet *without Hamlet*. Cambridge: Cambridge University Press, 2007.

Green, Thomas Andrew. *Verdict According to Conscience: Perspectives on the English Criminal Trial Jury, 1200–1800*. Chicago: University of Chicago Press, 1985.

Greenblatt, Stephen. *Marvelous Possessions: The Wonder of the New World*. Chicago: University of Chicago Press, 1991.

———. *Renaissance Self-fashioning from More to Shakespeare*. Chicago: University of Chicago Press, 1980.

———. *Shakespeare's Freedom*. Chicago: University of Chicago Press, 2010.

Greene, Gayle. "'The Power of Speech / To Stir Men's Blood': The Language of Tragedy in Shakespeare's *Julius Caesar*." *Renaissance Drama* 11 (1980): 67–93.

Grey, Patrick, and John D. Cox, eds. *Shakespeare and Renaissance Ethics*. Cambridge: Cambridge University Press, 2014.

Gries, Laura. *Still Life with Rhetoric: A New Materialist Approach for Visual Rhetorics*. Boulder: University Press of Colorado, 2015.

Grimaldi, William M. A. "Studies in the Philosophy of Aristotle's *Rhetoric*." *Hermes* 25 (1972): 1–151.

Guillory, John. *Cultural Capital: The Problem of Literary Canon Formation*. Chicago: University of Chicago Press, 1993.

Gumbrecht, Hans Ulrich. *Production of Presence: What Meaning Cannot Convey*. Stanford, CA: Stanford University Press, 2003.

Gunderson, Erik, ed. *The Cambridge Companion to Ancient Rhetoric*. Cambridge: Cambridge University Press, 2009.

Gurr, Andrew. *Playgoing in Shakespeare's England*. Cambridge: Cambridge University Press, 2004.

Habermas, Jürgen. *The Theory of Communicative Action, Volume 2: Lifeworld and System: A Critique of Functionalist Reason*, trans. Thomas McCarthy. Boston, MA: Beacon Press, 1985.

Hall, Edward T. "A System for the Notation of Proxemic Behavior." *American Anthropologist* 65 (1963): 1003–1026.

Hammill, Graham. *Sexuality and Form: Caravaggio, Marlowe, and Bacon*. Chicago: University of Chicago Press, 2000.

Hampton, Timothy. "Difficult Engagements: Private Passion and Public Service in Montaigne's *Essais*," in *Politics and the Passions, 1500–1850*, ed. Victoria Kahn, Neil Saccamano, and Daniela Coli. 30–48. Princeton, NJ: Princeton University Press, 2006.

Hanson, Donald W. *From Kingdom to Commonwealth: The Development of Civic Consciousness in English Political Thought*. Cambridge, MA: Harvard University Press, 1970.

Haraway, Donna. "Situated Knowledges: The Science Question in Feminism and the Privilege of Partial Perspective." *Feminist Studies* 14 (1988): 524–83.

Harkness, Deborah E. *The Jewel House: Elizabethan London and the Scientific Revolution*. New Haven, CT: Yale University Press, 2007.

Harman, Graham. *Guerrilla Metaphysics: Phenomenology and the Carpentry of Things*. Chicago: Open Court Press, 2005.

———. *Object-Oriented Ontology: A New Theory of Everything*. London: Penguin Books, 2018.

———. *Tool-Being: Heidegger and the Metaphysics of Objects*. Chicago: Open Court Press, 2002.

Hawkins, Harriett. *Likeness of Truth in Elizabethan and Restoration Drama*. Oxford: Clarendon Press, 1972.

Headlam-Wells, Robin. *Shakespeare on Masculinity*. Cambridge: Cambridge University Press, 2000.

Hegel, G. W. F. "Dramatic Poetry," in *Aesthetics: Lectures on Fine Art: Volume 2*, ed. T. M. Knox. 1158–1238. Oxford: Oxford University Press, 1998.

Heidegger, Martin. *Being and Time*, trans. Joan Stambaugh, rev. Dennis J. Schmidt. Albany: SUNY Press, 1996.

———. "Science and Reflection," in *The Question Concerning Technology and Other Essays*, trans. W. Lovitt. 155–82. New York: Harper and Row, 1977.

Herrup, Cynthia. *The Common Peace: Participation and the Criminal Law in Seventeenth-Century England*. Cambridge: Cambridge University Press, 1987.

Hesk, Jon. "Types of Oratory," in *The Cambridge Companion to Ancient Rhetoric*, ed. Erik Gunderson. 145–61. Cambridge: Cambridge University Press, 2009.

Holbrook, Peter. *Shakespeare's Individualism*. Cambridge: Cambridge University Press, 2010.

Holland, Norman H., Sidney Homan, and Bernard J. Paris, eds. *Shakespeare's Personality*. Berkeley: University of California Press, 1989.

Hudson, Joe, and Burt Gallaway, eds. *Restitution in Criminal Justice: A Critical Assessment of Sanctions*. Lexington, MA: Lexington Books, 1977.

Hunter, G. K. "The Marking of Sententiae in Elizabethan Printed Plays, Poems, and Romances." *The Library 5th ser.* 6 (1951): 171–88.

Husserl, Edmund. *The Crisis of European Sciences and Transcendental Phenomenology: An Introduction to Phenomenological Philosophy*. Evanston, IL: Northwestern University Press, 1970.

———. *Ideas Pertaining to a Pure Phenomenology and to a Phenomeno-logical Philosophy*, trans. F. Kersten. Dordrecht: Kluwer Academic Publishers, 1983.

———. *Logical Investigations*, trans. J. N. Findlay. Amherst, NY: Humanity Books, 2000.

Hutson, Lorna. *Circumstantial Shakespeare*. Oxford: Oxford University Press, 2015.

———. *The Invention of Suspicion: Law and Mimesis in Shakespeare and Renaissance Drama*. Oxford: Oxford University Press, 2007.

Hyman, Wendy Beth. "The Inner Lives of Renaissance Machines," in *Renaissance Personhood: Materiality, Taxonomy, Process*, ed. Kevin Curran. 44–61. Edinburgh, Edinburgh University Press, 2020.

Jones, Emrys. *The Origins of Shakespeare*. Oxford: Oxford University Press, 1977.

Jordan, Constance. "Interpreting Statute in *Measure for Measure*," in *Shakespeare and the Law: A Conversation Among Disciplines and Professions*, ed. Bradin Cormack, Martha C. Nussbaum, and Richard Strier. 101–20. Chicago: University of Chicago Press, 2013.

Jung, C. G. *Flying Saucers: A Modern Myth of Things Seen in the Sky*, trans. R. F. C. Hull. Princeton, NJ: Princeton University Press, 1978.

Kahn, Victoria. *Machiavellian Rhetoric: From the Counter-Reformation to Milton*. Princeton, NJ: Princeton University Press, 1994.

———. *Rhetoric, Prudence, and Skepticism in the Renaissance*. Ithaca, NY: Cornell University Press, 1985.

Kahn, Victoria, Neil Saccamano, and Daniela Coli, eds. *Politics and the Passions, 1500–1850*. Princeton, NJ: Princeton University Press, 2006.

Kant, Immanuel. *Critique of Judgment*, trans. Werner S. Pluhar. Indianapolis, IN: Hackett Publishing Company, 1987.

Kezar, Denis. *Solon and Thespis: Law and Theater in the English Renaissance*. Notre Dame, IN: University of Notre Dame Press, 2007.

Kierkegaard, Søren. *The Sickness Unto Death*, trans. Alastair Hannay. London: Penguin Books, 1989.

Kisery, Andras. *Hamlet's Moment: Drama and Political Knowledge in Early Modern England*. Oxford: Oxford University Press, 2016.

Knapp, James A. "'Ocular Proof': Archival Revelations and Aesthetic Response." *Poetics Today* 24 (2003): 695–727.

———. "Visual and Ethical Truth in *The Winter's Tale*." *Shakespeare Quarterly* 55 (2004): 253–78.

Kottman, Paul. *A Politics of the Scene*. Stanford, CA: Stanford University Press, 2008.

Kretzmann, Norman R., ed. *The Cambridge Companion to Thomas Aquinas*. Cambridge: Cambridge University Press, 1993.

——. "Philosophy of Mind," in *The Cambridge Companion to Thomas Aquinas*, ed. Norman R. Kretzmann. 128–59. Cambridge: Cambridge University Press, 1993.

Kwan, Roberta. *Shakespeare, the Reformation, and the Interpreting Self*. Edinburgh: Edinburgh University Press, 2023.

Lacan, Jacques. "On a Question Prior to Any Possible Treatment of Psychosis," in *Écrits*, trans. Bruce Fink. 445–88. New York: W. W. Norton & Co., 2006.

——. *The Seminars of Jacques Lacan, Book III: The Psychoses, 1955–56*, trans. Jacques-Alain Miller and Russell Grigg. New York: W. W. Norton & Co., 1997.

Lakoff, George, and Mark Johnson. *Philosophy in the Flesh: The Embodied Mind and Its Challenge to Western Thought*. New York: Basic Books, 1999.

Langbein, John. "The Criminal Trial Before the Lawyers." *University of Chicago Law Review* 45 (1978): 263–316.

——. *Prosecuting Crime in the Renaissance: England, Germany, France*. Cambridge, MA: Harvard University Press, 1974.

Langis, Unhae Park. *Passion, Prudence, and Virtue in Shakespearean Drama*. London: Bloomsbury, 2011.

Latour, Bruno. *Politics of Nature: How to Bring the Sciences into Democracy*. Cambridge, MA: Harvard University Press, 2004.

——. *Reassembling the Social: An Introduction to Actor-Network Theory*. Oxford: Open University Press, 2005.

Lee, John. *Shakespeare's* Hamlet *and the Controversies of Self*. Oxford: Clarendon Press, 2000.

Lemon, Rebecca. *Treason by Words: Literature, Law, and Rebellion in Shakespeare's England*. Ithaca, NY: Cornell University Press, 2006.

Lesser, Zachary, and Peter Stallybrass. "The First Literary *Hamlet* and the Commonplacing of Professional Plays." *Shakespeare Quarterly* 59 (2008): 371–420.

Levin, David Michael. *The Opening of Vision: Nihilism and the Postmodern Situation*. London: Routledge, 1988.

Levinas, Emmanuel. *Otherwise than Being, or Beyond Essence*, trans. Alphonso Lingis. Pittsburgh, PA: Duquesne University Press, 1998.

——. *Totality and Infinity: An Essay on Exteriority*, trans. Alphonso Lingis. Pittsburgh, PA: Duquesne University Press, 1969.

———. "The Trace of the Other," in *Deconstruction in Context: Literature and Philosophy*, ed. Mark Taylor. 345–59. Chicago: University of Chicago Press, 1986.

Lobkowicz, Nikolas. *Theory and Practice: History of a Concept from Aristotle to Marx*. Notre Dame, IN: University of Notre Dame Press, 1967.

Lupton, Julia Reinhard. "Judging Forgiveness: Hannah Arendt, W. H. Auden, and *The Winter's Tale*." *New Literary History* 45 (2014): 641–63.

———. *Shakespeare Dwelling: Designs for the Theater of Life*. Chicago: University of Chicago Press, 2018.

———. *Thinking with Shakespeare: Essays on Politics and Life*. Chicago: University of Chicago Press, 2011.

Lupton, Julia Reinhard, and Donovan Sherman, eds. *Shakespeare and Virtue: A Handbook*. Cambridge: Cambridge University Press, 2023.

Lyons, John. "Deixis, Space, and Time." *Semantics* 2 (1977): 636–724.

Lyotard, Jean-François. *Phenomenology*, trans. Brain Beakley. Albany: SUNY Press, 1991.

McIlwain, Charles Howard. *Constitutionalism: Ancient and Modern*. Ithaca, NY: Cornell University Press, 1940.

Mack, Peter. *Elizabethan Rhetoric: Theory and Practice*. Cambridge: Cambridge University Press, 2002.

Mahood, M. M. *Shakespeare's Wordplay*. London: Methuen, 1969.

Majeske, Andrew. "Equity's Absence: The Extremity of Claudio's Prosecution and Barnardine's Pardon in Shakespeare's *Measure for Measure*." *Law and Literature* 21 (2009): 169–84.

Manderson, Desmond. "Judgment in Law and the Humanities," in *Law and the Humanities: An Introduction*, ed. Austin Sarat, Matthew Anderson, and Catherine O. Frank. 496–516. Cambridge: Cambridge University Press, 2010.

———. *Proximity, Levinas, and the Soul of Law*. Montreal: McGill-Queen's University Press, 2006.

Marshall, Tristan. "'That's the Misery of Peace': Representations of Martialism in the Jacobean Public Theatre, 1608–13." *The Seventeenth Century* 13 (1998): 1–21.

Massumi, Brian, ed. *A Sock to Thought: Expression After Deleuze and Guattari*. London: Routledge, 2002.

Maus, Katharine Eisaman. *Inwardness and Theater in the English Renaissance*. Chicago: University of Chicago Press, 1995.

Merleau-Ponty, Maurice. *The Phenomenology of Perception*, trans. Colin Smith. London: Routledge, 2008.

Meyler, Bernadette. "'Our Cities Institutions' and the Institution of the Common Law." *Yale Journal of Law and the Humanities* 22 (2010): 441–66.

Moriarty, Michael. "Principles of Judgement: Probability, Decorum, Taste, and the *je ne sais quoi*," in *The Cambridge History of Literary Criticism, Volume 3: The Renaissance*, ed. Glyn P. Norton. 522–28. Cambridge: Cambridge University Press, 1999.

Moss, Ann. *Printed Commonplace-Books and the Structuring of Renaissance Thought*. Oxford: Clarendon Press, 1996.

Motha, Stewart. "Mabo: Encountering the Epistemic Limit of the Recognition of 'Difference.'" *Griffith Law Review* 7 (1998): 79–96.

Muir, Norman. "Middle-Class Heroism and the Cardinal Virtue Fortitude in Thomas Dekker's 'Honest Whore' Plays." *Explorations in Renaissance Culture* 15 (1989): 83–97.

Mullan, John. *Sentiment and Sociability: The Language of Feeling in the Eighteenth Century*. Oxford: Clarendon Press, 1988.

Nazar, Hina. *Enlightened Sentiments: Judgment and Autonomy in the Age of Sensibility*. New York: Fordham University Press, 2012.

Nevo, Ruth. *Tragic Form in Shakespeare*. Princeton, NJ: Princeton University Press, 1972.

Newstock, Scott. *How to Think Like Shakespeare: Lessons from a Renaissance Education*. Princeton, NJ: Princeton University Press, 2020.

Norton, Glyn P., ed. *The Cambridge History of Literary Criticism, Volume 3: The Renaissance*. Cambridge: Cambridge University Press, 1999.

Nunberg, Geoffrey. "Indexality and Deixis." *Linguistics and Philosophy* 19 (1993): 1–43.

Nussbaum, Martha. *Creating Capabilities: The Human Development Approach*. Cambridge, MA: Harvard University Press, 2011.

——. *Frontiers of Justice: Disability, Nationality, Species Membership*. Cambridge, MA: Harvard University Press, 2006.

——. *Poetic Justice: The Literary Imagination and Public Life*. Boston, MA: Beacon Press, 1995.

Nylund, Anna, Kaijus Ervasti, and Lin Adrian, eds. *Nordic Mediation Research*. New York: Springer, 2018.

Palmer, John. *Political Characters of Shakespeare*. London: Macmillan and Company, 1945.

Pasnau, Robert. *Theories of Cognition in the Later Middle Ages.* Cambridge: Cambridge University Press, 1997.

——. *Thomas Aquinas on Human Nature.* Cambridge: Cambridge University Press, 2002.

Paster, Gail Kern. *Humoring the Body: Emotions and the Shakespearean Stage.* Chicago: University of Chicago Press, 2004.

Pavis, Patrice. *Languages of the Stage: Essays in the Semiology of the Theatre.* New York: Performing Arts Journal Publications, 1982.

——. "Performance Analysis: Space, Time, Action," trans. Sinéad Rushe. *Gestos* 22 (1996): 11–32.

Peck, Linda Levy, ed. *The Mental World of the Jacobean Court.* Cambridge: Cambridge University Press, 1991.

Pedwell, Carolyn. "Mediated Habits: Images, Networked Affect and Social Change." *Subjectivity* 10 (2017): 147–69.

Pender, Stephen. "The Open Use of Living: Prudence, Decorum, and the 'Square Man.'" *Rhetorica: A Journal of the History of Rhetoric* 23 (2005): 363–400.

Peters, F. E. *Greek Philosophical Terms: A Historical Lexicon.* New York: New York University Press, 1967.

Peters, Julie Stone. *Law as Performance: Theatricality, Spectatorship, and the Making of Law in Ancient, Medieval, and Early Modern Europe.* Oxford: Oxford University Press, 2022.

Pfau, Thomas. *Minding the Modern: Human Agency, Intellectual Traditions, and Responsible Knowledge.* Notre Dame, IN: University of Notre Dame Press, 2013.

Pierce, Robert B. "'I stumbled when I saw': Interpreting Gloucester's Blindness in *King Lear.*" *Philosophy and Literature* 36 (2012): 153–65.

Pocock, J. G. A. *The Machiavellian Moment: Florentine Political Thought and the Atlantic Republican Tradition.* Princeton, NJ: Princeton University Press, 1975.

Poovey, Mary. *A History of the Modern Fact: Problems of Knowledge in the Sciences of Wealth and Society.* Chicago: University of Chicago Press, 1998.

Pye, Christopher, ed. *Political Aesthetics in the Era of Shakespeare.* Evanston. IL: Northwestern University Press, 2020.

——. *The Storm at Sea: Political Aesthetics in the Time of Shakespeare.* New York: Fordham University Press, 2015.

Radzik, Linda. *Making Amends: Atonement in Morality, Law, and Politics.* Oxford: Oxford University Press, 2009.

Raffield, Paul, and Gary Watt, eds. *Shakespeare and the Law*. Oxford: Hart Publishing, 2008.

——. *Shakespeare's Imaginary Constitutions: Late-Elizabethan Politics and the Theatre of Law*. Oxford: Hart Publishing, 2010.

Rancière, Jacques. *The Emancipated Spectator*, trans. Gregory Elliott. London: Verso, 2011.

——. *The Politics of Literature,* trans. Julie Rose. Cambridge: Polity Press, 2011.

Rawls, John. *A Theory of Justice*. Cambridge, MA: Harvard University Press, 1971.

Read, Alan. *Theatre and Law*. London: Bloomsbury, 2015.

Reiss, Timothy. *Knowledge, Discovery, and Imagination in Early Modern Europe*. Cambridge: Cambridge University Press, 1997.

Rice, Julian C. "*Julius Caesar* and the Judgment of the Senses." *Studies in English Literature, 1500–1900* 13 (1973): 238–55.

Ricoeur, Paul. *Oneself as Another*, trans. Kathleen Blamey. Chicago: University of Chicago Press, 1992.

Rollins, Lauren Leigh. "'Republicans' Behaving Badly: Anachronism, Monarchy, and the English Imperial Model in *Julius Caesar* and *Antony and Cleopatra*." *Medieval and Renaissance Drama in England* 30 (2017): 165–80.

Ruggieri, Davide. "Georg Simmel and the 'Relational Turn': Contributions to the Foundation of the Lebenssoziologie Since Simmel." *Simmel Studies* 21 (2017): 43–71.

Rutherford, Donald, ed. *The Cambridge Companion to Early Modern Philosophy*. Cambridge: Cambridge University Press, 2006.

Sachdev, Rachana. "Sycorax in Algiers: Cultural Politics and Gynaecology in Early Modern England," in *A Feminist Companion to Shakespeare*, ed. Dympna Callaghan. 226–43. Malden, MA: Wiley Blackwell, 2016.

Salinger, Leo. "Jacobean Playwrights and 'Judicious' Spectators.'" *Renaissance Drama* 22 (1991): 209–34.

Salmon, J. H. M. "Seneca and Tacitus in Jacobean England," in *The Mental World of the Jacobean Court*, ed. Linda Levy Peck. 169–88. Cambridge: Cambridge University Press, 1991.

Santner, Eric. *The Royal Remains: The People's Two Bodies and the Endgames of Sovereignty*. Chicago: University of Chicago Press, 2011.

Sarat, Austin. *Law and the Humanities: An Introduction*. Cambridge: Cambridge University Press, 2010.

Schmaltz, Ted. "The Science of Mind," in *The Cambridge Companion to Early Modern Philosophy*, ed. Donald Rutherford. 136–69. Cambridge: Cambridge University Press, 2006.

Schmitt, Charles B. *John Case and Aristotelianism in Renaissance England*. Montreal: McGill-Queen's University Press, 1983.

Schofield, Malcolm. *The Stoic Idea of the City*. Cambridge: Cambridge University Press, 1991.

Schütz, Alfred. *The Phenomenology of the Social World*. Evanston, IL: Northwestern University Press, 1967.

Scodel, Joshua. *Excess and the Mean in Early Modern English Literature*. Princeton, NJ: Princeton University Press, 2002.

Self, Lois S. "Rhetoric and Phronesis: The Aristotelian Ideal." *Philosophy & Rhetoric* 12 (1979): 130–45.

Serjeantson, R. W. "Testimony and Proof in Early Modern England." *Studies in the History and Philosophy of Science* 30 (1999): 195–236.

Shapin, Steven. *A Social History of Truth: Civility and Science in Seventeenth-Century England*. Chicago: University of Chicago Press, 1994.

Shapiro, Barbara. *A Culture of Fact: England, 1550–1720*. Ithaca, NY: Cornell University Press, 2000.

Sharpe, Kevin. "Virtues, Passions, and Politics in Early Modern England." *History of Political Thought* 32 (2011): 773–98.

Sharpe, Kevin, and Peter Lake, eds. *Culture and Politics in Early Stuart England*. Stanford, CA: Stanford University Press, 1993.

Sheen, Erica, and Lorna Hutson, eds. *Literature, Politics, and Law in Renaissance England*. Basingstoke: Palgrave Macmillan, 2005.

Sherman, Donovan. "Stoicism," in *Shakespeare and Virtue: A Handbook*, ed. Julia Reinhard Lupton and Donovan Sherman. 69–80. Cambridge: Cambridge University Press, 2023.

Shuger, Debora. "The 'I' of the Beholder: Renaissance Mirrors and the Reflexive Mind," in *Renaissance Culture and the Everyday*, ed. Patricia Fumerton and Simon Hunt. 21–41. Philadelphia: University of Pennsylvania Press, 1999.

Simmel, Georg. "The Problem of Sociology." *The American Journal of Sociology* 15 (1909): 289–320.

Sipiora, Philip, and James S. Baumlin, eds. *Rhetoric and Kairos: Essays in History, Theory, and Praxis*. Albany: SUNY Press, 2003.

Skinner, Quentin. *Forensic Shakespeare*. Oxford: Oxford University Press, 2014.

Smith, Adam. *The Theory of Moral Sentiments*, ed. D. D. Raphael and A. L. Macfie. Indianapolis, IN: Liberty Fund, 1982.

Smith, Bruce R. *The Key of Green: Passion and Perception in Renaissance Culture*. Chicago: University of Chicago Press, 2009.

———. "Outface and Interface," in *Face-to-Face in Shakespearean Drama: Ethics, Performance, Philosophy*, ed. Matthew James Smith and Julia Reinhard Lupton. 27–51. Edinburgh: Edinburgh University Press, 2019.

———. *Phenomenal Shakespeare*. Malden, MA: Wiley-Blackwell, 2010.

———. "Premodern Sexualities." *PMLA* 115 (2000): 318–29.

Smith, Matthew James, and Julia Reinhard Lupton, eds. *Face-to-Face in Shakespearean Drama: Ethics, Performance, Philosophy*. Edinburgh: Edinburgh University Press, 2019.

Smith, Valerie J. "Aristotle's Classical Enthymeme and the Visual Argumentation of the Twenty-First Century." *Argumentation and Advocacy* 43 (2007): 114–23.

Smuts, Malcolm. "Court-Centred Politics and the Uses of Roman Historians, c. 1590–1630," in *Culture and Politics in Early Stuart England*, ed. Kevin Sharpe and Peter Lake. 21–43. Stanford, CA: Stanford University Press, 1993.

Sokolowski, Robert. *Introduction to Phenomenology*. Cambridge: Cambridge University Press, 2000.

Soni, Vivasvan, ed. *The Eighteenth Century: Theory and Interpretation* 51 (2010). Special Issue: "The Crisis of Judgment."

Stallybrass, Peter, Roger Chartier, J. Franklin Mowery, and Heather Wolfe. "Hamlet's Tables and the Technologies of Writing in Renaissance England." *Shakespeare Quarterly* 55 (2004): 379–419.

Steele, Edward D. "The Role of the Concept of Choice in Aristotle's *Rhetoric*." *Western Speech* 27 (1963): 77–83.

Stern, Tiffany. *Documents of Performance in Early Modern England*. Cambridge: Cambridge University Press, 2009.

Stone, M. W. F. "Aristotelianism and Scholasticism in Early Modern Philosophy," in *The Blackwell Companion to Early Modern Philosophy*, ed. Stephen Nadler. 7–24. Malden, MA: Wiley-Blackwell, 2002.

———. "Scrupulosity, Probabilism, and Conscience: The Origins of the Debate in Early Modern Scholasticism," in *Contexts of Conscience in Early Modern Europe, 1500–1700*, ed. Harald Braun and Edward Vallance. 507–50. Basingstoke: Palgrave Macmillan, 2004.

Strain, Virginia Lee. "Preventive Justice in *Measure for Measure*," in *Shakespeare and Judgment*, ed. Kevin Curran. 21–44. Edinburgh: Edinburgh University Press, 2016.

———. "*The Winter's Tale* and the Oracle of the Law." *English Literary History* 78 (2011): 557–84.

Strier, Richard. "Shakespeare and Legal Systems: The Better the Worse (but Not Vice Versa)," in *Shakespeare and the Law: A Conversation Among Disciplines and Professions*, ed. Bradin Cormack, Martha C. Nussbaum, and Richard Strier. 174–200. Chicago: University of Chicago Press, 2013.

———. *The Unrepentant Renaissance: From Petrarch to Shakespeare to Milton*. Chicago: University of Chicago Press, 2011.

Summers, David. *The Judgment of Sense: Renaissance Naturalism and the Rise of Aesthetics*. Cambridge: Cambridge University Press, 1987.

Taminiaux, Jacques. *The Thracian Maid and the Professional Thinker: Heidegger and Arendt*. Albany: SUNY Press, 1997.

Taylor, Charles. *Sources of the Self: The Making of the Modern Identity*. Cambridge, MA: Harvard University Press, 1989.

Thompson, James. *Performance Affects: Applied Theatre and the End of Effect*. Basingstoke: Palgrave Macmillan, 2009.

Tilmouth, Christopher. *Passion's Triumph Over Reason: A History of the Moral Imagination from Spenser to Rochester*. Oxford: Oxford University Press, 2007.

Torrance, Thomas F. *Calvin's Doctrine of Man*. London: Lutterworth, 1952.

Turner, Henry S. *The English Renaissance Stage: Geometry, Poetics, and the Practical Spatial Arts, 1580–1630*. Oxford: Oxford University Press, 2006.

Tutu, Desmond. *No Future Without Forgiveness*. New York: Doubleday, 1999.

Vickers, Brian, ed. *English Renaissance Literary Criticism*. Oxford: Oxford University Press, 1999.

Warren, Christopher. *Literature and the Law of Nations, 1580–1680*. Oxford: Oxford University Press, 2015.

Weimann, Robert. *Author's Pen and Actor's Voice: Playing and Writing in Shakespeare's Theatre*. Cambridge: Cambridge University Press, 2000.

Weisberg, Richard H. *Poethics, and Other Strategies of Law and Literature*. New York: Columbia University Press, 1992.

Welsh, Andrew. *Hamlet in His Modern Guises*. Princeton, NJ: Princeton University Press, 2001.

Werner, Hans. "*The Hector of Germany or the Palsgrave Prime Elector* and Anglo-German Relations in Early Stuart England: The View from the Popular Stage," in *The Stuart Court and Europe: Essays in Politics and Political Culture*, ed. Malcolm Smuts. 113–32. Cambridge: Cambridge University Press, 1996.

West, William N. *Theaters and Encyclopedias in Early Modern Europe.* Cambridge: Cambridge University Press, 2002.

Wijffels, Alain. "Sir Julius Caesar and the Merchants of Venice," in *Geschichte der Zentraljustiz in Mitteleuropa: Festschrift für Bernhard Diestelkamp zum 65. Geburtstag*, ed. Bernhard Diestelkamp, Friedrich Battenberg, and Filippo Ranieri. 195–219. Weimar: Böhlau, 1994.

Williams, Raymond. *Keywords: A Vocabulary of Culture and Society.* Oxford: Oxford University Press, 1976.

Wilson, Jr., Robert F. "The Populist *Julius Caesar*." *Shakespeare Bulletin* 13 (1995): 37–38.

Wiseman, Rebecca. "A Poetics of the Natural: Sensation, Decorum, and Bodily Appeal in Puttenham's *Art of English Poesy*." *Renaissance Studies* 28 (2014): 33–49.

Witmore, Michael. *Culture of Accidents: Unexpected Knowledges in Early Modern England.* Stanford, CA: Stanford University Press, 2002.

Wood, Neal. "Cicero and the Political Thought of the Early English Renaissance." *Modern Language Quarterly* 51 (1990): 185–207.

Yachnin, Paul, and Marlene Eberhart, eds. *Forms of Association: Making Publics in Early Modern England.* Amherst: University of Massachusetts Press, 2015.

Yankelovitch, Daniel. *Coming to Public Judgment: Making Democracy Work in a Complex World.* Syracuse, NY: Syracuse University Press, 1991.

Zagorin, Perez. *Ways of Lying: Dissimulation, Persecution, and Conformity in Early Modern Europe.* Cambridge, MA: Harvard University Press, 1990.

Zaibert, Leo. "The Paradox of Forgiveness." *Journal of Moral Philosophy* 6 (2009): 365–93.

INDEX